Danish pocket dictionary

English-Danish & Danish-English

John Shapiro

Eric!
Best of luck on
your next adventure!
Don't forget your Reno
buddies ☺
Tillykke,
Sophie

Danish pocket dictionary
by John Shapiro

Copyright ©2015-2017 John Shapiro. All rights reserved.
Edited and published by Fluo!Languages.

First edition: March 2017

This dictionary includes processed information, partly based on data which forms part of the English Wiktionary project.

ENGLISH-DANISH

A

aardvark • *n* jordsvin *(n)*
abaca • *n* abaca
aback • *adv* bak, bagi
abacus • *n* kugleramme, abacus
abandon • *v* opgive, forlade, efterlade, forvise, udstøde • *n* løssluppenhed
abase • *v* ydmyge
abasia • *n* abasi
abbess • *n* abbedisse
abbey • *n* abbedi *(n)*
abbot • *n* abbed
abbreviate • *v* forkorte
abbreviation • *n* forkortelse
abdicate • *v* abdicere
abdication • *n* abdikation, abdicering
abdomen • *n* bug, bughule, bagkrop
abduct • *v* bortføre, kidnappe
abhorrence • *n* afsky
ability • *n* evne
ablaut • *n* aflyd
able • *adj* i stand til, have mulighed for, habil, kompetent, dygtig
abnormal • *adj* unormal, abnorm, anormal
abnormally • *adv* unormal, ualmindelig, anormal
aboard • *prep* om bord
abomination • *n* afskyelighed, pestilens, vederstyggelighed
aborigine • *n* aboriginer
abortion • *n* abort
about • *adv* omkring, cirka, næsten, omkreds • *prep* om, omkring, rundt om, cirka, til, på vej til, vedrørende, angående, på
above • *prep* ovenover, ovenpå, oppe over, over
abrade • *v* afskrabe
abridge • *v* forkorte, sammendrage
abridged • *adj* forkortet
abrogate • *v* ophæve, afskaffe
abrupt • *adj* brat, pludselig, uformodet
absence • *n* fravær, mangel
absent • *adj* fraværende
absinthe • *n* absint
absolutely • *adv* absolut, fuldstændig
abstain • *v* afholde sig fra, forhindre
abstemious • *adj* afholdende
abstract • *n* abstrakt, resume *(n)*
absurd • *n* absurditet • *adj* absurd
abuse • *n* misbrug *(n)*, vanrøgt, mishandling, seksuelt misbrug *(n)* • *v* misbruge, mishandle, krænke
abyss • *n* afgrund

academic • *n* akademiker
accelerate • *v* accelerere
acceleration • *n* acceleration
accent • *n* betoning, tryk *(n)*, accent
accident • *n* uheld *(n)*, ulykke, ulykkestilfælde, tilfælde *(n)*, tilfældighed, egenskab
accommodating • *adj* hjælpsom
accompanist • *n* akkompagnatør
accompany • *v* ledsage, gelejde
accomplish • *v* fuldende
accordion • *n* trækharmonika, harmonika, akkordeon
account • *n* konto
accountant • *n* bogholder
accounting • *n* regnskab *(n)*
accretion • *n* tilføjelse
accrue • *v* opsamle, indsamle, tilfalde, påløbe
accumulate • *v* akkumulere
accuracy • *n* nøjagtighed, præcision
accusation • *n* anklage, beskyldning
accusative • *n* akkusativ
ace • *n* es
achievement • *n* udførelse, præstation, resultat *(n)*, bedrift
acid • *n* syre • *adj* sur, -syre, syre-
acorn • *n* agern *(n)*
acoustic • *adj* akustisk
acquiesce • *v* slå sig til tåls med, indvillige
acquittal • *n* frikendelse
acrobat • *n* akrobat
acrobatics • *n* akrobatik
acronym • *n* akronym *(n)*
acrylic • *adj* akrylisk
act • *v* handle, agere, optræde, spille, opføre, virke • *n* handling, dåd, akt
actinium • *n* actinium
active • *adj* aktiv
activist • *n* aktivist
actor • *n* skuespiller, skuespillerinde
actress • *n* skuespillerinde
actually • *adv* egentlig
acupuncture • *n* akupunktur
add • *v* lægge sammen, addere, summere
adder • *n* hugorm
addict • *n* addict
address • *n* adresse
addressee • *n* adressat
adequate • *adj* tilstrækkelig
adequately • *adv* passende, betryggende, tilstrækkeligt, tilfredsstillende
adhere • *v* overholde
adjectival • *adj* adjektiv *(n)*

adjective • *n* tillægsord, adjektiv
adjustment • *n* justering, tilpasning
administrator • *n* administrator
admirable • *adj* beundringsværdig
admiral • *n* admiral
admirer • *n* beundrer
admittance • *n* admittans
adulator • *n* smigrer, spytslikker
adult • *n* voksen
adulterer • *n* horkarl
advantage • *n* fordel, fortrin *(n)*, nytte
advent • *n* komme *(n)*, ankomst
adverb • *n* adverbium, biord
advertise • *v* reklamere, annoncere
advertisement • *n* reklame
advice • *n* råd *(n)*
advise • *v* råde
aerial • *n* antenne
aerodrome • *n* aerodrom
aerodynamic • *adj* aerodynamisk
aerodynamics • *n* aerodynamik
aerology • *n* aerologi
aesthetic • *n* æstetik • *adj* æstetisk
aesthetics • *n* æstetik
aetiology • *n* ætiologi
affirm • *v* bejae
affix • *n* affiks
afraid • *adj* bange
after • *adv* efter, senere • *prep* efter, bagefter, som følge af, på trods af
afternoon • *n* eftermiddag
afterwards • *adv* bagefter, senere
again • *adv* igen
against • *prep* mod, imod, versus, i stedet, i stedet for
age • *n* levetid, alder, alderdom, myndig, epoke, tidsalder, generation
agent • *n* agent
aggression • *n* aggression
aggressive • *adj* aggressiv
agnostic • *n* agnostiker
agoraphobia • *n* agorafobia
agree • *v* være enig, stemme overens, overensstemme, rette sig efter
agreement • *n* aftale, samtykke *(n)*, enighed, overensstemmelse
agriculture • *n* landbrug
agronomist • *n* agronom
agronomy • *n* agronomi
aid • *n* hjælp, bistand, hjælper, hjælpemiddel • *v* hjælpe, bistå
aim • *v* rette
air • *n* luft, arie
air-conditioned • *adj* airconditioneret, luftkonditioneret
aircraft • *n* luftfartøj *(n)*, fly *(n)*, flyvemaskine

airline • *n* flyselskab *(n)*
airmail • *n* luftpost
airplane • *n* flyvemaskine, fly *(n)*
airport • *n* lufthavn
airtight • *adj* lufttæt
alabaster • *n* alabast *(n)*
alanine • *n* alanin
alarmingly • *adv* alarmerende
alas • *interj* ak
albatross • *n* albatros
albeit • *conj* omend, selv om
albino • *n* albino
albumen • *n* hvide, æggehvide
alchemist • *n* alkymist
alcohol • *n* alkohol
alcoholic • *n* alkoholiker
alcoholism • *n* alkoholisme
alcove • *n* alkove, niche
alder • *n* el
ale • *n* lyst øl
alga • *n* alge
algebra • *n* algebra
algorithm • *n* algoritme
alibi • *n* alibi
alien • *n* rumvæsen
alienate • *v* fremmedgøre
alimony • *n* hustrubidrag *(n)*
alkaline • *adj* alkalisk
alkalinity • *n* alkalitet
all • *n* alt • *adv* fuldstændig, aldeles, hver, per styk
allegation • *n* påstand
alleged • *adj* påstået, antaget
allegedly • *adv* angivelig
alley • *n* gyde
alliance • *n* forbund *(n)*, sammenslutning, alliance
alligator • *n* alligator
alliteration • *n* allitteration
allocation • *n* allokering
allow • *v* tillade, acceptere
alloy • *n* legering
allspice • *n* allehånde
allusion • *n* hentydning
almanac • *n* almanak
almighty • *adj* almægtig
almond • *n* mandel
almost • *adv* næsten
alongside • *adv* langskibs
alpaca • *n* alpaka
alpha • *n* alfa *(n)*
alphabet • *n* alfabet *(n)*
alphabetic • *adj* alfabetisk
alphanumeric • *adj* alfanumerisk
already • *adv* allerede
also • *adv* også
altar • *n* alter *(n)*

alternative • *adj* alternativ

although • *conj* selvom, selv om, skønt

altruistic • *adj* altruistisk, uegennyttig

always • *adv* altid

amanita • *n* fluesvamp

amateur • *n* amatør

ambassador • *n* ambassadør

amber • *n* rav *(n)*, gul

ambergris • *n* ambra

ambiguity • *n* tvetydighed

ambiguous • *adj* tvetydig, flertydig, dobbelttydig, dunkel, forblommet

ambitious • *adj* ambitiøs

ambrosia • *n* ambrosia

ambulance • *n* ambulance

amelioration • *n* forbedre, forbedring

amen • *adv* amen

amendment • *n* lovændring, tilføjelse, ændring

americium • *n* americium

amiable • *adj* elskværdig

amicable • *adj* venskabelig, fredelig

ammunition • *n* ammunition

amnesia • *n* amnesi, hukommelsestab *(n)*

amnesty • *n* amnesti

among • *prep* mellem, blandt

amorphous • *adj* amorf

amount • *v* beløbe, løbe op, det samme, ensbetydende • *n* antal *(n)*, sum, beløb *(n)*, mål *(n)*, mængde

ampersand • *n* og-tegn

amphibian • *n* amfibium *(n)*

amphitheater • *n* amfiteater *(n)*

ample • *adj* stor, vid, rigelig, fyldig

amplifier • *n* forstærker

amusement • *n* underholdning

amygdala • *n* mandelkerne

amylase • *n* amylase

an • *art* en, et *(n)* • *prep* pr., om

anabolism • *n* anabolisme

anagram • *n* anagram

analgesic • *n* lokalbedøvelse, analgetikum *(n)*

analysis • *n* analyse

anarchism • *n* anarkisme

anarchy • *n* anarki *(n)*

anatomically • *adv* anatomisk

anatomy • *n* anatomi

anchor • *n* anker

anchovy • *n* ansjos

ancillary • *adj* sekundær, underordnet

and • *conj* og

android • *n* androide • *adj* android

anemia • *n* blodmangel

anemone • *n* anemone

anesthesia • *n* anæstesi

angel • *n* engel

angelica • *n* kvan, kvaner

anger • *n* vrede

angle • *v* vinkle • *n* vinkel, hjørne *(n)*, synsvinkel, synspunkt *(n)*

angry • *adj* vred, sur

angstrom • *n* ångstrøm

animal • *n* dyr *(n)* • *adj* dyrisk

anime • *n* anime

anise • *n* anis

ankle • *n* kno, ankel

annex • *n* bilag

annexation • *n* annektion

annihilate • *v* annihilere, tilintetgøre

annoying • *v* irriterende

annual • *adj* årlig

annually • *adv* årlig, årligt

annulment • *n* annullation, annullering

anonymity • *n* anonymitet

anonymous • *adj* anonym, ukendt

anopia • *n* anopsi, anopi

anorexia • *n* anoreksi

answer • *n* svar *(n)* • *v* svare

ant • *n* myre

anteater • *n* myresluger

antelope • *n* antilope

antepenultimate • *adj* antepenultimær

anthology • *n* antologi

anthracite • *n* antracit

anthrax • *n* miltbrand

anthropological • *adj* antropologisk

anthropology • *n* antropologi

anthropomorphic • *adj* antropomorf

antibiotic • *n* antiobiotikum *(n)* • *adj* antibiotisk

anticipate • *v* forudse

antidepressant • *n* antidepressiv

antidote • *n* modgift

antimony • *n* antimon

antioxidant • *n* antioxidant

antonym • *n* antonym *(n)*

antonymy • *n* antonymi

anus • *n* endetarmsåbning, anus

anvil • *n* ambolt

anxiety • *n* angst, iver

anxious • *adj* urolig, urovækkende, ivrig, opsat, spændt

aorist • *n* aorist

aorta • *n* aorta, hovedpulsåre

apartment • *n* lejlighed

apathy • *n* apati

ape • *n* abe

aphasia • *n* afasi

aphorism • *n* aforisme

aphrodisiac • *n* afrodisiakum *(n)*

apnea • *n* apnø

apocope • *n* apokope

apologist • *n* undskylder, forsvarer,

apologet, skønmaler
apology • *n* undskyldning, forsvar *(n)*
aposiopesis • *n* aposiopese
apostrophe • *n* apostrof, apostrofe
apparatus • *n* apparat *(n)*, maskineri *(n)*
apparently • *adv* åbenbart, tilsyneladende, efter sigende
appendicitis • *n* blindtarmsbetændelse
appendix • *n* appendiks, blindtarm
appetite • *n* appetit
apple • *n* æble *(n)*
applicant • *n* ansøger
appoint • *v* udnævne
appraise • *v* vurdere
appreciate • *v* værdsætte, sætte pris på, forstå, stige i værdi
approach • *n* indflyvning, anflyvning
approval • *n* godkendelse, anerkendelse
approximately • *adv* omtrent, tilnærmelsesvis
apricot • *n* abrikos, abrikostræ *(n)* • *adj* abrikosfarvet
apron • *n* forklæde *(n)*
apropos • *adv* apropos • *prep* apropos
apse • *n* apsis *(m)*, korrunding *(m)*
aquarium • *n* akvarium *(n)*
aquavit • *n* akvavit, snaps, brændevin
arable • *adj* dyrkbar
arachnid • *n* spindler
arbitrary • *adj* arbitrær, vilkårlig
arc • *n* bue
arch • *n* bue
archaeologist • *n* arkæolog
archaeology • *n* arkæologi
archaic • *adj* gammeldags, fortidig, arkaisk
archaism • *n* arkaisme
archangel • *n* ærkeengel
archbishop • *n* ærkebiskop
archer • *n* bueskytte
archery • *n* bueskydning
archipelago • *n* øgruppe
architect • *n* arkitekt
architecture • *n* arkitektur
archive • *v* arkivere • *n* arkiv *(n)*
ardor • *n* iver
are • *n* ar
area • *n* areal *(n)*, flademål *(n)*
argent • *n* sølv
argentine • *n* guldlaks, strømsild
argon • *n* argon
arguably • *adv* velsagtens
argue • *v* argumentere
aria • *n* arie
aristocracy • *n* aristokrati *(n)*
arm • *n* arm, overarm, våben
armchair • *n* lænestol, armstol

armpit • *n* armhule
army • *n* hær, arme
arnica • *n* guldblomme *(n)*
aroma • *n* aroma, duft
arrange • *v* arrangere
arrest • *v* standse, stoppe, bremse, anholde, arrestere, pågribe • *n* anholdelse
arrival • *n* ankomst
arrive • *v* ankomme
arrogance • *n* arrogance
arrogant • *adj* arrogant, højrøvet
arrow • *n* pil
arsenic • *n* arsen *(n)*
art • *n* kunst
arthropod • *n* leddyr *(n)*
artichoke • *n* artiskok
article • *n* artikel, kendeord *(n)*, punkt *(n)*, paragraf
artist • *n* kunstner
artistic • *adj* kunstnerisk
as • *adv* så, lige så • *conj* som, da, mens, imens, siden, eftersom, idet • *prep* som
asexuality • *n* aseksualitet
ash • *n* aske
ashtray • *n* askebæger *(n)*
ask • *v* spørge, bede
asparagus • *n* asparges
aspartame • *n* aspartam
aspen • *n* asp, aspetræ *(n)*, esp, espetræ *(n)*
ass • *n* æsel *(n)*, røv
assassin • *n* attentatmand, morder, snigmorder
assassination • *n* attentat
asset • *n* aktiv
asshole • *n* røvhul *(n)*
assistance • *n* hjælp
assume • *v* antage, formode
assumption • *n* antagelse, formodning, optagelse i himlen, himmelfart
astatine • *n* astat
asterisk • *n* asterisk, stjerne
asteroid • *n* småplanet, asteroide, planetoide
asthma • *n* astma
astonish • *v* forbavse
astonishment • *n* forbavselse
astound • *v* forbløffe
astride • *adv* overskrævs
astrologer • *n* astrolog
astrology • *n* astrologi
astronaut • *n* astronaut
astronomer • *n* astronom
astrophysics • *n* astrofysik
astute • *adj* dreven, kvik, skarpsindig
asylum • *n* asyl *(n)*
asymmetrical • *adj* asymmetrisk

at • *prep* på, til
atavistic • *adj* atavistisk
athlete • *n* sportsudøver, atlet
atlas • *n* atlas
atmosphere • *n* atmosfære
atoll • *n* atol
atom • *n* atom *(n)*
atonal • *adj* atonal
atrium • *n* gårdhave, atrium
atrocious • *adj* grusom, oprørende, rædselsfuld
atrocity • *n* grusomhed
atrophy • *n* atrofi
attack • *v* angribe, overfalde • *n* angreb
attacker • *n* angriber
attempt • *v* forsøge, prøve • *n* forsøg *(n)*
attention • *n* opmærksomhed, bevågenhed
attentive • *adj* opmærksom
attic • *n* loftsrum
attitude • *n* attitude, positur, holdning, indstilling
attractive • *adj* tiltrækkende, tiltalende
attribute • *n* attribut
atypical • *adj* atypisk
auburn • *adj* kastanjebrun, kastanjerød
audiology • *n* audiologi
auditor • *n* revisor
aunt • *n* faster, moster, tante
aura • *n* aura
aurora • *n* polarlys *(n)*
authentic • *adj* autentisk

authenticate • *v* autentificere
authenticity • *n* autenticitet
author • *n* forfatter
authority • *n* myndighed
authorization • *n* autorisation
autism • *n* autisme
autistic • *adj* autistisk
autobiography • *n* selvbiografi
autocrat • *n* autokrat
autodidact • *n* autodidakt
autodidactic • *adj* autodidaktisk, autodidakt
autograph • *n* autograf
automatic • *adj* automatik
automatically • *adv* automatisk
autonomy • *n* autonomi *(n)*, selvstyre *(n)*
autopsy • *n* autopsi, obduktion
autumn • *n* efterår, høst
available • *adj* tilgængelig
avalanche • *n* lavine, sneskred *(n)*
avant-garde • *n* avantgarde
avenue • *n* allé, avenue
average • *n* gennemsnit *(n)*
aviary • *n* fuglehus *(n)*
avocado • *n* avocado, avokado
await • *v* afvente
awake • *v* vågne, vække • *adj* vågen
awe • *n* frygt, ærefrygt
awkward • *adj* akavet
aye-aye • *n* aye aye
azalea • *n* azalea

B

baa • *v* bræge • *interj* mæh, mæ
babble • *v* pludre, sludre, plapre, vrøvle • *n* pladder, pludren
baboon • *n* bavian
baby • *n* spædbarn, baby, pattebarn
babysitter • *n* barnepige, aftenvagt
babysitting • *n* babysitning, babysitting
baccarat • *n* baccarat
bachelor • *n* ungkarl, bachelor
back • *n* ryg, bagside • *adv* tilbage
backbone • *n* rygrad, fundament *(n)*, basis
backgammon • *n* backgammon *(n)*
backpack • *n* rygsæk
backside • *n* bagside, numse, bagdel
bacon • *n* flæsk *(n)*
bacteria • *n* bakterie
bacteriology • *n* bakteriologi
bacteriophage • *n* bakteriofag
bad • *adj* dårlig, ubehagelig, ond, slet, slem

badger • *n* grævling
badlands • *n* badland *(n)*
badminton • *n* badminton
bag • *n* pose, bærepose, sæk, taske
bagel • *n* bagel
bagpipes • *n* sækkepibe
bake • *v* bage, tørre
baker • *n* bager
bakery • *n* bageri *(n)*
baking • *n* bagning
baklava • *n* baklava
balaclava • *n* elefanthue
balalaika • *n* balalajka
balcony • *n* altan, balkon
bald • *adj* skaldet, nedslidt
ball • *n* bold, kugle, bal *(n)*
ballast • *n* ballast
ballet • *n* ballet
balloon • *n* ballon, luftballon

ballot • *n* afstemning
balmy • *adj* balsamisk
balsam • *n* balsam, balsamin
balustrade • *n* balustrade
bamboo • *n* bambus
banana • *n* banan
band • *n* band
bandage • *v* forbinde • *n* bandage
bandy • *n* bandy
bane • *n* bane
bang • *v* knalde, brage • *n* brag *(n)*, knald, pandehår • *interj* bang
banjo • *n* banjo
bank • *n* bank, bankfilial, -bank, bred, banke, vold, række, batteri
bankrupt • *adj* bankerot, fallit, konkurs
bankruptcy • *n* bankerot, fallit, konkurs
banner • *n* banner, bannerreklame, standart, rytterfane • *adj* fremragende
banquet • *n* middag, banket
baptism • *n* dåb
baptize • *v* døbe
bar • *n* bar
barbecue • *n* barbecue
bare • *adj* bar
barefoot • *adv* barfodet
barefooted • *adv* barfodet
barge • *n* pram
baritone • *n* baryton
barium • *n* barium
bark • *v* gø, bjæffe, råbe op, råbe, afbarke, skrubbe, tække • *n* gøen, bark, fartøj
barley • *n* byg
barn • *n* lade, stald
baroness • *n* baronesse
barrel • *n* tønde
barricade • *n* barrikade
barrier • *n* barrier, hindring
barter • *n* byttehandel
basalt • *n* basalt
baseball • *n* baseball
based • *v* baseret • *adj* baseret
basement • *n* kælder
basic • *adj* basal, grundlæggende, elementær, basisk
basil • *n* basilikum
basin • *n* bassin *(n)*
basis • *n* basis
basket • *n* kurv, indkøbskurv, ring, scoring
basketball • *n* basketball
bassoon • *n* fagot
bassoonist • *n* fagottist
bastard • *n* bastard, uægte barn *(n)*, røvhul *(n)*
bat • *n* flagermus
bath • *v* bade • *n* badekar *(n)*

bathe • *n* bad *(n)*
bathrobe • *n* badekåbe
bathroom • *n* badeværelse, toilet
bathtub • *n* badekar *(n)*
batik • *n* batik
baton • *n* depeche, stafet
battery • *n* batteri *(n)*, legemskrænkelse *(n)*
battle • *n* slag *(n)*, kamp
battleship • *n* slagskib *(n)*
bauxite • *n* bauxit
bay • *n* bugt
bayonet • *n* bajonet
bazaar • *n* basar
be • *v* være, finde sted, ske, være til, være her, være lig med, blive, ville
beach • *n* strand
beak • *n* næb
beaker • *n* bægerglas
beam • *v* stråle • *n* bjælke, drager
bean • *n* bønne, bønner
bear • *n* bjørn
bearberry • *n* melbærris, hede-melbærris
beard • *n* skæg *(n)*
bearded • *adj* skægget
bearing • *n* leje, pejling
beautiful • *adj* smuk
beauty • *n* skønhed
beaver • *n* bæver, mis
because • *adv* på grund af • *conj* fordi
become • *v* blive, passe
bed • *n* seng, bed *(n)*
bedbug • *n* væggelus
bedouin • *n* beduin
bedroom • *n* soveværelse *(n)*
bedspread • *n* sengetæppe
bee • *n* bi
beech • *n* bøg, bøgetræ *(n)*
beef • *n* oksekød *(n)*
beehive • *n* bikube
beekeeper • *n* biavler
beer • *n* øl
beeswax • *n* bivoks
beet • *n* bede
beetle • *n* bille
beetroot • *n* rødbede
before • *adv* før, tidligere, forud • *conj* før, inden, hellere • *prep* før, foran, inden
beforehand • *adv* på forhånd, i forvejen
beget • *v* afføde, skabe, avle
beggar • *n* tigger
begin • *v* begynde
behead • *v* halshugge
behind • *n* bagside, bagdel, rumpe • *adv* bagud, tilbage, bagefter, forsinket • *prep* bag ved, bagefter, efter, bag
beige • *n* beige

being • *n* væsen, opstå
belief • *n* tro
believe • *v* tro, mene
bell • *n* klokke
bellboy • *n* piccolo
bellow • *v* brøle, larme • *n* brøl *(n)*
belly • *n* mave
belong • *v* plads, passe, tilhøre, hjemme, høre, henhøre
belt • *v* omringe, omgive • *n* livrem, bælte *(n)*, sikkerhedssele, drivrem, slag, kæberasler, region
beluga • *n* hvidhval
bench • *n* bænk
beneficial • *adj* gavnlig
benefit • *n* hjælp
beriberi • *n* beriberi
berkelium • *n* berkelium
berry • *n* bær *(n)*
berserk • *n* bersærk
beryl • *n* beryl
beryllium • *n* beryllium
beseech • *v* bønfalde
besiege • *v* belejre
best • *adj* bedst
bestial • *adj* bestialsk, dyrisk
bet • *v* vædde • *n* væddemål *(n)*
beta • *n* beta *(n)*
betray • *v* forråde
betrayer • *n* angiver, forræder
better • *adj* bedre • *adv* bedre
between • *prep* mellem, imellem
betwixt • *prep* imellem
beverage • *n* drik
bewitched • *adj* forhekset
bibliography • *n* bibliografi
bicker • *v* skændes, mundhugges
bicycle • *n* cykel
bid • *n* bud
bidirectional • *adj* bidirektional, toretnings-
bigamy • *n* bigami
bigger • *adj* større
bikini • *n* bikini
bilberry • *n* blåbær
bile • *n* galde
bilingual • *adj* tosproget
bill • *n* næb
billiards • *n* billard
binary • *adj* binær
bind • *v* binde
bingo • *n* bingospil
binoculars • *n* kikkert
biochemist • *n* biokemiker
biochemistry • *n* biokemi
biography • *n* biografi
biological • *adj* biologisk

biology • *n* biologi
biomedical • *adj* biomedicinsk
biomedicine • *n* biomedicin
biopsy • *n* biopsi
biotic • *adj* biotisk
bipartite • *adj* todelt
bipolar • *adj* bipolar, bipolær
birch • *n* birk
bird • *n* fugl
birthday • *n* fødselsdag
birthmark • *n* modermærke *(n)*
bishop • *n* biskop, bisp, løber
bismuth • *n* vismuth *(n)*
bistro • *n* bistro
bitch • *n* tæve, kælling
bite • *v* bide • *n* bid *(n)*, bid
bitter • *n* bitter • *adj* bitter, bidende, forbitret
bittercress • *n* karse
bittern • *n* rørdrum
bittersweet • *n* Bittersød Natskygge
bivouac • *n* bivuak
biweekly • *adj* hver anden uge
bizarre • *adj* bizar
black • *n* sort, neger *(m)* • *adj* sort
blackberry • *n* brombær *(n)*
blackbird • *n* solsort
blackboard • *n* tavle
blackcap • *n* munk
blackleg • *n* skruebrækker
blackmail • *v* afpresse • *n* afpresning, pengeafpresning
blackshirt • *n* sortskjorte
blacksmith • *n* smed
bladder • *n* blære
blame • *v* skylde, bebrejde, dadle
bland • *adj* sød
blank • *v* strege • *n* løs patron, rubrik, råemne *(n)*, blanko-, mellemrum *(n)* • *adj* farveløs, tom, blank, hvid, ubeskrevet
blanket • *n* tæppe *(n)*
blaspheme • *v* bespotte
blasphemous • *adj* blasfemisk
blasphemy • *n* blasfemi
bleach • *v* blege • *n* blegemiddel *(n)*
bleed • *v* bløde
blender • *n* blender
bless • *v* velsigne, signe
blind • *v* blænde • *n* gardin *(n)*, rullegardin *(n)* • *adj* blind
blister • *n* vable, blære
block • *v* spærre, blokere • *n* karré, karre
blockade • *n* blokade
bloke • *n* fyr *(m)*
blond • *n* lyshåret, blondine
blood • *n* blod *(n)*, blodprøve
bloodbath • *n* blodbad *(n)*

bloodhound • n blodhund
bloodlust • n blodtørst
bloodroot • n blodurt
bloodthirsty • adj blodtørstig
bloody • adj blodig
blow • v blæse, puste
blowfish • n kuglefisk
blue • n blå • adj blå
blue-eyed • adj blåøjet
blueberry • n blåbær (n)
bluethroat • n blåhals
blunderbuss • n espingol
blunt • adj sløv
blush • n rouge
boar • n orne, galt
boast • v prale • n pral (n)
boat • n båd, skib (n)
boathouse • n bådehus (n), bådeskur (n)
body • n krop, lig (n)
bodybuilder • n bodybuilder
bodybuilding • n bodybuilding
bodyguard • n livvagt
bog • n mose, sump, lokum
bogeyman • n bussemand, bøhmand
bohemian • n boheme
bold • adj modig, fed
bolide • n ildkugle
bollard • n pullert
bollock • n nosse
bolster • n bolster
bomb • v bombe • n bombe
bone • n knogle, ben (n)
boner • n udbener, boner, stivert, stådreng
booger • n bussemand
book • v reservere, nedskrive, notere • n bog, album (n), bind (n)
bookbinder • n bogbinder
bookcase • n bogreol
bookkeeper • n bogholder
bookmobile • n bogbus
bookshop • n boghandel
bookworm • n bogorm
boomerang • n boomerang
boot • n støvle
border • v begrænse, grænse • n grænse
bore • v bore, kede
boredom • n kedsomhed
boring • adj kedelig
boron • n bor
borrow • v låne
borscht • n borsjtj
botanical • adj botanisk
botanist • n botaniker
botanize • v botanisere
botany • n botanik
botfly • n bremse, brems

both • conj både
bottle • n flaske
bottom • n bund
botulism • n botulisme, pølseforgiftning
bough • n gren
bouillon • n bouillon
boulder • n kampesten
bouncer • n dørvogter
bound • adj begrænset
boundary • n rand
bouquet • n buket, bouquet
bow • v stryge, bue, bøje, bukke • n bue, sløjfe, buk (n), bov
bowhead • n grønlandshval
box • v lægge, æske, pakke, kasse, slå, bokse • n kasse, æske, boks, skrin (n), loge, skilderhus (n), jagthytte, kuskesæde (n), buk, dåse, kassen, skridtbeskytter, bøsning, buksbom, slag (n)
boxing • n boksning
boy • n dreng, knægt, fyr, drengene • interj mand
boycott • v boykotte • n boykot
boyfriend • n kæreste
bra • n brystholder, bh, bøjle-bh
bracelet • n armbånd (n)
bracket • n parentes
brackish • adj brak, brakt vand, brakvand (n)
brag • v prale
braid • n fletning
braille • n punktskrift
brain • n hjerne
brake • n bremse
brambling • n kvækerfinke
branch • n gren, filial
brand • v brændemærke, indprente, stemple • n brændemærke, mærke (n), varemærke (n), kvalitet
brass • n messing
brat • n unge, møgunge
brave • adj modig
bravery • n mod (n), tapperhed
bravo • interj bravo
brawny • adj kraftig, muskuløs
bread • v panere • n brød (n)
breakable • adj skrøbelig
breakfast • n morgenmad
bream • n brasen
breast • n bryst (n)
breathe • v ånde, trække vejret
breeze • n brise
brethren • n broder
breviary • n breviar
brew • v brygge
brewer • n brygger
brewery • n bryggeri

bribe • *v* bestikke • *n* bestikkelse
brick • *n* mursten, sveske, knag • *adj* mursten
bricklayer • *n* murer
bride • *n* brud
bridegroom • *n* brudgom
bridesmaid • *n* brudepige
bridge • *n* bro, næseben *(n)*, stol, bridge
bridle • *n* bidsel
brief • *adj* kort, kortfattet
briefcase • *n* portefølje
brigand • *n* røver
bright • *adj* lys, funklende, klar, opvakt, kvik, munter, livlig
brimstone • *n* citronsommerfugl
bring • *v* bringe
brink • *n* kant, rand
bristle • *n* børste, børstehår *(n)*
brittle • *adj* skøre
broadband • *n* bredbånd
broadside • *n* skillingsvise
broccoli • *n* broccoli
brochure • *n* brochure
bromine • *n* brom
bronchitis • *n* bronkitis
bronze • *v* bronzere • *n* bronze • *adj* bronze, bronzefarvet
brooch • *n* broche
brood • *n* kuld *(n)*
broom • *n* kost
broomstick • *n* kosteskaft *(n)*
brothel • *n* bordel, horehus *(n)*
brother • *n* broder, bror
brother-in-law • *n* svoger
brotherhood • *n* broderskab *(n)*
brown • *v* brune • *n* brun • *adj* brun
browse • *v* gennemse, skimme, gennem-*(n)*, gennemrode, gennemsøge
brunette • *n* brunette • *adj* mørkhåret
brush • *v* børste • *n* børste
brusque • *adj* brysk
brute • *n* udyr *(n)*, bæst *(n)*
brutish • *adj* dyrisk, brutal
bubble • *n* boble
bucket • *n* spand
buckle • *n* spænde *(n)*
buckwheat • *n* boghvede
budgerigar • *n* undulat
budget • *n* budget *(n)*
buffalo • *v* jage, gå på jagt, forvirre, bringe ud af det, sætte til vægs • *n* bøffel, bison
bug • *n* insekt *(n)*, kryb *(n)*
build • *v* bygge
building • *n* byggeri, opførelse, bygning
built-in • *adj* indbygget
bull • *n* tyr *(m)*, han, haussespekulant,

haussist, strisser
bulldozer • *n* bulldozer
bullet • *n* kugle, projektil *(n)*, bullet, punkttegn *(n)*
bullfinch • *n* dompap
bully • *v* herse med, mobbe, tyrannisere • *n* bølle, tyran • *adj* fin, udmærket • *interj* fint, udmærket
bulwark • *n* bolværk *(n)*
bumblebee • *n* humlebi
bun • *n* bolle
bungalow • *n* bungalow
buoy • *n* bøje
buoyancy • *n* opdrift
burden • *n* byrde, læs *(n)*, belastning, last
burdock • *n* burre
bureaucracy • *n* bureaukrati
bureaucrat • *n* bureaukrat
bureaucratic • *adj* bureaukratisk
burette • *n* burette
burglary • *n* indbrud
burlesque • *n* varieté
burn • *v* brænde, brænde op • *n* brandsår, forbrænding, afbrænding, bæk, strøm
burned • *v* brændt
burp • *v* bøvse • *n* bøvs *(n)*
burrow • *n* jordhule
bury • *v* begrave
bus • *n* bus
bush • *n* busk
business • *n* forretning, branche
businessman • *n* forretningsmand
bust • *n* buste
bustard • *n* trappe
busy • *adj* travl
but • *conj* undtagen, uden, men
butcher • *n* slagter
butt • *n* røv *(m)*, skod *(n)*
butter • *v* smøre • *n* smør *(n)*
butterfly • *n* sommerfugl, sommerflue, skurvefugl
buttermilk • *n* kærnemælk
buttock • *n* balde, balle
button • *v* knappe • *n* knap
buttonhole • *n* knaphul *(n)*, knaphuls-blomst
buy • *v* købe
buzzard • *n* musvåge
buzzword • *n* modeord *(n)*
by • *adv* forbi • *prep* ved, omkring, af, ved at, efter, med
bye • *interj* farvel
byname • *n* tilnavn *(n)*
bypass • *n* omfartsvej
byre • *n* stald

C

cabaret • *n* kabaret
cabbage • *n* kål
cabin • *n* kahyt
cabriolet • *n* cabriolet
cacao • *n* kakao
cacophony • *n* kakofoni
cactus • *n* kaktus
cadaver • *n* kadaver
cadmium • *n* kadmium
caffeine • *n* koffein *(n)*
cage • *n* bur *(n)*
cake • *n* kage, lagkage, stykke
calcium • *n* kalcium *(n)*, calcium *(n)*
calculator • *n* lommeregner
calf • *n* kalv, unge, læg, lægmuskel
californium • *n* californium
caliper • *n* caliper
calipers • *n* skydelære
call • *v* kalde • *n* opkald *(n)*, telefonopkald *(n)*
calm • *v* berolige, blive stille, blive rolig • *n* ro, stilhed, vindstille • *adj* rolig, stille
calorie • *n* kalorie
calque • *n* oversættelseslån *(n)*
camel • *n* kamel
camera • *n* kamera
camouflage • *v* camouflere, sløre
campaign • *n* kampagne
can • *v* kunne, må, konservere, henkoge, smide ud, holde mund, afskedige, fyre • *n* dåse, kande, vandkande, toilet *(n)*, balder
canal • *n* kanal
canary • *n* kanariefugl, kanariegul • *adj* kanariegul
cancel • *v* strege ud, stryge, annullere, afbestille, aflyse, stemple, ophæve, forkorte • *n* aflysning, afbestilling, annullering, ophævningstegn
cancellation • *n* annullering
cancer • *n* kræft
candidate • *n* kandidat
candidiasis • *n* trøske
candle • *n* lys, stearinlys
candy • *n* slik
cannabis • *n* hamp, cannabis, hash, pot
cannon • *n* kanon
cannonball • *n* kanonkugle
canoe • *n* kano
canon • *n* kanon
cantaloupe • *n* kantalup
canton • *n* kanton
cantor • *n* kantor
canyon • *n* kløft

capacity • *n* kapacitet
cape • *n* kap *(n)*, kappe
caper • *n* kapers
capercaillie • *n* tjur
capon • *n* kapun
capricious • *adj* uberegnelig, uforudsigbar, uforutsigbar
capsize • *v* kuldsejle
capybara • *n* kapivar
car • *n* bil, automobil *(n)*, vogn, elevatorstol
caracal • *n* karakal
carafe • *n* karaffel
caramel • *n* karamel
caravan • *n* karavane *(f)*, campingvogn
caravel • *n* karavel
caraway • *n* kommen
carbohydrate • *n* kulhydrat
carbon • *n* carbon, karbon, kulstof *(n)*, kalkerpapir, karbonpapir, kul *(n)*, koks, trækul, stenkul
carcass • *n* kadaver
carcinogen • *n* carcinogen
card • *n* kort *(n)*
cardboard • *n* pap, karton
cardoon • *n* kardon
care • *n* omsorg
carefree • *adj* sorgløs, ubekymret
careful • *adj* forsigtig
carefully • *adv* forsigtig
caress • *v* kærtegne
cargo • *n* gods *(n)*
caricaturist • *n* karikaturtegner
carnation • *n* nellike
carnival • *n* karneval
carnivore • *n* kødæder, rovdyr *(n)*
carp • *n* karpe
carpenter • *n* tømrer, tømmermand
carpet • *n* tæppe *(n)*
carriage • *n* hestevogn, vogn, togvogn, holdning, slæde
carrot • *n* gulerod
carry • *v* bære
cartilage • *n* brusk
cartoon • *n* tegneserie, karikaturtegning, tegnefilm, tegning
cartouche • *n* kartouche
cartwheel • *n* vognhjul *(n)*, vejrmølle
cascade • *n* vandfald *(n)*, kaskade
case • *n* kasse
cash • *n* kontanter
casino • *n* kasino *(n)*
cassette • *n* kassette
cast • *v* kaste

caste • *n* kaste
castle • *v* rokere • *n* slot *(n)*, borg, herregård
castling • *n* rokade
cat • *v* katte, brække sig • *n* huskat, kat, fyr, ankerkat
cat-o'-nine-tails • *n* nihalet kat
catacomb • *n* katakombe
catalogue • *n* katalog *(n)*
catalyst • *n* katalysator
catamaran • *n* katamaran
cataplasm • *n* grødomslag
catastrophe • *n* katastrofe
catch • *v* fange
category • *n* kategori
caterpillar • *n* larve, kålorm
catfish • *n* malle
catharsis • *n* katarsis
cathedral • *n* domkirke
catnip • *n* katteurt, almindelig katteurt
cattle • *n* kvæg *(n)*
catty • *adj* sladrende
cauliflower • *n* blomkål
caulk • *v* kalfatring
cause • *v* forårsage
caution • *v* advare • *n* advarsel, forsigtighed, varsomhed, sikkerhed, garanti, kaution
cautious • *adj* varsom, forsigtig
cavalcade • *n* kavalkade
cave • *n* hule
caveat • *n* advarsel
caviar • *n* kaviar
cedar • *n* ceder, cedertræ *(n)*
ceiling • *n* loft *(n)*
celebrate • *v* prise, højtideligholde, fejre, feste
celebration • *n* fest, fejring
celery • *n* selleri
celestial • *adj* himmelsk
cell • *n* celle
cellar • *n* kælder
cello • *n* cello
cellophane • *n* cellofan *(n)*
cellulose • *n* cellulose
cement • *v* cementere • *n* cement
census • *n* folketælling
centaur • *n* kentaur
centenary • *adj* hundredåret
centennial • *n* hundredårsdag
center • *n* midte, centrum
centipede • *n* skolopender
centrifuge • *v* centrifugere • *n* centrifuge
century • *n* århundred, århundrede *(n)*
cereal • *n* korn, kornsort
cerebellum • *n* lillehjerne
cerebral • *adj* cerebral

cerebrum • *n* storhjerne
ceremony • *n* ceremoni
cerium • *n* cerium
certain • *adj* sikker, sikkert *(n)*, sikre
chafe • *n* gnavesår *(n)*
chaffinch • *n* bogfinke
chain • *n* kæde
chain-smoker • *n* kæderyger
chair • *n* stol
chalice • *n* kalk
chalk • *n* kridt *(n)*
challenge • *v* udfordre
challenging • *adj* udfordrende
chameleon • *n* kamæleon
chamois • *n* gemse
champagne • *n* champagne
champion • *v* forsvare, forfægte • *n* mester, champion • *adj* mesterlig, førsteklasses
championship • *n* mesterskab *(n)*
chancellor • *n* kansler
chandelier • *n* lysekrone
change • *v* ændre, forandre, skifte, udskifte, ombytte • *n* ændring, forandring, småpenge, vekselpenge, ombytning, udskiftning, skift *(n)*, omklædning
changeling • *n* skifting
channel • *v* kanalisere • *n* kanal
chanterelle • *n* kantarel
chaos • *n* kaos *(n)*
chaotic • *adj* kaotisk
chapel • *n* kapel
character • *n* figur, rolle, person, karakter, træk, natur, fasthed, viljestyrke, personlighed, tegn
characteristic • *n* karakteristik • *adj* kendemærke *(n)*, karakteristikum *(n)*, karakteristikon *(n)*
charcoal • *n* trækul
charge • *n* læs *(n)*, anklage, angreb *(n)*, ladning
charm • *v* charmere • *n* charme, charm
chase • *v* jagte • *n* jagt, forfølgelse
chassis • *n* chassis *(n)*
chasuble • *n* messehagel
chat • *v* snakke, sludre, chatte
chattel • *n* løsøre
chatter • *n* plapre, sludre, snakke, skræppe, hakke, klapre
chauvinism • *n* chauvinisme
cheaply • *adv* billigt
cheat • *v* snyde, svindle, bedrage, være utro, undgå
check • *n* skak
checkmate • *interj* skakmat
cheek • *n* kind, balde, frækhed, uforskammethed

cheerful • *adj* fornøjet, munter, lys, venlig
cheers • *interj* skål
cheese • *n* ost • *interj* appelsin
cheesecake • *n* ostekage
cheetah • *n* gepard
chemical • *n* kemikalie *(n)* • *adj* kemisk
chemist • *n* kemiker
chemistry • *n* kemi, kemiske, egenskab
cheque • *n* check
cherry • *n* kirsebær *(n)*, kirsebærtræ *(n)*, kirsebærfarvet
cherub • *n* kerub
chervil • *n* kørvel
chess • *n* skak
chessboard • *n* skakbræt
chest • *n* kiste
chestnut • *n* kastanje, kastanjebrun • *adj* kastanjebrun
chew • *v* tygge, gumle
chick • *n* fugleunge, ungfugl, kylling, pigebarn, sild
chickadee • *n* mejse
chicken • *n* kylling, høne, bangebuks
chickpea • *n* kikært, kikærter
child • *n* barn *(n)*, børn
childhood • *n* barndom, barndomstid
childless • *adj* barnløs
chili • *n* chili
chill • *v* chille
chimera • *n* kimære
chimney • *n* skorsten, skorstenspibe
chimpanzee • *n* chimpanse
chin • *n* hage
china • *n* porcelæn
chinchilla • *n* chinchilla
chintz • *n* chintz
chip • *n* jeton *(n)*, pomme frite, pomfrit, chips, fransk kartoffel
chipmunk • *n* jordegern
chiromancy • *n* kiromanti
chloride • *n* klorid *(n)*
chlorine • *n* klor
chlorophyll • *n* klorofyl, bladgrønt *(n)*
chloroplast • *n* grønkorn
chocolate • *n* chokolade
choice • *n* valg *(n)*, elite, bedste, del • *adj* udsøgt
choir • *n* kor *(n)*
choke • *n* kvælertag, reduceret
choking • *n* kvælning
cholera • *n* kolera
choose • *v* vælge, udvælge, foretrække, kåre, have lyst, finde for godt
chopstick • *n* spisepind
chord • *n* akkord
chorea • *n* sanktvejtsdans
chromatographic • *adj* kromatografisk

chromatography • *n* kromatografi
chromium • *n* krom
chromosomal • *adj* kromosomal
chromosome • *n* kromosom
chuck • *v* kaste
church • *n* kirke
churchgoer • *n* kirkegænger
churn • *n* kjerne
chutney • *n* chutney
cider • *n* æblemost
cigar • *n* cigar
cigarette • *n* cigaret
cinema • *n* biograf, bio
cinnamon • *n* kanel
circa • *prep* cirka
circle • *v* omkredse, sætte ring om • *n* cirkel, kredsløb *(n)*, kreds, poser under øjnene
circular • *adj* rund, cirkulær
circumcise • *v* omskære
circumcision • *n* omskæring, omskærelse
circumference • *n* omkreds
circumspect • *adj* varsom, forsigtig
circumstance • *n* omstændighed, detalje, omstændighed, kår *(n)*
circumvent • *v* omgå, omringe
circus • *n* cirkus *(n)*
cirrhosis • *n* skrumpelever
citation • *n* citation, citering
citizen • *n* borger
citizenship • *n* borgerskab, statsborgerskab
citron • *n* cedrat
city • *n* by
civil • *adj* civil
civilization • *n* civilisation, kultur, civilisering
clairvoyance • *n* clairvoyance, klarsyn *(n)*, synskhed
clairvoyant • *adj* clairvoyant, synsk
clapperboard • *n* klaptræet
clarinet • *n* klarinet
claustrophobia • *n* klaustrofobi
clavicle • *n* kraveben *(n)*, nøgleben *(n)*
claw • *n* klo, klosaks • *v* kradse, rive, gribe, klo
clay • *n* ler *(n)*
clean • *v* rense • *adj* ren
cleanliness • *n* renlighed
clear • *v* bane, opklare, rense, gå fri af, klare op, gennemføre • *adj* klar, gennemsigtig, fri, tydelig, god
clearly • *adv* tydelig, evident, indlysende, klart
cleavage • *n* kløft, kavalergang
cleave • *v* kløve
clef • *n* nøgle

cleft • *n* revne
clerk • *n* kontorassistent *(m)*, kontorfunktionær *(m)*, ekspedient *(m)*, ekspeditrice *(m)*
clever • *adj* kvik, rask, snild, smart, klog
click • *n* klik *(n)*
clientele • *n* klientel *(n)*
cliff • *n* klint
climate • *n* klima
climatology • *n* klimatologi
clinic • *n* klinik
clip • *v* clipse, klipse
clitoris • *n* klitoris
clobber • *v* slå til plukfisk, hamre ned, sable ned, banke
clock • *n* ur *(n)*
clog • *n* træsko
cloister • *n* kloster
close • *v* lukke • *adj* nær
closet • *n* skab *(n)*
closure • *n* afslutning
cloth • *n* stof *(n)*, tøj *(n)*, klæde *(n)*
clothes • *n* tøj *(n)*
clothesbrush • *n* klædebørste
clothing • *n* tøj *(n)*
cloud • *n* sky
cloudberry • *n* multebær, multebær *(n)*
cloudburst • *n* skybrud *(n)*
cloudy • *adj* overskyet
clove • *n* kryddernellike, fed *(n)*
clover • *n* kløver
clown • *n* klovn
club • *n* klub, kløver
clue • *n* spor *(n)*, holdepunkt *(n)*, fingerpeg *(n)*, nøgle
cluster • *v* flokkes • *n* klynge, klase, sværm, serie
clutch • *n* kobling, koblingspedal
coach • *n* træner
coachman • *n* kusk
coal • *n* kul *(n)*
coast • *n* bred, kyst, strand
coaster • *n* rullebord
coastline • *n* kystlinje
coat • *n* frakke, lag *(n)*, pels, fjerdragt
cobalt • *n* kobolt
cobblestone • *n* brosten
cocaine • *n* kokain
cock • *n* kok, han
cock-a-doodle-doo • *interj* kykkeliky
cockchafer • *n* oldenborre
cockerel • *n* hanekylling
cockroach • *n* kakerlak
cockscomb • *n* hanekam
cocoa • *n* kakao, kakaopulver *(n)*, chokolade
coconut • *n* kokosnød, kokos

cocoon • *n* kokon
cod • *n* torsk *(m)*
code • *n* kodeks *(n)*, kodex *(n)*
coefficient • *n* koefficient
coercion • *n* tvang
coffee • *n* kaffe, kaffebønne, kaffebusk, kaffetræ *(n)*
coffin • *n* kiste, ligkiste
cogent • *adj* overbevisende, slagkraftig
cognac • *n* cognac
cognition • *n* kognition, erkendelse
cognitive • *adj* kognitiv
cohesion • *n* kohæsion, sammenhæng, sammenhold, kohæsionskraft, sammenhængsevne
coif • *n* Danish
coin • *n* mønt
coinsurance • *n* selvrisiko
coke • *n* koks
cola • *n* cola, kola
cold • *n* kulde, forkølelse • *adj* kold
cold-blooded • *adj* koldblodig
collar • *n* krave
colleague • *n* kollega
collect • *v* samle
collection • *n* samling, indsamling
collector • *n* samler
collie • *n* collie
colloquial • *adj* dagligsprog
colloquy • *n* kollokvium
cologne • *n* kølnervand *(n)*, eau de Cologne
colon • *n* kolon *(n)*
colonel • *n* oberst
colonial • *adj* kolonial
colonialism • *n* kolonialisme
colonist • *n* kolonist
colony • *n* koloni
color • *v* farve, male, få kulør, få farve, rødme • *n* farve, farvetone, kulør, hudfarve • *adj* farve-
colored • *n* farvet • *adj* farvet, kulørt
colorful • *adj* farverig, blomstrende
colostrum • *n* råmælk
coltsfoot • *n* følfod
columbine • *n* akeleje
column • *n* søjle
coma • *n* koma
comb • *v* rede
combat • *n* kamp, slag, slagsmål, træfning
combative • *adj* kamplysten, krigerisk
combine • *v* kombinere, forene
combustion • *n* forbrænding
come • *v* komme
comedy • *n* komedie
comestible • *adj* spiselige

comet • *n* komet
comfort • *n* behagelighed, bekvemmelighed, komfort, trøst
comma • *n* komma *(n)*
commemorative • *n* særfrimærke
commence • *v* begynde
comment • *v* kommentere • *n* kommentar
commerce • *n* handel
commercial • *n* reklame
commissioner • *n* kommissær
commit • *v* begå
committee • *n* komité, komite
common • *n* fælled • *adj* fælles, almindelig, vanlig, sædvanlig, fælleskøn
commune • *n* kommune
communication • *n* kommunikation
communism • *n* kommunisme
communist • *n* kommunist
commute • *v* pendle, kommutere
company • *n* virksomhed
compare • *v* sammenligne, bøje, stemme overens
compass • *n* kompas *(n)*
compassion • *n* medlidenhed
compete • *v* konkurrere
competency • *n* kompetence, kompetens
competition • *n* konkurrence
complexity • *n* indviklethed, kompleksitet
compliment • *v* komplimentere • *n* kompliment
component • *n* bestanddel, komponent
composer • *n* komponist
composition • *n* sammensætning, komposition, blanding, essay
compost • *v* kompostere • *n* kompost
compote • *n* kompot
comprehensive • *adj* fyldestgørende, omfattende
computer • *n* regnemaskine, computer, datamat
comrade • *n* kammerat
conceal • *v* skjule
concede • *v* medgive
conceive • *v* forstå
concept • *n* begreb *(n)*, koncept *(n)*
concern • *n* Bekymring
concert • *n* koncert
concertina • *n* koncertina
concise • *adj* koncis
concrete • *v* gøre, til, en, fast, masse, størkne, blive hård, blive konkret, konkretisere • *n* beton • *adj* konkret, beton
concubine • *n* konkubine
concupiscence • *n* begær
condemn • *v* fordømme

condescending • *adj* nedladende
condition • *n* bekostning *(n)*
conditioning • *n* betingning
condom • *n* kondom, præservativ
condominium • *n* ejerlejlighed
condor • *n* kondor
conductor • *n* dirigent
cone • *n* kogle
confection • *n* godbid
conference • *n* konference
confess • *v* bekende, tilstå, indrømme
confessional • *n* skriftestol
confetti • *n* konfetti *(n)*
confidently • *adv* sikkert
confirm • *v* bekræfte
confiscate • *v* konfiskere
conflict • *v* være i modstrid med, overlappe • *n* konflikt
conformity • *n* konformitet
confuse • *v* forvirre, forlegenhed, forveksle
confused • *adj* forvirret
confusion • *n* forvirring, forvirrelse
congeal • *v* stivne, koagulere
congenital • *adj* medfødt
congratulate • *v* gratulere
congratulations • *interj* tillykke
conical • *adj* konisk
conjunction • *n* bindeord
conjurer • *n* tryllekunstner
connected • *adj* sammenhængende
connection • *n* forbindelse
connotation • *n* konnotation, medbetydning, bibetydning
conquer • *v* erobre, besejre, sejre
consanguinity • *n* konsangvinitet
conscience • *n* samvittighed
conscientious • *adj* samvittighedsfuld, pligtopfyldende
conscientiousness • *n* samvittighedsfuldhed, pligtopfyldendehed
consciousness • *n* bevidsthed
conscription • *n* værnepligt
consecutive • *adj* fortløbende, sekventiel
consensus • *n* konsensus
consequence • *n* konsekvens
conservation • *n* bevaring
conservative • *n* konservativ • *adj* konservativ
conservator • *n* konservator
conservatory • *n* konservatorium *(n)*, musikkonservatorium *(n)*
consistency • *n* konsistens
consonant • *n* konsonant
consternation • *n* bestyrtelse
constipation • *n* forstoppelse
constituency • *n* valgkreds

constitution • *n* forfatning, grundlov
constrain • *v* begrænse
construct • *v* konstruere, bygge
consulate • *n* konsulat *(n)*
contact • *v* kontakte • *n* kontakt, forbindelse
contaminate • *v* forurene, kontaminere
contemporary • *adj* samtidig, moderne, nutids-
content • *n* indhold *(n)* • *adj* tilfreds • *v* stille tilfreds, tilfredsstille
contest • *n* konkurrence
contestant • *n* konkurrent
continent • *n* kontinent
continuity • *n* kontinuitet
contortionist • *n* slangemenneske *(n)*
contraception • *n* prævention
contribute • *v* bidrage
contributor • *n* bidragyder, bidragsyder
control • *v* styre, kontrollere
controversial • *adj* kontroversiel, omstridt
conundrum • *n* gåde, ordgåde, hovedbrud *(n)*
conversation • *n* konversation, samtale
convertible • *n* cabriolet
convex • *adj* konveks
cook • *n* kok
cookbook • *n* kogebog
cool • *adj* kølig, kold, Kølig, cool, koldblodig, ok, fint, rolig
cooperate • *v* samarbejde
cooperation • *n* samarbejde *(n)*
coordinate • *v* koordinere • *n* koordinat *(n)*
coordination • *n* koordination
copper • *n* kobber
copula • *n* kopula *(n)*
copy • *v* kopiere, efterligne • *n* kopi, eksemplar *(n)*
copyright • *n* ophavsret
coquet • *v* kokettere
coral • *n* koral
corduroy • *n* jernbanefløjl *(n)*, fløjl *(n)*
coriander • *n* koriander
corkscrew • *n* proptrækker
cormorant • *n* skarv, storskarv, ålekrage
corncrake • *n* engsnarre
cornea • *n* hornhinde
cornflower • *n* kornblomst
corollary • *n* korollar *(n)*
coronation • *n* kroning
corporal • *n* korporal
corpse • *n* lig *(n)*, kadaver *(n)*
correct • *adj* korrekt, rigtig
corruption • *n* korruption
corset • *n* korset *(n)*, snørliv *(n)*

corvette • *n* korvet
cosmetologist • *n* kosmetiker
cosmology • *n* kosmologi
cosmopolite • *n* verdensborger
cosmos • *n* kosmos
cosy • *adj* hyggelig
cotton • *n* bomuld • *adj* bomuld
couch • *v* lægge, affatte, udtrykke • *n* sofa, briks, leje
cougar • *n* puma
cough • *v* hoste • *n* hoste
council • *n* råd *(n)*
count • *v* tælle • *n* tælling, optælling, nedtælling, greve
countenance • *v* billige, støtte, tolerere • *n* ansigt *(n)*, mine
counter • *n* jeton, brik, disk, skranke, tæller, optæller, køkkenbord *(n)*
countess • *n* grevinde
countless • *adj* utallig, talløs
country • *n* land *(n)*
county • *n* amt *(n)*
couple • *n* par *(n)*
courage • *n* mod *(n)*, tapperhed
courageous • *adj* modig
courier • *n* kurer
course • *v* rulle, jage • *n* forløb *(n)*, gang, rute, bane, kursus *(n)*, ret, kurs, undersejl *(n)*, skifte *(n)*, løb *(n)*
court • *n* domstol
courthouse • *n* retsbygning
courtyard • *n* gårdsplads
cousin • *n* fætter, kusine
covenant • *n* pagt
cover • *v* dække
cow • *n* ko, hun
coward • *n* bangebuks
cowardice • *n* fejhed
cowboy • *n* cowboy
coyote • *n* prærieulv
cozy • *adj* hyggelig
crab • *n* krabbe
crack • *n* sprække
cradle • *n* vugge
craft • *v* håndlavet, bygge, konstrukere • *n* håndværk *(n)*, fartøj *(n)*, håndværker
cranberry • *n* tranebær, tranebær *(n)*
crane • *n* trane, kran
crankcase • *n* krumtaphus
crankshaft • *n* drivaksel
cranky • *adj* gnaven
crash • *v* crashe, overnatte • *n* sammenstød *(n)*, flystyrt *(n)*, crash *(n)*, nedbrud *(n)*, krash, brag *(n)* • *adj* forceret, lyn-
crawl • *v* kravle, krybe • *n* crawl
crayfish • *n* krebs
crazy • *adj* skør

creak • *n* knagen, knirken
cream • *v* purere, røre, creme • *n* fløde,
creme • *adj* cremefarvet
create • *v* skabe, kreere
creature • *n* væsen, væsener
creep • *v* krybe, liste
crematorium • *n* krematorium *(n)*, krematorie *(n)*
crescent • *n* halvmåne, horn *(n)*
crime • *n* forbrydelse, kriminalitet
criminal • *n* kriminel, forbryder
criminology • *n* kriminologi
crippled • *adj* forkrøblet
crisis • *n* vendepunkt *(n)*, krise, krisetilstand
criterion • *n* kriterium *(n)*
critic • *n* kritiker
criticism • *n* kritik, dadel
croak • *n* kvæk *(n)*
crocodile • *n* krokodille
crop • *n* afgrøde
cross • *n* kryds *(n)*
crossbill • *n* korsnæb
crossbow • *n* armbrøst
crossroads • *n* vejkryds *(n)*
crotch • *n* skridt *(n)*
crotchet • *n* fjerdedelsnode
crow • *n* krage
crowbar • *n* koben *(n)*, brækjern *(n)*
crowberry • *n* revling, almindelig revling
crown • *n* krone, isse
crucial • *adj* afgørende
crucible • *n* smeltedigel, ildprøve
crucifix • *n* krucifiks
cruel • *adj* grusom
crumb • *n* krumme
crumble • *v* forvitre, smuldre, hensmuldre
cry • *v* græde, råbe, skrige, udbryde, bekendtgøre • *n* gråd, klage, råb, skrig, udbrud *(n)*, udråb *(n)*
cryptography • *n* kryptografi
crystallize • *v* krystallisere, kandisere
cube • *n* kubus
cubism • *n* kubismen
cuckold • *n* hanrej
cuckoo • *n* gøg
cucumber • *n* agurk
cuddle • *v* kæle, knuse, putte
cuff • *n* manchet
cufflink • *n* manchetknap
cuisine • *n* køkken *(n)*

culinary • *adj* kulinarisk
cult • *n* kult, sekt
cultivate • *v* dyrke, pleje
cultural • *adj* kulturel
culture • *n* kultur
cumin • *n* spidskommen
cunt • *n* kusse, fisse
cup • *n* kop, pokal, cup, skål
cur • *n* køter, sjover
curfew • *n* udgangsforbud *(n)*, spærretid
curiosity • *n* nysgerrighed
curious • *adj* nysgerrig, besynderlig, mærkværdig, kuriøs
curium • *n* curium *(n)*
currant • *n* solbær
currency • *n* valuta
current • *adj* aktuel, nuværende
currently • *adv* i øjeblikket
curse • *n* forbandelse
curtail • *v* forkorte, begrænse
curtain • *n* gardin *(n)*, tæppe *(n)*
curve • *n* kurve, kurver
cushion • *v* polstre, afbøde • *n* pude, hynde, bande
cusk • *n* brosme
custom • *n* skik, sædvane
customer • *n* kunde
customs • *n* told
cut • *v* skære, snitte, udskære, udelukke, snyde, beskære, nedsætte, slibe, tilskære, tilhugge, krydse, pjække • *n* snitsår *(n)*, skramme, hug *(n)*, snit *(n)*, aftagning, mode, nedsættelse, udskæring, stykke *(n)* • *adj* skære, slebet
cute • *adj* nuttet, sød
cutlery • *n* bestik
cuttlefish • *n* blæksprutte
cyanide • *n* cyanid
cycle • *v* cykle, køre på cykel, tænde for, slå til, slukke for, slå fra • *n* cyklus, kredsløb, (vaske)-program
cycling • *n* cykle *(n)*
cyclist • *n* cyklist
cyclone • *n* orkan
cylinder • *n* cylinder
cylindrical • *adj* cylindrisk
cynic • *n* kyniker
cynical • *adj* kynisk
cynicism • *n* kynisme
cyst • *n* cyste
cysteine • *n* cystein

D

dacha • *n* datja
daffodil • *n* påskelilje
dagger • *n* dolk
daikon • *n* Kinaradisen, Japan-Ræddike
daily • *adj* daglig • *adv* dagligt
dairy • *n* mejeri *(n)*, mejeriprodukt *(n)*
daisy • *n* tusindfryd
dale • *n* dal
dam • *n* dæmning
damage • *v* beskadige, skade, tilføje • *n* skade, beskadigelse
damask • *n* damask *(n)*
damn • *v* fordømt • *adv* pokkers, hulens, forbandet • *interj* pokkers, sørens, hulens
damp • *adj* fugtig
damsel • *n* ungmo
dance • *v* danse • *n* dans
dancer • *n* danser, danserinde
dandelion • *n* mælkebøtte, løvetand • *adj* mælkebøtte, løvetand
dandruff • *n* skæl *(n)*
danger • *n* fare
dangerous • *adj* farlig
danish • *n* wienerbrød
dark • *n* mørke, uvidenhed, skumring • *adj* mørk, dunkel, hemmelighedsfuld, skummel, mørke-
dark-haired • *adj* mørkhåret
darkness • *n* mørke
darling • *n* elskede
data • *n* data
database • *n* databank, database
date • *n* daddel, datering, tidspunkt *(n)*, dato, stævnemøde *(n)*, date, ledsager, rendezvous *(n)* • *v* datere, tidsbestemme, tidsfæste, gå ud med, komme sammen med
dated • *adj* dateret, forældet, ugyldig, anakronistisk, umoderne, udgået
dauber • *n* klatmaler
daughter • *n* datter
daughter-in-law • *n* svigerdatter
davit • *n* david
dawn • *v* daggry • *n* daggry *(n)*, solopgang
day • *n* døgn *(n)*, dag
deacon • *n* diakon
dead • *n* døde • *adj* død • *adv* lige, direkte, død
deaf • *adj* døv
dear • *adj* kære, dyrebar, dyr
death • *n* død, Døden
debate • *n* debat
debt • *n* gæld, skyldighed
debut • *n* debut
decade • *n* årti, dekade
decant • *v* dekantere

decapitate • *v* halshugge
decapitation • *n* halshugning
decathlon • *n* tikamp
deceive • *v* bedrage
decide • *v* afgøre, beslutte
deciduous • *adj* løvfældende
decimal • *n* decimal
decision • *n* beslutning, beslutsomhed, afgørelse
decisive • *adj* afgørende, beslutsom
deck • *n* dæk *(n)*
deed • *n* dåd
deep • *n* dyb *(n)* • *adj* dyb, dybsindig, dybttænkende, bred, mørk • *adv* dybt
deer • *n* hjort
default • *n* standard
defeat • *v* besejre, overvinde • *n* usejr, tab *(n)*
defecate • *v* defækere
defend • *v* forsvare
defender • *n* forsvar, forsvarer
defense • *n* forsvar
deference • *n* ærbødighed
defiant • *adj* trodsig
deficiency • *n* mangel, utilstrækkelighed
definition • *n* definition, opløsningsevne, opløsning, gengivelse
definitive • *n* dagligmærke
degree • *n* grad, valens
deism • *n* deisme
dejection • *n* modløshed, nedtrykthed
deliberate • *v* overveje • *adj* bevidst, overlagt, velovervejet, gennemtænkt, langsom, sindig, rolig
deliberately • *adv* bevidst, med vilje, langsomt, roligt, sindigt
deliberation • *n* overvejelse, drøftelse, rådslagning
delicious • *adj* delikat, liflig, lækker, yndig, herlig, velsmagende, smagfuld
deliver • *v* befri, udfri, barsle, nedkomme, forløse, tage imod, levere, aflevere, indlevere, overlevere, overbringe, udbringe, ombære, omdele, udlevere, overgive, holde
delta • *n* delta, delta *(n)*
deluge • *n* overflod
delusion • *n* indbildning, vrangforestilling
delve • *v* grave, dykke ned i
demand • *v* kræve • *n* efterspørgsel, krav
demarcation • *n* grænsedragning, afgrænsning, demarkationslinje, faggrænse, grænse
demeanor • *n* opførsel, optræden
dementia • *n* demens
demijohn • *n* vinballong

democracy • *n* demokrati, demokrati *(n)*
demon • *n* dæmon
demonstrate • *v* demonstrere
demonstration • *n* demonstration
demoralize • *v* demoralisere
den • *n* hule, værelse *(n)*, hybel, hummer *(n)*
denominator • *n* nævner
denounce • *v* bekendtgøre, beskylde, anklage, opsige
dense • *adj* kompakt, tæt
dentist • *n* tandlæge
deoxyribose • *n* deoxyribose
departure • *n* afgang, afvigelse, død, bortgang
depend • *v* afhænge
depiction • *n* afbildning
depleted • *adj* udtømme, formindske, reducere
derive • *v* udlede, opstå
derogatory • *adj* nedsættende
describe • *v* beskrive
description • *n* beskrivelse
desecrate • *v* vanhellige
desert • *n* fortjeneste, ørken
deserve • *v* fortjene
designation • *n* betegnelse, benævnelse
desire • *v* ønske, begære, attrå • *n* ønske, begær, lyst
desk • *n* skrivebord *(n)*
despite • *prep* på trods af
despondency • *n* modløshed
despondent • *adj* knuget, forknyt
despotic • *adj* despotisk
despotism • *n* despoti
dessert • *n* dessert
destiny • *n* skæbne
destroy • *v* ødelægge, aflive
destruction • *n* ødelæggelse
detached • *adj* fritstående
detail • *n* detalje, detaljer
detergent • *n* vaskemiddel *(n)*
determination • *n* opsigelse
detonation • *n* brag, eksplosion, knald
detour • *n* omvej
detrimental • *adj* skadelig
develop • *v* udvikle
developer • *n* udvikler, programmør
development • *n* udvikling, udbygning, udvidelse
deviate • *v* deviere
deviation • *n* afvigelse
devil • *n* djævel, djævlen, fanden, satan
devise • *v* opfinde, udtænke, finde på, udarbejde, testamentere
devour • *v* grovæde
devout • *adj* from

dew • *n* dug
dewberry • *n* korbær *(n)*
dexterity • *n* fingerfærdighed
dextrose • *n* druesukker
diabetic • *n* diabetiker
dialect • *n* dialekt
dialogue • *n* dialog, samtale, konversation
diamond • *n* diamant, ruder
diaper • *n* ble
diarrhea • *n* diare, diaré, diarre, diarré
diary • *n* dagbog
dibs • *n* helle for
dick • *n* pik, gren, dolk, diller, kødfløjte
dictatorship • *n* diktatur *(n)*
dictionary • *n* ordbog
didactic • *adj* didaktisk, belærende, docerende
die • *v* dø, udånde, opgive, ophøre • *n* terning
diencephalon • *n* mellemhjernen
diesel • *n* diesel
difference • *n* forskel, differens
different • *adj* forskellig, anderledes, ulig
differentiable • *adj* differentiabel
differentiation • *n* differentiering
difficult • *adj* vanskelig
difficulty • *n* sværhed, vanskelighed, besvær *(n)*
dig • *v* grave, kunne, lide, forstå, være med • *n* udgravning
digest • *v* fordøje
digit • *n* ciffer, nummer
dignified • *adj* værdig
dignity • *n* værdighed
dike • *n* dige *(n)*
dildo • *n* dildo, vibrator
diligent • *adj* flittig, ihærdig, arbejdsom
dill • *n* dild
dimension • *n* dimension, side, aspekt *(n)*
diminutive • *n* diminutiv *(n)* • *adj* diminutiv
dine • *v* spise
dinghy • *n* jolle
dinner • *n* middag, aftenmad
diocese • *n* stift *(n)*
diode • *n* diode
diphtheria • *n* difteri, difteritis
diphthong • *n* diftong, tvelyd
diploma • *n* diplom *(n)*
diplomacy • *n* diplomati *(n)*
diplomat • *n* diplomat
dire • *adj* ildevarslende, ondskabsfuld, skrækkelig
direct • *v* dirigere, lede, rette
direction • *n* retning

dirty • *adj* beskidt, uren, grumset
disappear • *v* forsvinde, få til at forsvinde
disaster • *n* katastrofe
disband • *v* afskaffe, nedlægge
discoloration • *n* misfarvning
discount • *n* rabat
discover • *v* opdage
discovery • *n* opdagelse
discuss • *v* diskutere
discussion • *n* diskussion
disdain • *n* despekt, foragt
disease • *n* sygdom
disgust • *v* fremkalde, væmmelse • *n* afsky, væmmelse
dish • *n* tallerken
dishwasher • *n* oppvaskemaskine
disintegrate • *v* opløse, desintegrere
disk • *n* skive
disorder • *n* uorden, forstyrrelse
disparaging • *adj* nedsættende
dispel • *v* henvejre
dissect • *v* dissekere
distance • *n* afstand
distant • *adj* fjern
distortion • *n* fordrejelse, forvridning, forvrængning, distortion
distress • *n* ubehag (*n*), nødsituation
district • *n* distrikt (*n*)
disturbance • *n* forstyrrelse
diver • *n* dykker, lom
diversity • *n* diversitet
dividend • *n* udbytte (*n*)
divine • *adj* guddommelig
divisible • *adj* delelig
do • *v* gøre, udføre, gå an, klare sig, være nok
do-it-yourself • *adj* gør-det-selv
dobra • *n* dobra
doctor • *v* doktorere, forfalske • *n* læge, doktor
document • *n* dokument (*n*)
documentary • *n* dokumentarfilm
documentation • *n* dokumentation
dodecahedron • *n* dodekaeder
dodo • *n* dronte
doe • *n* hind, då, rå
dog • *n* hund
doge • *n* doge
dogma • *n* dogme (*n*)
dogsled • *n* hundeslæde
dogwood • *n* kornel
doldrums • *n* kalmebælte (*n*)
doll • *n* dukke
dollar • *n* dollar
dolor • *n* smerte
dolphin • *n* delfin, duc d'albe
dome • *n* kuppel

donkey • *n* æsel (*n*)
door • *n* dør, låge
doorbell • *n* dørklokke
doormat • *n* dørmåtte
dopamine • *n* dopamin
dormouse • *n* syvsover, hasselmus
double-edged • *adj* tveægget
doublet • *n* vams, dublet
doubt • *v* tvivle • *n* tvivl
doubtful • *adj* tvivlende, usikker, tvivlsom
dough • *n* dej
doughnut • *n* donut, munkering, berliner
dove • *n* due, handue, hundue
down • *n* højdedrag, bane, dun • *v* sluge, hælde ned, tabe, lade falde • *adj* langt nede, nede, deprimeret, lav, nedadgående, aftagende • *adv* ned, nedad, nede • *prep* ned ad, hen ad
dozen • *n* dusin (*n*)
draft • *n* kladde
dragon • *n* drage, lindorm
dragonfly • *n* guldsmed
drain • *v* bortlede, dræne, udtørre, tømme, tappe • *n* dræn, rende, afløb, spild
drake • *n* andrik
dramaturgic • *adj* dramaturgisk
draughts • *n* dam
draw • *v* tegne, trække, trække for • *n* remis, lodtrækning
drawbridge • *n* vindebro
drawer • *n* skuffe, tegner
dreadfully • *adv* forfærdelig, frygtelig, skrækkelig
dream • *v* drømme • *n* drøm
dress • *v* beklæde, klæde, afrette, afpudse, behandle, ordne, pudse, tilhøvle, tilhugge • *n* kjole, beklædning, påklædning, dragt
dressmaker • *n* syerske
drill • *v* bore • *n* bor (*n*), dril
drink • *v* drikke • *n* drink, tår, alkohol, spiritus
drip • *v* dryppe
drive • *v* køre, drive
driver • *n* chauffør
driving • *n* kørsel
dromedary • *n* dromedar
drool • *v* savle • *n* savl (*n*)
drop • *v* falde
drought • *n* tørke
drug • *n* stof (*n*)
drum • *v* tromme, banke • *n* tromme, tromle, tønde
drunk • *adj* fuld
drunken • *adj* beruset, fuld

drunkenness • *n* fuldskab
dry • *adj* tør
dryer • *n* tørretumbler
dual • *n* dualis
dubious • *adj* tvivlsom, usikker, tvivlende, tvivlrådig
duchess • *n* hertuginde
duchy • *n* hertugdømme
duck • *v* dukke, dykke, smyge, uden om, undvige • *n* and
duckling • *n* ælling
duckweed • *n* andemad
duct • *n* kanal
ductile • *adj* stækbar, smidig, sej, føjelig
dude • *n* fyr, starut, fætter
duel • *v* duellere • *n* duel, tvekamp
duke • *n* hertug
dulcimer • *n* hakkebræt
dull • *adj* sløv, kedelig, mat, dum
duma • *n* dumaen
dumb • *adj* dum, åndssvag, fordummende
dumbfounded • *adj* målløs
dune • *n* klit
dung • *n* gødning, møg
dungeon • *n* fangekælder
duodenum • *n* tolvfingertarm
durian • *n* durian *(n)*
during • *prep* i, gennem, i løbet af, under
dusk • *n* skumring
dust • *n* støv *(n)*
dustpan • *n* fejebakke
duty • *n* pligt, tjeneste, told
dwarf • *n* dværg
dwell • *v* leve, forblive, bebo, bo, dvæle
dye • *v* farve
dyke • *n* lebbe
dynamite • *n* dynamit
dynasty • *n* dynasti *(n)*
dyslexia • *n* ordblindhed
dysprosium • *n* dysprosium *(n)*

E

eagle • *n* ørn, eagle
ear • *n* øre *(n)*, aks *(n)*
earache • *n* ørepine
earl • *n* greve *(m)*, jarl
early • *adj* tidlig
earring • *n* ørering
earth • *v* jordforbinde, jorde, begrave • *n* jord, jordart, jordforbindelse, jordet forbindelse, rævegrav
earthquake • *n* jordskælv *(n)*
earthworm • *n* regnorm
earwig • *n* ørentvist
easel • *n* staffeli *(n)*
easement • *n* servitut
easiness • *n* lethed, enkelhed
east • *n* øst
easy • *adj* let, nem, let på tråden
eat • *v* spise, æde, plage, fortære
ebb • *n* ebbe
ebony • *n* ibenholt
ecclesiology • *n* ekklesiologi, ecclesiologi
echidna • *n* myrepindsvin
echo • *n* ekko
eclectic • *n* eklektiker • *adj* eklektisk
ecliptic • *n* ekliptika
ecological • *adj* økologisk
ecology • *n* økologi
econometrics • *n* økonometri
economics • *n* økonomi
economy • *n* økonomi, husholdning
ectoplasm • *n* ektoplasma
ecumenical • *adj* økumenisk
ecumenism • *n* økumeni
eczema • *n* eksem *(n)*
edge • *n* rand, kant
edible • *adj* spiselig
edit • *v* redigere
education • *n* uddannelse
eel • *n* ål, ålefisk
eelgrass • *n* Almindelig Bændeltang
efflorescence • *n* forvitring
egg • *n* æg *(n)* • *v* ægge
eggnog • *n* æggelikør
eggplant • *n* aubergine
eggshell • *n* æggeskal
eider • *n* edderfugl
eiderdown • *n* ederdun, ederdunsdyne
eidetic • *adj* eidetisk
eight • *n* ottetal *(n)*, otter
eighteenth • *n* attener, attendedel • *adj* attende
eighth • *adj* ottende
eightieth • *adj* firsindstyvende
einsteinium • *n* einsteinium
ejaculation • *n* udløsning, ejakulation
elaborate • *adj* detaljeret
elbow • *v* albue • *n* albue
elder • *n* hyld, hyldetræ *(n)*
elderberry • *n* hyldebær *(n)*
elect • *v* vælge
election • *n* valg *(n)*
electrician • *n* elektriker

electricity • *n* elektricitet, el
electromagnetic • *adj* elektromagnetisk
electromagnetism • *n* elektromagnetisme
electron • *n* elektron
electronics • *n* elektronik
elegant • *adj* elegant
elegy • *n* elegi, klagesang, sørgedigt *(n)*
element • *n* element *(n)*, grundstof *(n)*, elementer
elementary • *adj* elementær, folkeskole-, elementar-
elephant • *n* elefant
eleventh • *n* ellevtedel • *adj* ellevte
elixir • *n* eliksir
ell • *n* alen
elm • *n* elm, elmetræ *(n)*
else • *adv* ellers
elsewhere • *adv* andetsteds
elucidate • *v* uddybe
embassy • *n* ambassade
embed • *v* indlejre i
ember • *n* glød
embodiment • *n* legemliggørelse
embolism • *n* emboli
emerald • *n* smaragd
emigrate • *v* emigrere, udvandre
emission • *n* emission
emmer • *n* emmer
emotion • *n* følelse
empathy • *n* empati
emperor • *n* kejser, Keiseren
empire • *n* imperium *(n)*, kejserrige *(n)*, kejserdømme *(n)*
empirical • *adj* empirisk
employ • *v* ansætte
employee • *n* ansat
employer • *n* arbejdsgiver
emporium • *n* varehus *(n)*
empress • *n* kejserinde, enkekejserinde
emptiness • *n* tomhed
empty • *v* tømme • *adj* tom
emu • *n* emu
enamel • *n* emalje
encourage • *v* opmuntre, anbefale
encroach • *v* krænke
encyclopedia • *n* encyklopædi, leksikon *(n)*
end • *n* ende, afslutning
endogamy • *n* endogami, indgifte *(n)*
endoscopy • *n* endoskopi
endurance • *n* udholdenhed
enemy • *n* fjende • *adj* fjendtlig
energy • *n* energi
engaged • *adj* forlovet, optaget
engine • *n* motor
engineer • *n* ingeniør
engobe • *n* engobe

enjoin • *v* påbyde, pålægge
enjoy • *v* nyde
enter • *v* gå ind, gå ind i, indgå i, indtaste
enterprise • *n* virksomhed, foretagende, bedrift, foretagsomhed, initiativ
entertainment • *n* underholdning
enthusiast • *n* entusiast, sværmer
entomologist • *n* entomolog
entomology • *n* entomologi, insektlære
entrance • *n* indgang
envelope • *n* kuvert, konvolut
envious • *adj* misundelig
environment • *n* miljø *(n)*, omgivelser
envy • *n* misundelse
enzyme • *n* enzym
epic • *adj* episk, storslået
epicycle • *n* epicykel
epilepsy • *n* epilepsi
epileptic • *n* epileptiker • *adj* epileptisk
episode • *n* afsnit
epithelium • *n* epitel
epitome • *n* indbegrebet
equality • *n* lighed
equation • *n* ligning
equator • *n* ækvator
equilibrium • *n* ligevægt, sindsligevægt
equinox • *n* jævndøgn
equipment • *n* udstyr *(n)*
equity • *n* aktie, billighedsret, friværdi, egenkapital, rimelighed, retfærdighed
equivalent • *n* ækvivalent *(n)*
era • *n* æra
erase • *v* slette, viske, fjerne
eraser • *n* viskelæder *(n)*
erbium • *n* erbium
erection • *n* erektion, rejsning
ermine • *n* hermelin, lækat
erotic • *adj* erotisk
eroticism • *n* erotik
err • *v* fejle
errand • *n* ærinde *(n)*
error • *n* fejl, fejltagelse, forseelse, afvigelse
esoteric • *adj* esoterisk
espionage • *n* spionage
espresso • *n* espresso
essay • *v* prøve, forsøge
essence • *n* essens, koncentrat *(n)*
establishment • *n* etablering, oprettelse
estimate • *v* estimere • *n* estimat
eternity • *n* evighed
ethics • *n* etik
ethnic • *adj* etnisk, hedning, eksotisk, fremmed
ethology • *n* etologi
etiquette • *n* etikette *(f)*
etymology • *n* etymologi

euphemism • *n* eufemisme
euphoria • *n* eufori
euphoric • *adj* euforisk
eureka • *interj* heureka
europium • *n* europium
euthanasia • *n* dødshjælp
evacuate • *v* evakuere
evaporate • *v* fordampe
evaporation • *n* fordampning, inddampning
even • *adj* jævn
evening • *n* aften
event • *n* begivenhed, hændelse
evergreen • *adj* stedsegrøn
everyone • *pron* alle
everything • *pron* alt
everywhere • *adv* overalt
evidence • *v* vidne, godtgøre, bevise • *n* bevis *(n)*, vidneudsagn *(n)*
evident • *adj* indlysende
evil • *n* ond, ondskab • *adj* ond, slem, slet, dårlig, skadelig, umoralsk
evoke • *v* fremmane, fremkalde, vække
evolution • *n* udvikling, evolution
ewe • *n* moderfår
exactly • *adv* præcis
exaggerate • *v* overdrive
examination • *n* eksamen
example • *n* eksempel
excavator • *n* gravemaskine, gravko
exceed • *v* overskride, overgå
exception • *n* undtagelse
exceptionally • *adv* undtagelsesvis
excited • *adj* spændt, ophidset, eksalteret
exciting • *adj* spændende
exclude • *v* eksludere
excoriate • *v* skælde ud, hudflette
execute • *v* afvikle, udføre, eksekvere, starte, påbegynde
execution • *n* henrettelse
executioner • *n* bøddel
exempt • *n* fritaget
exhausted • *adj* udkørt, udmattet, opbrugt, udtømt

exhibitionist • *n* ekshibitionist
exist • *v* eksistere
existence • *n* eksistens
exit • *n* udgang, udvej
exorbitant • *adj* eksorbitant
expanse • *n* vidde
expatriate • *v* forvise, udvandre • *n* udvandrer, udvist • *adj* udvandrer
expensive • *adj* dyr
experience • *v* opleve, erfare • *n* oplevelse, erfaring, rutine, øvelse
expire • *v* udløbe
explanation • *n* forklaring
explicit • *adj* tydelig, bestemt, udstrykkelig, eksplicit
explode • *v* sprænge, afsløre, forkaste, eksplodere, springe
exploit • *v* udnytte
explore • *v* udforske, undersøge, opdagelsesrejse, eksplorere
exponent • *n* eksponent, potenseksponent
express • *v* udtrykke
expression • *n* udtryk *(n)*
extension • *n* forlængelse
extensive • *adj* ekstensiv
exterminate • *v* udrydde
extinct • *adj* uddød
extinction • *n* uddøen, tilintetgørelse, udslettelse
extinguish • *v* slukke, udslukke, udrydde
extortion • *n* afpresning
extra • *adj* ekstra
extraordinary • *adj* ekstraordinær
extreme • *adj* ekstrem
eye • *n* øje *(n)*, nåleøje
eyeball • *n* øjeæble *(n)*
eyebrow • *n* øjenbryn *(n)*
eyelash • *n* øjenvippe
eyelid • *n* øjelåg *(n)*, øjenlåg *(n)*
eyesight • *n* syn *(n)*

F

fable • *v* fable, fabulere • *n* fabel
fabric • *n* struktur, system *(n)*, stof *(n)*, sammensætning
fabulous • *adj* fabelagtig, fantastisk
fabulously • *adv* fabelagtig
face • *v* vende, mod, være, vendt, konfrontere, se i øjnene, trodse • *n* ansigt *(n)*, ansigtsudtryk *(n)*, facade, flade, yderside,

kæft
facet • *v* facettere • *n* facet, flade, side
facilitate • *v* facilitere
fact • *n* kendsgerning, faktum, virkelighed
factor • *v* faktorisere • *n* agent, faktor
factory • *n* fabrik, fabriksbygning, virksomhed, anlæg *(n)*

factotum • *n* altmuligmand, faktotum *(n)*
fade • *v* falme
faience • *n* fajance
fail • *v* dumpe, fejle, mislykkes, slå fejl, forsømme, undlade, svigte
fail-safe • *adj* vandtæt
failure • *n* fiasko, nedbrud *(n)*, svigt *(n)*
faint • *v* besvime • *n* besvimelse
fair • *adj* smuk, lys, blond, retfærdig, rimelig • *n* marked *(n)*
fairy • *n* fe, alf, bøsse
faith • *n* tro
fakir • *n* fakir
falcon • *n* falk
fall • *v* falde, kaste sig, blive • *n* fald *(n)*
fallacy • *n* fejlslutning
false • *adj* falsk, kunstig
fame • *n* berømmelse
familiar • *adj* bekendt
family • *n* familie, æt, familie-
famine • *n* hungersnød
famished • *adj* udhungret
fan • *v* vifte, spredes i vifteform • *n* vifte, ventilator
fang • *n* hugtand
fantastic • *adj* fantastisk
far • *adj* langt borte, fjern
fare • *n* billetpris, kunde
farewell • *n* farvel *(n)* • *interj* farvel
farm • *v* drive landbrug, dyrke • *n* gård
farmer • *n* landmand, bonde
farrier • *n* beslagsmed
farrow • *v* få grise, fare
fart • *v* fjærte, prutte, fise • *n* fjært, prut, fis
fascinating • *adj* fascinerende, betagende, fængslende
fascism • *n* fascisme
fascist • *n* fascist
fast • *adj* fast, dyb, farvefast, hurtig • *adv* foran, fast, dybt • *v* faste
fat • *v* opfede • *n* fedt *(n)* • *adj* fed
fate • *n* skæbne
father • *v* være far for • *n* far, fader
father-in-law • *n* svigerfar
fatherland • *n* fædreland *(n)*
fathom • *v* begribe, fatte • *n* favn
fathomable • *adj* begribelig
fatigue • *n* udmatning
faultless • *adj* fejlfri
favor • *n* god vilje
fawn • *n* kalv, roe, lam, dådyr • *adj* lysebrun, dådyrfarvet • *v* logre, sleske
faze • *v* skræmme
fealty • *n* troskab, lensed
fear • *n* angst, frygt
feasible • *adj* mulig

feast • *n* festmåltid *(n)*
feat • *n* præstation
feather • *n* fjer
feature • *n* feature, træk *(n)*, ansigtstræk *(n)*
febrile • *adj* febersyg, febril
feces • *n* afføring
feckless • *adj* hjælpeløs, initiativløs, uduelig
federation • *n* føderation
fee • *n* gebyr *(n)*
feed • *v* fodre, indføre • *n* foder *(n)*
feel • *v* føle, mærke
feeler • *n* følehorn *(n)*, føletråd, føler, prøveballon
feeling • *n* følelse
feign • *v* simulere
fellatio • *n* fellatio
felon • *n* forbryder
felt • *v* filte • *n* filt *(n)*, filthat
female • *n* kvinde • *adj* hun-, hunlig, kvindelig
feminine • *n* femininum *(m)* • *adj* kvindelig, kvinde, feminin, hunkøn
feminism • *n* feminisme
fencing • *n* fægtning
fender • *n* fender
fennel • *n* fennikel
fenugreek • *n* bukkehorn
ferment • *v* gære, fermentere
fermentation • *n* fermentering, gæring
fermium • *n* fermium
fern • *n* bregne
ferret • *n* fritte
ferry • *n* færge
fertile • *adj* frugtbar
fertility • *n* frugtbarhed, fertilitet
fertilizer • *n* gødning, kunstgødning
festival • *n* festival
festive • *adj* festlig
festoon • *n* guirlande, lyskæde
fetch • *v* hente
fetus • *n* foster *(n)*
fever • *n* feber
fiasco • *n* fiasko
fickle • *adj* lunefuld, vankelmodig, vægelsindet
fiction • *n* fiktion, skønlitteratur, fantasi, opspind
fictional • *adj* opdigtet
fiddle • *n* violin
fiddler • *n* spillemand
field • *n* felt, mark, ager, felt *(n)*, område, legeme *(n)*, bane, spilleplads
fieldfare • *n* sjagger
fiend • *n* djævel, dæmon, entusiast
fierce • *adj* voldeligt, aktivt, truende

fife • *n* marchfløjte
fifteenth • *adj* femtende
fifth • *n* femte • *adj* femte
fifties • *n* halvtredserne
fiftieth • *n* den halvtredsindstyvende, nr. halvtreds, halvtredsindstyvendedel • *adj* halvtredsindstyvende
fifty • *n* halvtredser
fig • *n* figentræ *(n)*, figen
fight • *v* slås, kæmpe, udkæmpe, bekæmpe • *n* kamp, slag, slagsmål, ballade
fighter • *n* kriger, kampfly *(n)*
figure • *v* beregne, slutte • *n* figur, skikkelse, ciffer, tal
file • *v* arkivere • *n* arkivalie *(n)*, fil, kø
filibuster • *n* fribytter
filigree • *n* filigran *(n)*
film • *v* filme • *n* film
fin • *n* finne, halefinne
final • *n* finale • *adj* endelig, endegyldig
finale • *n* finale
finance • *v* finansiere
financial • *adj* finansiel
finch • *n* finke
find • *v* finde, træffe, udpege, dømme • *n* fund
finger • *v* udpege, pege, fingerere, famle, fingersætning • *n* finger, tå
fingerboard • *n* gribebræt *(n)*
fingernail • *n* negl, fingernegl
fingerprint • *n* fingeraftryk *(n)*, digitalt fingeraftryk
fingertip • *n* fingerspids
finish • *n* slutning, finish
fir • *n* ædelgran
fire • *v* opvarme, fyre, afskedige, fritstille, affyre • *n* ild, bål *(n)*, brand, ovn *(m)*, ildsted *(n)*
firearm • *n* ildvåben *(n)*, skydevåben *(n)*
fireball • *n* ildkugle, kuglelyn *(n)*, meteor
firefly • *n* ildflue
firewall • *n* brandmur
firework • *n* fyrværkeri
fireworks • *n* fyrværkeri *(n)*
first • *n* først, forrest • *adj* første • *adv* først
fiscal • *adj* fiskal, skattemæssig, skatte-, financiel, finans-
fish • *n* fisk • *v* fiske
fisherman • *n* fisker
fishhook • *n* fiskekrog
fishing • *n* fiskeri *(n)*, lystfiskeri *(n)* • *adj* fiske
fishmonger • *n* fiskehandler, fiskemand
fishy • *n* småfisk • *adj* fiskeagtig, lusket
fissure • *n* revne, sprække

fist • *n* næve, knytnæve
fit • *adj* passende, i form • *v* passe sammen, tilpasse, passe til • *n* pasform, slagtilfælde *(n)*
fitness • *n* egnethed
fitted • *v* tilpassede, tilpasset
five • *n* femtal *(n)*, femmer
fizzle • *v* bruse, ebbe ud • *n* brusen
fjord • *n* fjord
flag • *v* signalere, standse, vinke ad, flage, svækkes, belægge, flise • *n* flag *(n)*, fane, flaggivning, sværdlilje, flise
flagpole • *n* flagstang
flagship • *n* flagskib *(n)*
flail • *n* stridsplejl
flamboyant • *adj* flamboyant
flame • *v* flamme, blusse • *n* flamme, lue
flamethrower • *n* flammekaster
flamingo • *n* flamingo
flange • *n* flange
flank • *v* flankere • *n* flanke
flare • *n* udfladning
flash • *v* lyse, skinne, blinke, glimte, glimt, blotte • *n* glimt *(n)*, lyn *(n)* • *adj* flot
flashlight • *n* stavlygte
flat • *n* flade • *adj* flad, død • *adv* jævnt, helt
flatfish • *n* fladfisk
flatten • *v* jævne
flatulence • *n* fjært, vind, fis
flax • *n* hør
flaxen • *adj* hørfarvet
flea • *n* loppe
fleabite • *n* loppebid *(n)*
flee • *v* flygte, fly
fleet • *n* flåde
flesh • *v* opfede • *n* kød, krop, hud, frugtkød, kødfarve
fleur-de-lis • *n* lilje
flexible • *adj* fleksibel *(n)*, smidig, fleksibel, føjelig
flight • *n* flyvning
flightless • *adj* ikke flyvedygtig
flint • *n* ildsten, flint
flock • *n* flok
flood • *v* oversvømme • *n* oversvømmelse
floor • *v* lægge gulv, nedlægge • *n* gulv *(n)*
flotsam • *n* drivgods *(n)*
flounder • *n* skrubbe, flynder
flour • *n* mel *(n)*
flow • *v* strømme • *n* strøm, flod
flower • *v* blomstre • *n* blomst
flowerbed • *n* blomsterbed *(n)*
flu • *n* influenza

fluctuation • *n* fluktuation
flue • *n* røgrør *(n)*
fluent • *adj* flydende
fluently • *adv* flydende
fluid • *n* væske • *adj* flydende, om-skiftelig
fluorine • *n* fluor
flute • *n* fløjte
flux • *n* forandring, flusmiddel *(n)*, flux
fly • *n* flue, gylp
flying • *v* flyvende
foal • *v* fole • *n* føl *(n)*
foam • *n* skum *(n)*, skumgummi *(n)*
focus • *v* fokusere, koncentrere • *n* fokus *(n)*
fodder • *n* foder *(n)*
foehn • *n* føn
fog • *n* tåge
foible • *n* dårskab, svaghed, manér
foliation • *n* foliering
folklore • *n* folklore
follow • *v* følge
follower • *n* efterfølger, ledsager, følgesvend, tilhænger, medløber, efter-snakker, forfølger, madkæreste
following • *n* følge *(n)* • *adj* følgende, næste • *prep* efter
fond • *v* glad, holde af, kunne lide • *adj* øm, kærlig, eftergivende, eksotisk, aparte
fondue • *n* fondue
font • *n* skrifttype
food • *n* mad, føde, ædelse
foodstuff • *n* fødevare, levnedsmiddel *(n)*, madvare
fool • *n* fjols *(n)*, nar
foolish • *adj* tåbelig, dum
foolishness • *n* tåbelighed
foolproof • *adj* idiotsikker
foot • *v* sparke, betale • *n* fod, fødder, versefod, versfod, versefødder, versfød-der
football • *n* fodbold, australsk fodbold, rugby, fodboldspil
footprint • *n* fodspor
footwear • *n* fodtøj *(n)*, skotøj *(n)*
for • *conj* for, fordi, thi • *prep* til, mod, for, i
forbid • *v* forbyde
forbidden • *adj* forbudt
force • *v* tvinge, fremtvinge • *n* kraft, styrke, magt
forcemeat • *n* fars
ford • *n* vadested *(n)*
foreclose • *v* tvangsauktionere
forefinger • *n* pegefinger
forehead • *n* pande
foreign • *adj* fremmed, fremmede, udlænding, udenlandsk
forenoon • *n* formiddag
foreplay • *n* forspil
foresee • *v* forudse
foreseeable • *adj* forudsigeligt
forest • *n* skov
forever • *adv* for altid
forge • *n* esse, smedje, smedeværksted *(n)* • *v* smede, forfalske
forger • *n* forfalsker
forget • *v* glemme
forget-me-not • *n* forglemmigej
forgive • *v* tilgive, forlade
forgotten • *adj* glemt
fork • *v* gafle • *n* fork, greb, høtyv, gaffel, skillevej, vejgaffel
form • *v* forme • *n* form, formular, blan-ket
formal • *adj* formel
formaldehyde • *n* formaldehyd
fortieth • *adj* fyrretyvende
fortify • *v* befæste
fortress • *n* fæstning
fortunate • *adj* heldig
forum • *n* forum *(n)*
fossil • *n* fossil *(n)*, oldtidslevning
fossilized • *adj* fossil
foster • *v* opfostre
foundation • *n* grundlæggelse, funda-ment *(n)*, grundlag *(n)*
fountain • *n* springvand
four • *n* firtal *(n)*
fourteenth • *adj* fjortende
fourth • *adj* fjerde
fox • *n* ræv, steg
foxglove • *n* fingerbøl
fraction • *n* brøkdel, brøk
fragile • *adj* skrøbelig, spinkel
fragment • *n* fragment *(n)*
fragrance • *n* duft
francium • *n* francium
frankincense • *n* røgelse
freckle • *n* fregne
free • *v* befri, fritage, løslade • *adj* fri
freedom • *n* frihed
freestanding • *adj* fritstående
freethinker • *n* fritænker
frenzy • *n* vanvid, raseri
frequency • *n* hyppighed, frekvens *(n)*
fresco • *n* freske, fresko, freskomaleri *(n)*
fresh • *adj* frisk, ny, forfriskende, fersk, fræk
fret • *n* bånd *(n)*
friend • *n* ven, veninde, kammerat, kam-meratinde, bekendt
friendless • *adj* venneløs
friendly • *n* venskabskamp • *adj* venlig,

venligsindet, venskabelig • *adv* venligt
friendship • *n* venskab *(n)*
frigate • *n* fregat
frightened • *adj* bange
frisk • *v* kropsvisitere • *adj* kåd, livlig, sprælsk
frog • *n* frø
from • *prep* fra, mod
frost • *n* frost
frown • *v* skule
frozen • *adj* frossen
fructose • *n* fruktose
fruit • *n* frugt
fruitful • *adj* frugtbar
frustrated • *adj* frustreret
frustrating • *adj* frustrerende
fuchsia • *n* fuchsia
fuck • *v* kneppe, bolle, pule, knalde • *n* knald *(n)*
fuel • *n* brændstof
fugitive • *n* flygtning • *adj* flygtig
fulcrum • *n* understøttelsespunkt *(n)*
full • *adj* fuld, fyldt, fuldstændig, komplet, mæt, fyldt op, vid, fuldtonet • *v*

valke, stampe
fulmar • *n* mallemuk, isstormfugl
fume • *v* ryge
fun • *adj* sjov
function • *v* fungere, virke • *n* funktion
fundamental • *adj* fundamental, grundlæggende
funeral • *n* begravelse, bisættelse • *adj* begravelses-
fungible • *adj* fungibel
fungicide • *n* svampemiddel
fungus • *n* svamp
funnel • *n* tragt
funny • *adj* morsom, sjov, besynderlig, underlig
fur • *n* pels
furniture • *n* møbel *(n)*, inventar *(n)*
fury • *n* raseri *(n)*
fuse • *n* sikring
fussy • *adj* pertentlig, nøjeregnende
futile • *adj* nytteløs
future • *n* fremtid • *adj* fremtidig

G

gadfly • *n* provokatør, urostifter
gadget • *n* gadget
gadolinium • *n* gadolinium
gaffe • *n* fejltagelse
gaffer • *n* gammel mand, formand
gaiter • *n* gamache
galactose • *n* galaktose
galaxy • *n* galakse
gale • *n* kuling, pors
galena • *n* blyglans
galleon • *n* galeon
galley • *n* køkken *(n)*, kabys
gallium • *n* gallium *(n)*
gallop • *v* galopere • *n* galop
gallows • *n* galge
galosh • *n* galoche
gambit • *n* gambit
game • *n* spil
gamete • *n* kønscelle
gander • *n* gase, hangås
gangrene • *n* koldbrand, gangræn *(n)*
gape • *v* gabe
garage • *n* garage
garbage • *n* affald *(n)*
garden • *v* havearbejde • *n* have, park, anlæg
gardener • *n* gartner
garganey • *n* atlingand

garlic • *n* hvidløg *(n)*
garner • *v* indhøste, indsamle • *n* kornkammer *(n)*, magasin *(n)*
garrison • *n* garnison
gas • *n* gas *(n)*
gasoline • *n* benzin
gate • *n* port
gather • *v* samle
gatherer • *n* samler
gawk • *v* glane, glo, måbe
gay • *n* bøsse, homo • *adj* glad, livlig, sjov, farverig
gear • *n* udstyr *(n)*
gearbox • *n* gearkasse
geek • *n* geek, nørd
gem • *n* ædelsten, perle
gendarmerie • *n* gendarm
gender • *n* køn *(n)*
general • *n* general • *adj* generel, almindelig, almen
generation • *n* generation, slægtled *(n)*
genial • *adj* genial
genitive • *n* ejefald
genius • *n* geni
genocide • *n* folkedrab
genome • *n* genom *(n)*
genotype • *n* genotype
genre • *n* genre

genuine • *adj* ægte, original
genus • *n* slægt, genus *(n)*, genus
geochemistry • *n* geokemi
geodesy • *n* geodæsi
geography • *n* geografi
geologist • *n* geolog
geomancy • *n* geomanti
geometry • *n* geometri
geophysics • *n* geofysik
geranium • *n* storkenæb, pelargonie, geranium
gerbil • *n* ørkenrotte
germane • *adj* relevant, relevante
germanium • *n* germanium
gerund • *n* gerundium *(n)*
gestalt • *n* gestalt
gesticulate • *v* gestikulere
get • *v* få fat i, få, modtage, blive, forstå
geyser • *n* gejser
gherkin • *n* asie
ghost • *n* spøgelse *(n)*, genganger, gen-færd *(n)*, gespenst, ånd, draug, sjæl
ghostwriter • *n* neger
gibberish • *n* vrøvl *(n)*, volapyk *(n)*, kaud-ervælsk *(n)*, nonsens *(n)*
gift • *n* gave
gigantic • *adj* gigantisk
gill • *n* gælle
ginger • *n* ingefær
gingerly • *adv* varsomt, forsigtigt
ginseng • *n* ginseng, ginsengrod
giraffe • *n* giraf
girdle • *n* hofteholder, strømpeholder
girl • *n* pige
girlfriend • *n* kæreste, veninde
give • *v* give, give efter
gizzard • *n* kråse
glacier • *n* gletsjer, jøkel, bræ
glad • *adj* glad
gladiator • *n* gladiator
glans • *n* agernet
glare • *v* stirre, glo, skinne, blænde • *n* skin
glass • *n* glas *(n)*
glassworks • *n* glasværk
global • *adj* kuglerund, kugleformet, sfærisk, global
globe • *n* klode, jordklode, globus
glogg • *n* gløgg
glory • *n* pragt
glossary • *n* glosar, glossar, glosarium, glossarium, glosebog, ordliste, termliste, gloseliste, glossehæfte
glove • *n* handske, vante
glucose • *n* glukose, druesukker
glue • *n* lim
gluttony • *n* fråseri *(n)*

glycine • *n* glycin
gnat • *n* myg
gneiss • *n* gnejs
gnu • *n* gnu
go • *v* gå, blive, passe
goal • *n* mål
goalkeeper • *n* målmand, målvogter
goat • *n* ged, buk
goatee • *n* fipskæg *(n)*
goblin • *n* nisse, trold
god • *n* gud, afgud, idol *(n)*
godchild • *n* gudbarn *(n)*
goddaughter • *n* guddatter
goddess • *n* gudinde
godfather • *n* fadder, gudfar, gudfader
godless • *adj* gudløs
godlike • *adj* gudelig
godmother • *n* gudmor, gudmoder
godparent • *n* fadder
godson • *n* gudsøn
gold • *n* guld *(n)*, guldmønt, gylden farve, centrum *(n)*, guld, guldmedalje, rigdom • *adj* guld *(n)*, gylden
golden • *adj* gylden
goldeneye • *n* hvinand
goldfinch • *n* stillids, stillits
goldfish • *n* guldfisk
goldsmith • *n* guldsmed
golf • *n* golf
golfer • *n* golfer, golfspiller
gong • *n* gongong
gonorrhea • *n* gonoré
good • *adj* god *(m)*, godt *(n)*, sund, god, fin, dygtig • *n* godhed, gode
goodbye • *interj* farvel
goof • *n* tumpe
goosander • *n* stor skallesluger
goose • *n* gås
gooseberry • *n* stikkelsbær *(n)*
gorge • *v* æde
gory • *adj* blodig
goshawk • *n* duehøg
gospel • *n* evangelium *(n)*
gossip • *n* sladder
goulash • *n* gullasch
govern • *v* regere, beherske, styre, bestemme, lede, herske
government • *n* regering
governor • *n* guvernør
grade • *n* karakter
gradually • *adv* gradvis
graduate • *n* akademiker
grammar • *n* grammatik
gramophone • *n* grammofon
grandchild • *n* barnebarn *(n)*
granddaughter • *n* sønnedatter, datter-datter

grandfather • *n* bedstefar, forfader
grandmother • *n* bedstemor
grandson • *n* sønnesøn, dattersøn
granite • *n* granit
grape • *n* drue, vindrue
grapefruit • *n* grapefrugt, grape
grapevine • *n* vinstok
graph • *n* graf
graphite • *n* grafit
grasp • *v* gribe, begribe
grass • *n* græs *(n)*, græsplæne, plæne *(n)*, græs, stikker
grasshopper • *n* græshoppe
grateful • *adj* taknemmelig, taknemlig
grater • *n* rivejern
gratis • *adv* gratis
grave • *n* grav, begravelse
gravedigger • *n* graver
gravel • *n* grus *(n)*, ral *(n)*
gravestone • *n* gravsten
gravy • *n* sovs
gray • *v* gråne • *n* grå • *adj* grå
great • *interj* fedt, super, nice
green • *n* grøn • *adj* grøn
greenhouse • *n* drivhus *(n)*
greeting • *n* hilsen
grenade • *n* granat
griffin • *n* grif
grimace • *v* grimassere • *n* grimasse
gristle • *n* brusk
groan • *v* stønne
groin • *n* lyske, skridt *(n)*
grotesque • *adj* grotesk
grotto • *n* grotte
group • *n* gruppe
grove • *n* lund

grow • *v* vokse, udvikle, gro, dyrke
growth • *n* vækst
grudge • *v* ikke unde, misunde • *n* nag, uvilje
grudging • *adj* modstræbende, modvillig
grunt • *v* fnyse, grynte • *n* fnys *(n)*, grynt *(n)*, fodtusse
guarantee • *v* garantere, kautionere, sikre • *n* garanti, garant
guarantor • *n* garant, kautionist
guard • *v* bevogte, holde vagt • *n* vagt, livvagt, skærm, afskærmning
guava • *n* guava
guess • *n* gæt *(n)*
guest • *v* gæste • *n* gæst
guide • *n* guide, vejledning, vejviser
guideline • *n* retningslinje
guild • *n* lav
guilt • *n* skyld
guitar • *n* guitar
guitarist • *n* guitarist
gulf • *n* bugt
gull • *n* måge
gum • *n* tandkød *(n)*
gunboat • *n* kanonbåd
gunfire • *n* geværild
gunpowder • *n* krudt
gymnasium • *n* gymnasium *(n)*
gymnastics • *n* gymnastik
gynecology • *n* gynækologi
gypsum • *n* gips
gypsy • *n* sigøjner
gyrfalcon • *n* jagtfalk
gyroscope • *n* gyroskop

H

ha • *interj* ha
habit • *n* vane
habitat • *n* levested *(n)*, habitat *(n)*, udbredelsesområde *(n)*
hackberry • *n* nældetræ *(n)*
haddock • *n* kuller
hafnium • *n* hafnium *(n)*
haggle • *v* prutte, købslå
hagiography • *n* hagiografi
haha • *interj* ha, ha ha, hæhæ
haiku • *n* haiku *(n)*
hail • *n* hagl *(n)* • *v* hil
hair • *n* hår *(n)*
hairbrush • *n* hårbørste
hairdresser • *n* frisør
hairy • *adj* håret, behåret, lodden

hajj • *n* hajj
half • *n* halvdel • *adj* halv
half-moon • *n* halvmåne
halibut • *n* helleflynder
hallelujah • *interj* halleluja
hallow • *n* helgen • *v* hellige, helliggøre
halo • *n* halo, glorie
halyard • *n* fald *(n)*
ham • *n* skinke
hamburger • *n* hamburger
hamlet • *n* landsby
hammer • *v* hamre • *n* hammer, geværhane
hammerhead • *n* hammerhaj
hammock • *n* hængekøje
hamster • *n* hamster

hamstring • *n* hase

hand • *n* hånd, viser, håndskrift, håndfuld

hand-me-down • *n* aflagt, stykke, tøj

handball • *n* håndbold

handcuff • *n* håndjern

handcuffs • *n* håndjern

handful • *n* håndfuld, håndsbred

handkerchief • *n* lommetørklæde

handle • *n* håndtag *(n)*

handlebar • *n* styr *(n)*

handshake • *n* håndtryk *(n)*

handwriting • *n* håndskrift

hang • *v* hænge

hanger • *n* bøjle

hangover • *n* tømmermænd

hapless • *adj* ulykkelig

happen • *v* ske, hænde, indtræffe

happiness • *n* lykke, glæde

happy • *adj* glad, lykkelig, heldig

harassment • *n* chikane

hard • *adj* vanskelig

hardly • *adv* knap

hardware • *n* udstyr *(n)*, isenkram *(n)*, hardware, maskinel *(n)*, isenkram, maskine, våben *(n)*

hardy • *adj* hårdfør, modstandsdygtig

hare • *n* hare

harebell • *n* blåklokke

harelip • *n* hareskaar

harlot • *n* skøge

harm • *n* skade

harmful • *adj* skadelig

harmonica • *n* mundharmonika, mundharpe

harp • *n* harpe

harpoon • *n* harpun

harpsichord • *n* cembalo

harpsichordist • *n* cembalist

harrow • *n* harve

harsh • *adj* ru, grov

harvestman • *n* mejere

hashish • *n* hashish, hash

hassle • *v* chikanere, genere, plage • *n* besvær *(n)*, bøvl *(n)*, mas *(n)*, skænderi *(n)*, slagsmål *(n)*

hat • *n* hat, kasket

hate • *v* hade

hateful • *adj* Hadefuld

hatred • *n* had

haulm • *n* halm

have • *v* have, få, skulle

haven • *n* havn, tilflugtssted *(n)*, refugium *(n)*, fristed *(n)*

hawk • *n* høg, mørtelbræt *(n)* • *v* falbyde, harke, rømme sig

hawser • *n* trosse

hawthorn • *n* tjørn

hay • *v* slå hø • *n* hø *(n)*

haystack • *n* høstak

hazelnut • *n* hasselnød

he • *pron* han

head • *n* hoved *(n)*

headache • *n* hovedpine

headboard • *n* hovedgærde *(n)*

headmistress • *n* rektor

headscarf • *n* tørklæde

headstone • *n* gravsten

health • *n* sundhed

healthy • *adj* sund

hear • *v* høre

hearse • *n* ligvogn, rustvogn

heart • *n* hjerte *(n)*, hjerter

heartless • *adj* hjerteløs

hearts • *n* hjerter

heat • *n* varme, hede, løbetid, heat, runde, opvarmning, hedebølge • *v* opvarme, tænde

heatstroke • *n* hedeslag

heavy • *adj* tung

heckle • *v* håne, fornærme

hedge • *n* hæk

hedgehog • *n* pindsvin *(n)*

hedonism • *n* hedonisme

heel • *n* hæl

heifer • *n* kvie eller skældsord (fede ko) om en tyk kvinde

heinous • *adj* afskyelig, frygtelig, grufuld, motbydelig

heir • *n* arving

heiress • *n* arving

heirloom • *n* arvestykke *(n)*

helicopter • *n* helikopter

helium • *n* helium *(n)*

helix • *n* skruelinje

hello • *interj* hej, dav, god dag, hallo

helmet • *n* hjelm

help • *n* hjælp • *v* hjælpe • *interj* hjælp

helpful • *adj* hjælpsom

helpless • *adj* hjælpeløs

hemisphere • *n* halvkugle

hemlock • *n* hemlock, skarntydegran, skarntyde

hemp • *n* hamp

hen • *n* høne

henbane • *n* bulmeurt

hence • *adv* heden, derfor

henceforth • *adv* fra nu af, for fremtiden, fremover

henpecked • *adj* i sin hule hånd, tøffelhelt

hepatitis • *n* leverbetændelse, hepatitis

her • *pron* hende

heraldry • *n* heraldik

herb • *n* urt
herbaceous • *adj* urteagtig
herbivore • *n* planteæder
herd • *n* hjord, flok, hob, hyrde
here • *adv* her, herhen
hereditary • *adj* arvelig
heresy • *n* kætteri *(n)*
heretic • *n* kætter • *adj* kættersk
heretical • *adj* kættersk
hermaphrodite • *n* hermafrodit • *adj* tvekønnet, hermafroditisk
hernia • *n* brok
hero • *n* helt
heroic • *adj* heltemodig, heroisk
heroin • *n* heroin
heroine • *n* heltinde
heroism • *n* heltemod
heron • *n* hejre
herring • *n* sild
hers • *pron* hendes
hertz • *n* hertz
hesitate • *v* stamme, hakke
heterosexual • *n* heteroseksuel • *adj* heteroseksuel
hetman • *n* hetman
heuristic • *n* heuristik • *adj* heuristisk
hex • *n* forbandelse, heks
hexadecimal • *n* hexadecimale talsystem *(n)*, sekstentalssystem *(n)* • *adj* hexadecimal
hey • *n* hej
heyday • *n* blomstringstid, storhedstid, velmagtsdage
hi • *interj* hallo, goddag, hej, dav
hiccup • *v* hikke • *n* hikke *(m)*, hik *(n)*
hide • *v* gemme, skjule, gemme sig • *n* skind
hideout • *n* skjulested *(n)*, tilflugtssted *(n)*, gemmested *(n)*
hierarchical • *adj* hierarkisk
hierarchy • *n* hierarki *(n)*, rangorden
hieroglyph • *n* hieroglyf
high • *adj* høj, skæv
hight • *v* hedde
highway • *n* motorvej
highwayman • *n* landevejsrøver
hilarious • *adj* hylende morsom
hill • *n* bakke
hinder • *v* hindre • *adj* bagest, bag-
hindsight • *n* bagklogskab
hinge • *n* hængsel *(n)*
hinny • *n* muldyr *(n)*
hip • *n* hofte, hyben *(n)*
hippopotamus • *n* flodhest
hire • *v* ansætte
his • *pron* hans
hiss • *v* hvæse • *n* hvæse

historical • *adj* historisk
history • *n* historie, beretning
hit • *v* slå
hitchhiker • *n* tomler, blaffer
hither • *adv* herhen, hid
hitherto • *adv* hidtil
hoard • *v* samle, hamstre, puge • *n* forråd, skat
hobby • *n* hobby *(n)*, lærkefalk
hog • *n* svin *(n)*
hogshead • *n* oksehoved
hold • *v* holde
hole • *n* hul *(n)*
holiday • *n* helligdag, fridag, ferie
hollow • *adj* hul, dyb
holly • *n* kristtorn
holmium • *n* holmium
holy • *adj* hellig
homage • *n* lenshyldning, hyldest, tribut
home • *n* hjem *(n)*, hjemland *(n)* • *adv* hjemme, hjem, hjemad
homeless • *adj* hjemløs
homelessness • *n* hjemløshed
homesickness • *n* hjemve
homestead • *n* hjemsted *(n)*
hometown • *n* hjemby
homework • *n* lektier, hjemmearbejde *(n)*
homogeneity • *n* homogenitet
homophobia • *n* homofobi
homosexual • *n* homoseksuel • *adj* homoseksuel
homosexuality • *n* homoseksualitet
honest • *adj* ærlig
honesty • *n* ærlighed
honey • *n* honning
honeymoon • *n* hvedebrødsdage, bryllupsrejse
honor • *n* ære
hood • *n* hætte
hoof • *n* hov
hook • *v* hænge, få på krogen, få til at bide på, koble • *n* krog, knage, hage, hook
hooker • *n* luder, prostitueret
hop • *n* humle
hope • *n* håb • *v* håbe
hopeless • *adj* håbløs
horde • *n* horde
horizon • *n* horisont
horizontal • *adj* vandret
hormone • *n* hormon
horn • *n* horn *(n)*
hornet • *n* hveps, gedehams
horny • *adj* liderlig
horoscope • *n* horoskop *(n)*
horse • *n* hest, hingst, hoppe, kavaleri *(n)*
horsefly • *n* klæg
horsemeat • *n* hestekød *(n)*

horsepower • *n* hestekraft
horseradish • *n* peberrod
horseshoe • *n* sko
horsetail • *n* padderokke, padderok
hose • *n* slange *(n)*
hospital • *n* hospital *(n)*, sygehus *(n)*
hospitality • *n* gæstfrihed
host • *n* vært
hostage • *n* gidsel *(n)*
hostess • *n* værtinde
hostility • *n* fjendtlighed
hot • *adj* varm, hot, lækker
hotbed • *n* varmebed, drivbænk
hotel • *n* hotel
hound • *n* hund
hour • *n* time
hourglass • *n* timeglas *(n)*
house • *n* hus *(n)*
houseboat • *n* husbåd
housewife • *n* husfru
housework • *n* husholdningsarbejde
how • *adv* hvor, hvordan, hvorledes • *conj* hvordan, hvorledes
however • *adv* dog
howitzer • *n* haubits
howl • *n* hyl *(n)*
hubris • *n* hybris, overmod
hue • *n* farve, skær *(n)*, afskygning, farvetone
hug • *v* omfavne, kramme, knuse • *n* kram, omfavnelse, knus
huge • *adj* enorm, kæmpestor
huh • *interj* æh
human • *n* menneske • *adj* menneskelig, human
humanism • *n* humanisme
humble • *v* nedgøre, ydmyge, ringagte • *adj* jordnær, ydmyg
humility • *n* ydmyghed
hunger • *n* sult

hungry • *adj* sulten
hunk • *n* stort stykke, luns, tyr
hunt • *v* jage, gå på jagt efter, søge, lede • *n* jagt
hunter • *n* jæger
hurricane • *n* orkan
hurry • *v* skynde sig
husband • *v* spare • *n* mand, ægtemand, husbond
hush • *n* stilhed
hyacinth • *n* hyacint
hydrangea • *n* hortensia
hydrate • *v* hydrere • *n* hydrat *(n)*
hydraulics • *n* hydraulik
hydrocarbon • *n* kulbrinte, karbonhydrid *(n)*
hydrogen • *n* brint, hydrogen
hydrophilic • *adj* hydrofil
hydrophobia • *n* rabies, hundegalskab, hydrofobi
hyena • *n* hyæne
hygiene • *n* hygiejne
hygienic • *adj* hygiejnisk
hygrometer • *n* hygrometer
hymen • *n* jomfruhinde, mødomshinde, mødom
hymn • *n* hymne
hyperbola • *n* hyperbel
hyperbole • *n* hyperbel
hyperbolic • *adj* hyperbolsk
hypertext • *n* hypertekst
hyphen • *n* bindestreg
hypnosis • *n* hypnose
hypnotist • *n* hypnotisør
hypocrite • *n* hykler
hypotenuse • *n* hypotenuse
hypothesis • *n* hypotese
hyrax • *n* klippegrævling
hyssop • *n* isop

I

ibex • *n* stenbuk
ice • *n* is
iceberg • *n* isbjerg
icebreaker • *n* isbryder
icicle • *n* istap
icing • *n* glasur
icon • *n* ikon
icosahedron • *n* ikosaeder *(n)*
identical • *adj* identisk
identity • *n* identitet
ideogram • *n* ideogram *(n)*
ideology • *n* ideologi

idiocy • *n* idioti
idiom • *n* idiom
idiomatic • *adj* idiomatisk
idiosyncrasy • *n* idiosynkratisk, overfølsomhed, idiosynkrasi, særhed, særegenhed, særpræg *(n)*
idiot • *n* idiot
idolatry • *n* afgudsdyrkelse
idolize • *v* idolisere
idyll • *n* idyl
idyllic • *adj* idyllisk
if • *conj* hvis, om, dersom, nærmest,

snarere, hvorvidt
igloo • *n* iglo
ignorance • *n* uvidenhed
ignore • *v* ignorere
ill • *adj* syg, kvalm
illegitimate • *adj* uretmæssig, uberettiget, illegitim, ulogisk
illiterate • *n* analfabet
illness • *n* syg
illusion • *n* illusion
image • *n* billede *(n)*
imaginary • *adj* fantasi-, imaginær
imagine • *v* forestille sig
imam • *n* imam
imitation • *n* imitation, efterligning
immaculate • *adj* pletfri
immature • *adj* umoden, infantil
immediate • *adj* øjeblikkelig, tæt
immediately • *adv* øjeblikkeligt, med det samme
immigrant • *n* indvandrer
immigration • *n* indvandring
immortal • *adj* udødelig
impala • *n* impala
impale • *v* spidde
impartial • *adj* upartisk
impatience • *n* utålmodighed
impatient • *adj* utålmodig
impetuous • *adj* impulsiv, opfarende, heftig, fremfusende
implacable • *adj* stædig
implant • *n* implantat *(n)*
implicit • *adj* implicit
implore • *v* bønfalde, trygle
important • *adj* vigtig
imposing • *adj* imposant, imponerende, statelig, monumental
impossible • *n* umulighed • *adj* umuligt, umulig
imprecise • *adj* upræcis
imprison • *v* fængsle
imprisonment • *n* fangenskab *(n)*
improvement • *n* forbedring
impudent • *adj* næsvis
impulsive • *adj* impulsiv
in • *adv* inde, ind
inadvertent • *adj* utilsigtet
inane • *adj* intetsigende, åndsforladt
incarcerate • *v* indespære, fængsle
incense • *n* røgelse, virak
incest • *n* incest, blodskam
inch • *n* tomme
incident • *n* begivenhed
income • *n* indtægt, indkomst
incomplete • *adj* ukomplet
incontinence • *n* inkontinens
increase • *n* stigning

indecisive • *adj* ubeslutsom
indeclinable • *adj* ubøjelig
indeed • *adv* sandelig, sandhed, søreme
independence • *n* uafhængighed, selvstændighed
index • *v* indeksere • *n* indeks *(n)*, indholdsfortegnelse
indium • *n* indium *(n)*
industrious • *adj* arbejdsom, ihærdig, flitig
industry • *n* industri
inebriated • *adj* beruset, fuld
inequality • *n* ulighed
inexcusable • *adj* utilgivelig
inexorable • *adj* ubønhørlig
infallible • *adj* ufejlbarlig
infamous • *adj* berygtet, infamøs
infant • *n* spædbarn, mindreårig
infantry • *n* infanteri
infection • *n* infektion *(f)*
infelicitous • *adj* uheldig
inferno • *n* inferno *(n)*
infinitive • *n* infinitiv
infinity • *n* uendelighed
inflammation • *n* betændelse
inflation • *n* inflation
inflect • *v* bøje
inflection • *n* modulation, vendepunkt, afvigelse
influence • *n* indflydelse
influential • *adj* indflydelsesrig
informant • *n* informant
information • *n* information, informationer
infrared • *n* infrarød stråling • *adj* infrarød
infrequently • *adv* ualmindelig, sjælden
ingenious • *adj* opfindsomt
ingenuity • *n* snedighed
inherent • *adj* naturlig, iboende
inheritable • *adj* arvelig
injury • *n* sår
ink • *n* blæk *(n)*
inn • *n* kro
innovative • *adj* opfindsom, nyskabende
innuendo • *n* hentydning, insinuation
insane • *adj* sindssyg
insanity • *n* sindssyge, galskab, vanvid *(n)*
insatiable • *adj* umættelig
insect • *n* insekt
insectivore • *n* insektæder
insecure • *adj* usikker, utryg
insecurity • *n* usikkerhed
insertion • *n* indkast *(n)*
insinuation • *n* insinuation
insomnia • *n* søvnløshed

inspiration • n inspiration
instant • n øjeblik, han, døde, øjeblikkeligt
instead • adv i stedet, i stedet for
institute • n institut
instruction • n vejledning, vejlederen
insulin • n insulin
insult • n fornærmelse
insurance • n forsikring
integer • n heltal (n)
intelligence • n intelligens, efterretninger, efterretningstjeneste
intelligentsia • n intelligentsia
intensify • v intensivere
intercession • n forbøn
interest • v interessere • n interesse, interessant
interested • adj interesseret
interesting • adj interessant
interjection • n udråbsord (n)
intermittent • adj periodisk optrædende, uregelmæssig, afbrudt
interpersonal • adj interpersonelle
interpreter • n tolk
interrupt • v afbryde
intersection • n kryds (n), skæring, skæringspunkt (n), fællesmængde
intervention • n intervention
interview • n interview
intestine • n tarm
intonation • n intonation
intoxicated • adj beruset, fuld, drukken
intramuscular • adj intramuskulær
intravenous • adj intravenøs
intravenously • adv intravenøst
intrinsic • adj indre, egentlig

invade • v invadere, krænke, oversvømme
invasion • n invasion
invention • n opfindelse
invest • v investere
invisible • adj usynlig
invite • v invitere, indbyde
iodine • n jod
ionosphere • n ionosfære
irascible • adj opfarende
iridium • n iridium (n)
iris • n iris, regnbuehinde
iron • v stryge • n jern (n), strygejern (n) • adj jern-
ironic • adj ironisk
irony • n ironi
irrational • adj irrationel, irrational
irresolute • adj tvivlrådig, ubeslutsom, vankelmodig
irrevocable • adj uigenkaldelig
irrigation • n vanding, overrisling, udskyldning
irritation • n irritation
is • v er
island • n ø, holm, skær
islander • n øbo, øboer
isolate • v isolere
isomorphism • n isomorfi
isotropic • adj isotropisk
isthmus • n landtange
it • pron det
item • n stykke (n), punkt (n)
its • pron dens, dets (n)
ivory • n elfenben (n)
ivy • n efeu

J

jack • n donkraft, knægt, æselhingst, stik, gøs
jackal • n sjakal
jackass • n idiot
jackdaw • n allike
jacket • n jakke
jackfruit • n brødfrugttræ (n), brødfrugt
jade • n jade (n), jadegrøn
jaeger • n kjove
jaguar • n jaguar
jam • n marmelade, syltetøj (n), knibe
jammed • adj propfuld, smækfuld
jaundice • n gulsot
jaw • n kæbe
jay • n skovskade
jazz • n jazz

jealous • adj jaloux, ejekær, misundelig
jellyfish • n gople, vandmand, brandmand
jet • n dyse
jeweler • n juveler, guldsmed
jewellery • n smykker
jihad • n jihad
joke • v spøge • n vittighed, spøg
jotun • n jætte
joule • n joule
journal • n tidsskrift (n)
journalism • n journalistik
journalist • n journalist
journalistic • adj journalistisk
journey • n rejse
journeyman • n svend

joy • *n* lykke
jubilee • *n* jubilæum *(n)*
judge • *n* dommer
judo • *n* judo
juggle • *v* jonglere
juggler • *n* jonglør
juggling • *n* jonglering
juice • *n* saft, juice
juicy • *adj* saftig
jukebox • *n* jukeboks, grammofonautomat
jump • *v* springe, hoppe, spjætte, fare sammen, springe over • *n* spring *(n)*, hop *(n)*, spjæt *(n)*
jungle • *n* jungle
juniper • *n* ene, enebær
junk • *v* kassere, smide ud • *n* bras, ragelse, affald, junke
jurisprudence • *n* jura, retsvidenskab
jurist • *n* retslærd
justice • *n* ret, retfærdighed
jute • *n* jute
juvenile • *adj* barnlig

K

kale • *n* grønkål
kaleidoscope • *n* kaleidoskop *(n)*
kangaroo • *n* kænguru
kaput • *adj* kaput
kayak • *n* kajak *(n)*
keelhaul • *v* kølhale
keelson • *n* kølsvin *(n)*
keep • *n* kernetårn *(n)*, borgtårn *(n)*, barfred
keepsake • *n* minde *(n)*
kelp • *n* kelp
keratin • *n* keratin
kernel • *n* kerne
kestrel • *n* falk, tårnfalk
kettle • *n* kedel
key • *n* nøgle, signaturforklaring, tast, tangent
keyboard • *n* tastatur
kick • *v* sparke • *n* spark *(n)*
kid • *n* gedekid, kid *(n)*, barn, unge
kidney • *n* nyre
kill • *n* drab *(n)*, bytte *(n)*, offer *(n)*
killer • *n* morder
kilogram • *n* kilogram *(n)*
kind • *n* slags, art, natur, naturalier • *adj* rar, venlig
kindergarten • *n* børnehave
kindle • *v* tænde, fænge, vække, sætte i brand, ophidse
kindly • *adv* venlig, venligst
kindness • *n* venlighed, velvilje, imødekommenhed, elskværdighed, godhed, tjeneste
king • *n* konge, kong
kingdom • *n* kongerige *(n)*, kongedømme *(n)*, rige *(n)*
kinship • *n* slægtskab *(n)*
kiosk • *n* kiosk, automat
kiss • *v* kysse • *n* kys
kitchen • *n* køkken
kite • *n* glente, drage
kitten • *n* killing
kittiwake • *n* ride
kitty • *n* kattekilling, killing
kiwi • *n* kiwi
kleptomania • *n* kleptomani
knead • *v* ælte
knee • *n* knæ
knife • *v* skære, stikke, kniv • *n* kniv
knight • *n* ridder, springer
knit • *v* strikke
knot • *n* knude, hårdknude, knast, knob, islandsk ryle
know • *v* vide, kende, forstå sig på, kende til
knowledge • *n* viden, kundskab, kendskab
known • *adj* kendt
knuckle • *n* kno
koala • *n* koala
kohlrabi • *n* kålrabi
kolkhoz • *n* kolkhoz
krypton • *n* krypton *(n)*

L

laborer • *n* arbejder, arbejdsmand, landarbejder
lackey • *n* lakaj
laconic • *adj* lakonisk, kortfattet
lacquer • *v* lakere • *n* lak
lacrosse • *n* lacrosse
lactose • *n* laktose, mælkesukker
ladder • *n* stige
ladle • *n* øse
lagoon • *n* lagune, strandsø
lahar • *n* lahar
lake • *n* sø
lamb • *n* lam *(n)*
lame • *adj* lam, lamt
lamp • *n* lampe, olielampe
lamppost • *n* lygtepæl, gadelygte
lampshade • *n* lampeskærm
lance • *n* lanse
land • *v* lande • *n* land *(n)*, land
landlocked • *adj* indlands-
landlubber • *n* landkrabbe
landscape • *n* landskab *(n)*
landslide • *n* bjergskred *(n)*, jordskred *(n)*
language • *n* sprog *(n)*, mål, tunge, sprogbeherskelse, terminologi, ordvalg
languish • *v* trættes
lanthanum • *n* lanthan
lap • *n* skød *(n)*
lapel • *n* jakkerevers
laptop • *n* bærbar computer
lapwing • *n* vibe
larboard • *n* bagbord
larch • *n* lærk, lærketræ *(n)*
lark • *n* lærke
larynx • *n* strubehoved *(n)*
lasagna • *n* lasagne
laser • *n* laser
lash • *n* piskesnert, piskeslag *(n)*
last • *adj* sidste, sidst, senest
late • *adj* salig • *adv* sen
latent • *adj* latent
later • *adv* senere
latex • *n* latex, saft
latrine • *n* latrin *(n)*
laugh • *v* le, grine, smile, le ad, gøre, sig,
lystig, over • *n* latter
laughable • *adj* latterlig, komisk
laughter • *n* latter, grin *(n)*
launch • *v* søsætte
launching • *n* søsætning
launderette • *n* møntvaskeri
laundry • *n* vasketøj *(n)*
laurel • *n* laurbær *(n)*, laurbærkrans
lava • *n* lava
lavender • *n* lavendel
law • *n* lov, jura
lawless • *adj* lovløs

lawlessness • *n* lovløshed
lawn • *n* græsplæne, plæne
lawrencium • *n* lawrencium
lawyer • *n* advokat, sagfører
lay • *v* lægge • *adj* læg, læg-
lazy • *adj* doven
lead • *n* bly *(n)*
leaf • *n* blad *(n)*, løv *(n)*
leak • *v* lække
leap • *v* springe, hoppe • *n* spring *(n)*,
hop *(n)*
learn • *v* lære, studere, erfare
leash • *n* hundesnor
leather • *n* læder *(n)* • *adj* læder-
leave • *n* tilladelse, permission, frihed,
orlov, afsked
leech • *n* blodigle, igler
leek • *n* porre
left • *n* venstre, venstrefløjen • *adj* venstre, venstreorienteret • *adv* til venstre, på
venstre hånd
left-handed • *n* kejthåndet, venstrehåndet
leg • *n* ben, etape, runde
legal • *adj* lovlig
legally • *adv* lovligt, lovmæssigt
legible • *adj* læselig
legislative • *adj* lovgivende
lemon • *n* citron • *adj* citrongul
lend • *v* låne
length • *n* længde
lens • *n* linse
lentil • *n* linse
leonine • *adj* løve-
leper • *n* spedalsk
leprosy • *n* spedalskhed
leprous • *adj* spedalsk
lesbian • *n* lesbisk • *adj* lesbisk
lesbianism • *n* lesbianisme
let • *v* tillade, lade
letter • *n* bogstav *(n)*, brev *(n)*
lettuce • *n* salat
leucine • *n* leucin
leukemia • *n* leukæmi
level • *v* nivellere, jævne, planere • *n*
vaterpas *(n)*, nivelleringsinstrument *(n)*,
niveau *(n)*, højde, etage, plan, sal • *adj*
jævn, plan, vandret, i vater, ensformig,
nøgtern, sindig
leveret • *n* killing, harekilling
levin • *n* lynglimt *(n)*
levitation • *n* levitation
lexicography • *n* leksikografi
liana • *n* lian
liar • *n* løgner
libation • *n* drikoffer
libel • *v* bagtale, bagvaske

liberalism • *n* liberalisme
liberate • *v* befri, frigøre
liberty • *n* frihed
libidinous • *adj* liderlig
librarian • *n* bibliotekar
library • *n* bibliotek *(n)*
lichen • *n* lav *(n)*
lick • *v* slikke
lickspittle • *v* spytslikker
licorice • *n* lakrids *(n)*
lid • *n* låg
lie • *v* ligge, lyve • *n* løgn
lieutenant • *n* løjtnant
life • *n* liv *(n)*, livstid, levetid
lift • *v* løfte, hæve, ophæve, stjæle • *n* elevator, lift *(n)*, kørelejlighed, løft *(n)*
ligature • *n* ligatur
liger • *n* liger
light • *n* lys *(n)*, lyskilde *(n)*, flamme *(n)* • *v* antænde, tænde, belyse, oplyse • *adj* lys, belyst, oplyst, bleg, mælk, fløde, melk, let, kalorielet, banal, triviel
lighthouse • *n* fyr *(n)*, fyrtårn *(n)*
lightning • *n* lyn *(n)*, lynglimt *(n)*, lynnedslag *(n)*
lignite • *n* brunkul *(n)*
like • *v* kan lide, synes om • *adj* som
likely • *adj* sandsynlig
likewise • *adv* i lige måde
lilac • *n* syren
lily • *n* lilje
lime • *n* lime
limestone • *n* kalksten
limitation • *n* begrænsning
limousine • *n* limousine
limpet • *n* albueskæl *(n)*
line • *n* line
linear • *adj* lineær
linen • *n* hør
lingonberry • *n* tyttebær, tyttebær *(n)*
linguist • *n* lingvist *(f)*
linguistics • *n* lingvistik, sprogforskning
link • *v* forbinde, kæde, sammenkæde • *n* forbindelse, led, link
linseed • *n* hørfrø *(n)*
lion • *n* løve, løvinde *(f)*
lioness • *n* hunløve, løvinde
lip • *n* læbe
lipstick • *n* læbestift
liqueur • *n* likør
liquid • *n* væske • *adj* flydende
liquidity • *n* likviditet
liquor • *n* likør, spiritus
list • *n* liste
listen • *v* lytte, høre efter
literary • *adj* litterær
literature • *n* litteratur

lithium • *n* lithium
litter • *n* kuld *(n)*
little • *adj* lille, små
liturgical • *adj* liturgisk
liturgy • *n* liturgi
livable • *adj* til at leve med, beboelig
live • *v* leve, bo, overleve • *adj* direkte
livelihood • *n* levebrød *(n)*
liver • *n* lever
livid • *adj* rasende
lizard • *n* firben *(n)*, øgle
load • *v* lade
loam • *n* ler *(n)*
loanword • *n* låneord *(n)*, fremmedord *(n)*
loathe • *v* afsky
lobby • *v* lobbye • *n* lobby
lobbyist • *n* lobbyist
lobe • *n* lap, hjernelap
lobscouse • *n* labskovs, skipperlabskovs
lobster • *n* hummer
local • *adj* lokal
localize • *v* lokalisere
lock • *n* lås, lok
lockout • *n* lockout
locomotive • *n* lokomotiv
locust • *n* vandregræshoppe
loess • *n* løss
loft • *n* loft *(n)*
logarithm • *n* logaritme
logistics • *n* logistik, forsyningstropper
lollipop • *n* slikkepind, slikpind
loneliness • *n* ensomhed
lonely • *adj* ensom
long • *adj* lang • *adv* længe • *v* længes
longbow • *n* langbue
longitude • *n* længdegrad, meridian
look • *v* kikke, se, se ud, synes, virke, kikke efter, se efter
lookout • *n* udkig, udkigspost, udkigspunkt, udkigsmand, vagtpost
loom • *n* væv
loon • *n* lom
lord • *v* spille, herre • *n* herre, godsejer, lensherre, hersker, lord
lose • *v* tabe, miste
lost • *adj* vildfaren, faret vild, forsvundet
lot • *n* grundstykke *(n)*
loud • *adj* høj
loudspeaker • *n* højtaler
louse • *n* lus
love • *n* kærlighed, romantik, skat, søde, elskede, kæreste, nul
lovely • *adj* dejlig
lover • *n* elsker *(m)*, elskerinde *(f)*
low • *adj* lav, nede
lowland • *n* lavland *(n)*

loyal • *adj* loyal
loyalty • *n* loyalitet
luck • *n* held *(n)*
lucky • *adj* heldig
luggage • *n* bagage
lukewarm • *adj* lunken
lullaby • *n* godnatsang
lumpsucker • *n* almindelig stenbider, kulso, kvabso, stenbider
lunch • *v* spise, frokost • *n* frokost
lung • *n* lunge
lure • *v* lokke • *n* lokkemiddel *(n)*, lokke-

mad, blink *(n)*
lust • *v* tørste, begære, føle, begær • *n* begær *(n)*, lyst, liderlighed
lustrous • *adj* glansfuld
lute • *n* lut
lutefisk • *n* ludfisk, ludefisk
lutetium • *n* lutetium
lye • *n* lud
lymph • *n* lymfe
lynx • *n* los
lyre • *n* lyre

M

macadamia • *n* macademia, macademiatræ
macaroon • *n* makron
macaw • *n* ara
machine • *n* maskine
mackerel • *n* makrel
macro • *n* makro
mad • *adj* vanvittig, skør, sindssyg, gal, vred
madness • *n* galskab, sindssyge, vanvid *(n)*
maelstrom • *n* malstrøm
magazine • *n* tidsskrift, magasin *(n)*
mage • *n* mager, magiker, troldmand
maggot • *n* maddike
magic • *n* magi
magician • *n* tryllekunstner
magma • *n* magma
magnanimous • *adj* storsindet
magnate • *n* magnat
magnesium • *n* magnesium *(n)*
magnet • *n* magnet
magnetism • *n* magnetisme
magpie • *n* skade, husskade
mahogany • *n* mahogni *(n)*
mailbox • *n* postkasse
mailman • *n* postbud
maim • *v* lemlæste
mainland • *n* fastland *(n)*
mainmast • *n* stormast
mainsail • *n* storsejl
maintain • *v* vedligeholde
maintenance • *n* vedligeholdelse, hævdelse, forsvar *(n)*
make • *v* lave, udføre, fremstille, skabe, gøre, få til • *n* mærke *(n)*, fabrikat *(n)*
maker • *n* fabrikant
makeup • *n* makeup, sminke
malaria • *n* malaria
mallard • *n* gråand

malnourished • *adj* fejlernæret, underernæret
malnutrition • *n* fejlernæring, underernæring
mammal • *n* pattedyr
mammoth • *n* mammut
man • *n* menneske *(n)*, mand • *interj* mand
manacle • *n* håndjern
manager • *n* bestyrer, leder, chef, promotor
manatee • *n* søko
mandarin • *n* mandarin
mandola • *n* mandola
mandrake • *n* alrune
mane • *n* manke, man
manganese • *n* mangan
mango • *n* mango
mania • *n* mani
manic-depressive • *adj* maniodepressiv
manifold • *n* mangfoldighed
mankind • *n* menneskehed
manly • *adj* mandig
manticore • *n* manticore
manual • *n* manual
manure • *v* gøde, gødske • *n* møg, gødning
manuscript • *n* håndskrift *(n)*, manuskript *(n)*
map • *n* kort *(n)*, afbildning
maple • *n* ahorn *(n)*, løn, ær
marathon • *n* maraton *(n)*, maratonløb *(n)*
marathoner • *n* maratondeltager, maratonløber
marble • *n* marmor *(n)*
march • *v* marchere, udvikle sig, rykke frem • *n* march, gang, udvikling
mare • *n* hoppe
margrave • *n* markgreve

marigold • *n* morgenfrue, tagetes, fløjls-blomst

market • *v* markedsføre • *n* marked *(n)*, markedsplads, torv *(n)*, handel, markeds-

marksman • *n* finskytte *(n)*

marl • *n* mergel

marmalade • *n* syltetøj

marmot • *n* murmeldyr

maroon • *n* maron

marriage • *n* ægteskab *(n)*, giftermål *(n)*, bryllup *(n)*, vielse, forbindelse, forening

married • *adj* gift

marrow • *n* marv

marry • *v* gifte sig

marsh • *n* mose

marshmallow • *n* skumfidus, skumfidus *(n)*, marshmallow

marsupial • *n* pungdyr *(n)*

marten • *n* mår

marzipan • *n* marcipan

mascara • *n* mascara

masculine • *adj* mandlig, maskulin, mandig, hankøn

mash • *n* grød, mæsk

mask • *n* maske

massacre • *v* massakrere • *n* massakre

massage • *n* massage

masseur • *n* massør

mast • *n* mast

masterpiece • *n* mesterværk *(n)*

masturbation • *n* masturbation, onani

mat • *n* måtte

match • *n* kamp, tændstik

material • *n* materiale *(n)*, stof *(n)* • *adj* materiel

mathematical • *adj* matematisk

mathematics • *n* matematik

matrix • *n* matrix

mattress • *n* madras

maxim • *n* maksime

may • *v* må, måske

maybe • *adv* måske

mayonnaise • *n* mayonnaise, majonæse

mayor • *n* borgmester

maypole • *n* majstang, midsommerstang

me • *pron* mig, min, jeg

mead • *n* mjød

meadow • *n* eng

meadowlark • *n* englærke

meal • *n* måltid

mean • *v* betyde, mene • *n* middel *(n)*

meaning • *n* betydning, mening

measles • *n* mæslinger

meat • *n* kød *(n)*

mechanic • *n* mekaniker

mechanism • *n* mekanisme

medal • *n* medalje

medicine • *n* medicin

medieval • *adj* middelalderlig

mediocre • *adj* middelmådig

meditation • *n* meditation

medium • *n* medium

medley • *n* medley *(n)*

meerkat • *n* surikat

meet • *v* møde, træffe, mødes, opfylde

meeting • *n* møde *(n)*

megalomania • *n* storhedsvanvid *(n)*, megalomani

megawatt • *n* megawatt

melancholy • *n* melankoli • *adj* melankolsk

melanoma • *n* melanom

melee • *n* nærkamp, håndgemæng, sammenstød

melodious • *adj* melodiøs

melon • *n* melon

member • *n* medlem *(n)*

membership • *n* medlemskab *(n)*, medlemskab

memory • *n* hukommelse

mend • *v* reparere, fikse, lappe, forbedre

mendacity • *n* uhæderlighed, løgnagtighed

mendelevium • *n* mendelevium *(n)*

menopause • *n* overgangsalder

menstruation • *n* menstruation

mentality • *n* mentalitet

menthol • *n* mentol

menu • *n* spisekort *(n)*, menu

meow • *interj* mjav, miav

mercenary • *n* lejesoldat

merchant • *n* købmand

mercury • *n* kviksølv *(n)*

mercy • *n* barmhjertighed, nåde

merlin • *n* dværgfalk

mermaid • *n* havfrue

mesh • *n* net *(n)*, maske

mesmerize • *v* hypnotisere

mess • *n* messe, rod

message • *n* budskab *(n)*, besked, bud *(n)*

messenger • *n* bud *(n)*

messiah • *n* messias

messianic • *adj* messianske

metabolism • *n* stofskifte

metal • *n* metal *(n)*

metallurgy • *n* metallurgi

metamorphosis • *n* metamorfose

metaphor • *n* metafor

metastasis • *n* metastase

meteor • *n* meteor *(n)*

method • *n* metode

metic • *n* metoik

metro • *n* metro, tunnelbane, T-bane, undergrundsbane, U-bane

metrology • *n* metrologi
metropolitan • *n* metropolit
microbe • *n* mikrobe
microorganism • *n* mikroorganisme
microphone • *n* mikrofon
microscope • *n* mikroskop *(n)*
microscopic • *adj* mikroskopisk
microsecond • *n* mikrosekund *(n)*
microwave • *n* mikrobølge
midbrain • *n* mesencephalon, midthjernen
middle • *n* midte
midfield • *n* midtbane
midnight • *n* midnat *(n)*
midwife • *n* jordemoder, jordemor, fødselshjælper
migraine • *n* migræne
mildew • *n* meldug, mug *(n)*
mile • *n* mil
milestone • *n* milepæl
milieu • *n* miljø *(n)*
mill • *n* mølle
miller • *n* møller
millet • *n* hirse
milligram • *n* milligram *(n)*
millionaire • *n* millionær
millionth • *n* milliontedel
millipede • *n* tusindben *(n)*
millisecond • *n* millisekund
millstone • *n* møllesten
mind • *n* sind *(n)*, sjæl, indstilling
mine • *pron* min *(m)* • *n* mine
miner • *n* minearbejder, grubearbejder
mineral • *adj* mineralsk
mineralogy • *n* mineralogi
mining • *n* minedrift
minion • *n* håndlanger
minister • *n* minister
ministry • *n* ministerium *(n)*, regering, kabinet *(n)*, præsteembede *(n)*
minium • *n* mønje
minor • *n* mindreårig, bifag *(n)* • *adj* ubetydelig, mol
minority • *n* mindretal
mint • *n* mønt, mynte • *adj* postfrisk
minute • *n* minut *(n)*
miracle • *n* mirakel *(n)*, under *(n)*
mirage • *n* luftspejling
mirror • *n* spejl *(n)*
misanthropic • *adj* misantropisk, menneskefjendsk
miscarry • *v* mislykkes
miscellaneous • *adj* diverse, blandet
miser • *n* gnier
miserly • *adj* gnieragtig, gerrig, nærig
misery • *n* elendighed
mislead • *v* vildlede

miss • *v* savne • *n* forbier, frøken
missile • *n* missil
missionary • *n* missionær
misspell • *v* stave forkert
misspelling • *n* stavefejl *(n)*
mistake • *v* misforstå • *n* fejl
mistletoe • *n* mistelten
misunderstand • *v* misforstå
misuse • *n* misbrug *(n)*
mite • *n* mide
mitten • *n* luffe, vante
mix • *v* blande, mikse, røre • *n* blanding
mixer • *n* mikser, håndmikser, blender
mizzenmast • *n* mesanmast
moa • *n* moa
moat • *n* voldgrav
mocha • *n* mokka
moderately • *adv* moderat
modest • *adj* beskeden, moderat, blufærdig, anstændig, sømmelig, ærbar
modify • *v* modificere
modulate • *v* modulere, regulere
modulation • *n* modulation
molasses • *n* melasse
mold • *n* mug *(n)*
mole • *n* modermærke *(n)*, muldvarp
molecule • *n* molekyle *(n)*
molybdenum • *n* molybdæn *(n)*
moment • *n* øjeblik
monarch • *n* monark
monarchy • *n* monarki *(n)*
monastery • *n* kloster *(n)*
money • *n* betalingsmiddel *(n)*, valuta, møntenhed, penge, rede penge, pengesum, velstand, værdigenstand, pengemand
monk • *n* munk
monkey • *n* abe, abekat
mononucleosis • *n* mononukleose, kyssesyge
monopolize • *v* monopolisere
monopoly • *n* monopol *(n)*, monopolist
monotheism • *n* monoteisme
monotonous • *adj* enstonig, monoton, ensformig
monotony • *n* monotoni
monster • *n* uhyre
monstrosity • *n* skrummel
month • *n* måned
monument • *n* monument, mindesmærke
moo • *v* brøle • *n* muh • *interj* muh
moon • *n* månen, måne, måned
moonlight • *n* måneskin *(n)*
moor • *n* hede • *v* fortøje
mooring • *n* fortøjning
moose • *n* elg, elsdyr *(n)*

moped • *n* knallert
moraine • *n* moræne
morality • *n* moral
moratorium • *n* moratorium *(n)*
more • *adv* mere
morgue • *n* morgue
morning • *n* morgen
morphism • *n* morfi
morsel • *n* bid, godbid, stump
mortal • *adj* dødelig
mortality • *n* dødelighed
mortar • *n* mørtel
mortgage • *n* pant
mosque • *n* moské, moske
mosquito • *n* stikmyg
moss • *n* mos
moth • *n* møl
mother • *v* mor, tage sig ordentlig af • *n* moder, mor
mother-in-law • *n* svigermor
mother-of-pearl • *n* perlemor
motherhood • *n* moderskab
motion • *n* bevægelse
motive • *n* bevæggrund, motiv *(n)*
motorboat • *n* motorbåd
motorcycle • *n* motorcykel
motorist • *n* bilist
motto • *n* motto *(n)*
mouflon • *n* muflon
mountain • *n* bjerg *(n)*
mourn • *v* sørge
mouse • *n* mus
mousetrap • *n* musefælde
moustache • *n* overskæg *(n)*
mouth • *n* mund, kæft, udmunding
move • *v* bevæge sig, flytte sig, sætte i bevægelse, flytte, trække, bevæge, tilskynde, foreslå, fremsætte forslag om • *n* bevægelse, skridt, flytning, træk
movement • *n* bevægelse
movie • *n* film, biograf
mow • *v* meje, slå, klippe
mu • *n* my
mucus • *n* slim *(n)*
mud • *n* ælte *(n)*
mudguard • *n* skærm

mudslide • *n* mudderstrøm
muesli • *n* mysli
muezzin • *n* muaddhin
muffin • *n* muffin
mug • *n* krus *(n)*, fjæs *(n)*, fæ *(n)*, tosse
mugwort • *n* bynke, grå-bynke
mulatto • *n* mulat
mulberry • *n* morbær *(n)*
mullet • *n* multe, svenskerhår *(n)*
multilingual • *adj* flersproget
multiple • *adj* flere
mumble • *v* mumle • *n* mumlen
mummy • *n* mumie
municipality • *n* kommune
murder • *v* myrde, smadre, slå ihjel, kvæle • *n* mord *(n)*
murderer • *n* morder
murmur • *v* mumle • *n* mumlen, susen, rislen
muscle • *n* muskel
muscular • *adj* muskulær, muskuløs
muse • *n* muse
museum • *n* museum
mushroom • *n* svamp
music • *n* musik, node
musical • *n* musical, musikal
musician • *n* musiker
musket • *n* musket
musketeer • *n* musketer
muskrat • *n* bisamrotte
must • *v* skulle
mustard • *n* sennep
mutation • *n* mutation
mute • *adj* stum, umælende
mutilate • *v* lemlæste
mutiny • *n* mytteri *(n)*
mutual • *adj* gensidig, fælles
myopia • *n* nærsynethed
myriad • *n* myriade
myrrh • *n* myrra
myrtle • *n* myrte
mystery • *n* mysterium *(n)*
myth • *n* myte
mythology • *n* mytologi

N

nag • *n* pony, øg, krikke, nasser • *v* stikke til, hakke på, skænde på
nail • *n* negl, nagle, søm *(n)* • *v* sømme
naive • *adj* naiv, enfoldig
naked • *adj* nøgen, bar, blottet, utilsløret, åben, uafskærmet

nakedness • *n* nøgenhed
name • *v* døbe, navngive, nævne, vælge • *n* navn
namely • *adv* navnlig
nape • *n* nakke
napkin • *n* serviet

narcissus • *n* påskelilje
narcolepsy • *n* narkolepsi
narcoleptic • *n* narkoleptiker • *adj* narkoleptisk
narrate • *v* fortælle
narrative • *adj* fortællende, berettende
narrator • *n* fortæller
narrow • *v* snævres • *adj* snæver, tæt, smal
narwhal • *n* narhval
nasalization • *n* nasalitet
nation • *n* nation, stat
national • *adj* national
naturalism • *n* naturalisme
nature • *n* natur
naughty • *adj* slem, uartig
nausea • *n* kvalme
nave • *n* skib *(n)*
navel • *n* navle
navy • *n* marine, marineblå
near • *adj* nær
nebula • *n* stjernetåge
necessary • *adj* nødvendig
neck • *v* elske • *n* hals
necklace • *n* halskæde
necktie • *n* slips *(n)*
necromancy • *n* nekromanti
necrophilia • *n* nekrofili
necropsy • *n* obduktion
nectar • *n* nektar, saftevand *(n)*
nectarine • *n* nektarin
need • *n* behov *(n)* • *v* behøve
needle • *n* nål
neem • *n* neemtræ
neglect • *v* negligere, forsømme, ignorere • *n* negligering, forsømmelse, forsømthed
negligible • *adj* ubetydelig
neighborhood • *n* kvarter *(n)*, nabolag *(n)*
neither • *conj* hverken
neoclassicism • *n* nyklassicisme
neodymium • *n* neodym *(n)*
neologism • *n* neologisme
neon • *n* neon *(n)*
neophyte • *n* begynder, Nybegynder
nephew • *n* nevø
neptunium • *n* neptunium *(n)*
nerve • *n* nerve
nervous • *adj* nervøs, nervesvag, nerve-
nervously • *adv* nervøst
nervousness • *n* nervøsitet
ness • *n* næs *(n)*
nest • *v* bygge rede • *n* rede, fuglerede
net • *n* net *(n)*, garn, vod
nettle • *n* nælde, brændenælde
network • *n* net *(n)*, netværk *(n)*

neurotic • *n* neurotiker • *adj* neurotisk
neuter • *v* kastrere • *n* intetkøn, neutrum, intetkøn *(n)*, intetkønsord *(n)*, neutrum *(n)* • *adj* intetkøn, intransitiv, ukønnet, kønsløs
neutrino • *n* neutrino
never • *adv* aldrig
new • *adj* ny, frisk, nuværende, nyfødt
newborn • *adj* nyfødt
newcomer • *n* nybegynder
newfangled • *adj* nymodens
news • *n* nyt, nyheder
newspaper • *n* avis, dagblad *(n)*, tidsskrift, avispapir
next • *adj* næste
nexus • *n* sammenhæng, bindeled *(n)*, forbindelse, kæde, gruppe, række, schankel, nexus
nice • *adj* pæn
nickel • *n* nikkel
nickname • *n* øgenavn *(n)*, kælenavn *(n)*, tilnavn *(n)*
nicotine • *n* nikotin *(n)*
niece • *n* niece
nigger • *n* nigger, abekat
night • *n* nat, aften, overnatning, nattesøvn, skumring, mørke
nightfall • *n* skumring
nightingale • *n* sydlig nattergal
nightmare • *n* mareridt *(n)*
nihilism • *n* nihilisme
nilpotent • *adj* nilpotent
nincompoop • *n* fjols, skvadderhoved, idiot, knallert
nine • *n* nital *(n)*, nier
nineteenth • *n* nittener, nittendedel • *adj* nittende
ninetieth • *adj* halvfemsindstyvende
ninth • *adj* niende
niobium • *n* niobium *(n)*
nipple • *n* brystvorte
nit • *n* luseæg *(n)*, fjols *(n)*, kvaj *(n)*
nitrate • *n* nitrat *(n)*
nitrogen • *n* nitrogen *(n)*, kvælstof *(n)*
nix • *n* niks
no • *n* nej *(n)*
nobelium • *n* nobelium *(n)*
noise • *n* støj, larm, spektakel, lyd
nominate • *v* nominere
none • *pron* ingen
nonexistent • *adj* ikkeeksisterende
nonsense • *n* nonsens *(n)*
nonsensical • *adj* absurd
noodle • *n* nudel
nook • *n* hjørne *(n)*, krog
noon • *n* middag
noose • *n* løkke

norm • *n* norm
normal • *adj* normal, almindelig, rask
north • *n* nord • *adj* nordlig
north-northeast • *n* nordnordøst
north-northwest • *n* nordnordvest
northeast • *n* nordøst
northwest • *n* nordvest
nose • *v* liste, snuse • *n* næse, snude, spids, tud
nosebleed • *n* næseblod
nostril • *n* næsebor *(n)*
not • *adv* ikke, ej • *interj* ikke
notary • *n* notar
note • *n* node
notebook • *n* skrivehæfte
nothing • *pron* intet, ingenting
notice • *v* bemærke • *n* notits, opsigelsesfrist
notorious • *adj* berygtet
noun • *n* hovedord *(n)*, substantiv *(n)*, navneord *(n)*
novel • *n* roman
now • *n* nu *(n)* • *adv* nu • *conj* nu
nowadays • *adv* nu om stunder, nu til dags

nowhere • *adv* ingensteds, intetsteds
nu • *n* ny *(n)*
nude • *adj* nøgen
nudity • *n* nøgenhed
nugget • *n* klump
nuke • *v* lave mad i mikron
number • *n* tal
numerator • *n* tæller
numismatist • *n* numismatiker
nun • *n* nonne
nurse • *n* barneplejerske, nurse, sygeplejerske
nut • *n* nød
nutcracker • *n* nøddeknækker *(n)*
nutmeg • *n* muskat, muskatnød
nutrition • *n* ernæring
nutritional • *adj* ernæring-, ernæringmæssig
nutshell • *n* nøddeskal
nyctophobia • *n* mørkeræd, nyktofobi
nymph • *n* nymfe
nymphomania • *n* nymfomani
nymphomaniac • *n* nymfoman • *adj* nymfoman

O

oak • *n* eg, egetræ *(n)*
oakum • *n* værk
oar • *n* åre
oasis • *n* oase
oat • *n* havre
oath • *n* ed, løfte
oatmeal • *n* havregryn *(n)*
oats • *n* havregryn
obedience • *n* lydighed
obese • *adj* fed
obesity • *n* fedme, overvægt
object • *v* indvende • *n* objekt, ting
obligation • *n* pligt
oblivious • *adj* uvidende *(n)*
oboe • *n* obo
obsequious • *adj* underdanig, servil, slesk
observatory • *n* observatorium *(n)*
observe • *v* betragte, iagttage, observere, overholde, følge, bemærke
observer • *n* observatør
obsession • *n* tvangstanke, besættelse, fiks ide
obsolescence • *n* forældelse
obsolete • *adj* gået af brug, forældet
obstetrics • *n* obstetrik
obvious • *adj* tydelig, åbenbar, oplagt,

indlysende
obviously • *adv* naturligvis
occasion • *v* foranledige, forårsage • *n* begivenhed, anledning, lejlighed, grund, behov *(n)*
occult • *n* okkultisme • *adj* okkult, esoterisk
occupation • *n* arbejde *(n)*, beskæftigelse, erhverv *(n)*, besættelse, okkupation
occupational • *adj* arbejdsmæssig
occur • *v* forekomme
ocean • *n* ocean *(n)*
octagon • *n* ottekant
octave • *n* oktav
octet • *n* oktet
octopus • *n* blæksprutte
ode • *n* ode
of • *prep* i, af
offer • *n* bud *(n)*, tilbud *(n)*, udbud *(n)*, udbudsforretning • *v* tilbyde, foreslå, udlove, udsætte
office • *n* kontor, bureau
offside • *n* offside
often • *adv* ofte, hyppig
oil • *v* smøre • *n* olie, råolie
ointment • *n* salve *(n)*
old • *adj* gammel, tidligere

old-fashioned • *adj* gammeldags
oligarchy • *n* oligarki *(n)*, fåmandsvælde *(n)*
olive • *n* oliven
ombudsman • *n* ombudsmand
ominous • *adj* varslende, ildevarslende, uheldsvanger
omit • *v* udelade
omniscient • *adj* alvidende
omnivore • *n* altæder
on • *adj* på
once • *adv* en gang, engang • *conj* så snart, bare, når først
oncology • *n* onkologi
one • *n* et, én, ener, ettal *(n)*, endollarseddel • *adj* en, et, den, det, ene, eneste • *pron* man, en, én
one-eyed • *adj* enøjet
onion • *n* løg *(n)*
only • *adj* eneste
onomatopoeia • *n* onomatopoietikon, lydord
onomatopoeic • *adj* onomatopoietisk
onyx • *n* onyks
opera • *n* opera
operator • *n* operatør, telefonist, telefonistinde, operator
ophthalmologist • *n* øjenlæge
opinion • *n* mening
opportune • *adj* passende, opportun, belejlig
opposite • *adj* modsat • *prep* over for
oppress • *v* undertrykke
oppression • *n* undertrykkelse
optional • *adj* valgfrit
or • *conj* eller
orange • *n* appelsintræ, appelsin, orange • *adj* orange
orc • *n* ork
orchestra • *n* orkester *(n)*, orchestra, orkestergrav
ordain • *v* ordinere
order • *n* ordre
orderly • *n* portør, ordonnans, oppasser • *adj* ordentlig, velordnet
ordinal • *n* ordenstal *(n)*, ordinaltal *(n)*
ore • *n* malm
oregano • *n* oregano, almindelig merian
organ • *n* organ, orgel *(n)*

organic • *adj* økologisk
organism • *n* organisme
organization • *n* organisation
organize • *v* organisere
orgasm • *n* orgasme
orgy • *n* orgie *(n)*
orient • *v* orientere
original • *adj* oprindelig
ornithology • *n* ornitologi
orphan • *n* forældreløst barn *(n)*, hittebarn *(n)*
orphanage • *n* børnehjem *(n)*
orthodox • *adj* ortodoks, rettroende, almindelig anerkendt
orthodoxy • *n* ortodoksi
orthogonal • *adj* ortogonal, vinkelret
osmium • *n* osmium *(n)*
osprey • *n* fiskeørn
ostrich • *n* struds
other • *adj* andre
otherwise • *adv* anderledes, ellers
otology • *n* otologi
otter • *n* odder
ouch • *interj* av
ought • *v* burde
outbreak • *n* udbrud *(n)*, bølge
outskirt • *n* udkant
ovary • *n* æggestok
oven • *n* ovn
over • *adj* forbi
overboard • *adv* over bord
overestimate • *v* overvurdere
overhear • *v* overhøre
overload • *n* overbelastning
overnight • *adv* natten over, i nattens løb, pludselig, straks
overpopulation • *n* overbefolkning
overseer • *n* opsynsmand
overshadow • *v* overskygge
overtake • *v* overhale
overwhelm • *v* overmande, overvælde
ovum • *n* ægcelle
owl • *n* ugle
own • *v* eje • *adj* egen
owner • *n* ejer
oxygen • *n* ilt, oxygen *(n)*
oystercatcher • *n* strandskade, tjald
ozone • *n* ozon *(n)*

P

package • *v* pakke • *n* pakke, pakning
pact • *n* pagt
paddle • *n* paddel, padle, padleåre, pagaj
paddy • *n* rismark *(n)*
padlock • *n* hængelås
page • *n* side
pagoda • *n* pagode
pain • *n* smerte
painful • *adj* smertefuld
paint • *v* male
painter • *n* maler, kunstmaler
painting • *n* malerkunst
pajamas • *n* pyjamas
palace • *n* palads *(n)*
palatable • *adj* velsmagende, spiselig, acceptabel
palaver • *n* palaver
pale • *adj* bleg, blegt
paleontology • *n* palæontologi
paletot • *n* frakke
palindrome • *n* palindrom
palladium • *n* palladium
pallet • *n* palle
pallid • *adj* bleg
palm • *n* håndflade
palmistry • *n* håndlæsning
pancake • *n* pandekage
pancreas • *n* bugspytkirtel
pandemic • *n* pandemi
panegyric • *n* lovtale
panegyrical • *adj* panegyrisk
panic • *n* panik
panther • *n* panter
pants • *n* bukser, buks
paper • *n* papir
parachute • *n* faldskærm
parade • *n* parade, optog *(n)*
paradise • *n* paradis
paragraph • *n* paragraf
parallax • *n* parallakse
parallelepiped • *n* parallelepipedum
paramedic • *n* paramediciner
paranoia • *n* paranoia
parasite • *n* parasit *(m)*
parent • *n* forælder, ophav
parish • *n* sogn
park • *n* park
parliament • *n* parlament, ting *(n)*
parody • *v* parodiere • *n* parodi
parrot • *n* papegøje
parsimony • *n* sparsomhed
parsley • *n* persille
parsnip • *n* pastinak
part • *n* del
partial • *adj* partiel, partisk
participate • *v* deltage, participere
particle • *n* partikel, lille del, elemen-

tarpartikel
partisan • *n* partisoldat
partner • *v* samarbejde • *n* partner, kompagnon, kavaler, medspiller
partnership • *n* partnerskab
partridge • *n* agerhøne
party • *n* parti *(n)*, fest
pasha • *n* sværmeri
passenger • *n* passager
passionate • *adj* lidenskabelig
passport • *n* pas *(n)*
password • *n* kodeord *(n)*, løsen *(n)*, feltråb *(n)*, adgangskode, password *(n)*
pastiche • *n* pastiche, potpourri *(n)*
pastry • *n* bagværk *(n)*
patch • *n* lap, bed *(n)*, jordstykke *(n)*
path • *n* sti, havegang, passage, retning, vej
pathetic • *adj* medynkvækkende, sørgelig, ynkelig, patetisk
pathological • *adj* patologisk
patience • *n* tålmod *(n)*, tålmodighed
patient • *n* patient • *adj* tålmodig
patio • *n* teresse, gårdhave
patriarchal • *adj* patriakalsk
patriot • *n* patriot
patrol • *n* patrulje
patronymic • *n* patronym *(n)*
pavement • *n* fortov, vejbelægning
paw • *n* pote
pawn • *n* bonde
pay • *v* betale, betale sig • *n* betaling
payday • *n* lønningsdag
pea • *n* ært
peace • *n* fred, ro, sindsro, sjælefred
peaceable • *adj* fredelig, fredsommelig
peacetime • *n* fredstid
peach • *n* ferskentræ *(n)*, fersken
peacock • *n* påfugl
peanut • *n* jordnød, peanut
pear • *n* pære
pearl • *n* perle
peasant • *n* bonde
peat • *n* tørv
pebble • *n* ral
peckish • *adj* brødflov, sulten, irritabel
pectin • *n* pektin
pedagogue • *n* pædagog
pedal • *n* pedal
pedant • *n* pedant
pederast • *n* pæderast
pederasty • *n* pæderasti
pedicure • *n* fodpleje
pee • *v* tisse, pisse
peel • *v* skrælle • *n* skræl
peerless • *adj* mageløs
pelican • *n* pelikan

pelvis • *n* bækken *(n)*
pen • *n* pen, hunsvane
penalty • *n* straf
pencil • *n* blyant
penguin • *n* pingvin
penicillin • *n* penicillin
peninsula • *n* halvø
penis • *n* penis, pik, tissemand, diller, javert
pensive • *adj* eftertænksom, tankefuld, tungsindig
pentagon • *n* pentagon, femkant
penultimate • *adj* næstsidst
peony • *n* pæon
people • *n* folk, folk *(n)*, slægt
pepper • *n* peber *(n)*, chili, paprika
peppermint • *n* pebermynte
perceive • *v* begribe
perdition • *n* evig, fordømmelse, undergang
perennial • *adj* helårlig, evig, flerårig, tilbagevendende
perfectionist • *n* perfektionist
perforate • *v* perforere
perfume • *n* perfume
perfunctory • *adj* skødesløs, overfladisk
perhaps • *adv* måske
peril • *n* fare, risiko
perilous • *adj* farlig
perineum • *n* mellemkød *(n)*
periodic • *adj* periodisk
periodically • *adv* periodisk
periphery • *n* periferi, udkant
periscope • *n* periskop *(n)*
peristalsis • *n* peristaltik
perjure • *v* mened
permanent • *n* permanent
permanganate • *n* permanganat, kaliumpermanganat
permission • *n* tilladelse
permit • *v* tillade
perpetrate • *v* begå
perpetrator • *n* gerningsmand
perpetual • *adj* vedvarende
persimmon • *n* kaki
person • *n* person, legeme *(n)*
personal • *adj* personlig
personality • *n* personlighed, skikkelse, karisma
perspicacious • *adj* klarsynet
perspicacity • *n* skarpsindighed
persuade • *v* overbevise
pervert • *n* perverst menneske
pest • *n* skadedyr, plage, plageånd, pestilens
pet • *v* kæle • *n* kæledyr *(n)*
petrel • *n* stormfugl

petrify • *v* forstene
pettifogger • *n* ordkløver
petty • *adj* ubetydelig
pew • *n* kirkestol
pewter • *n* tin, tintøj
phalanx • *n* falanks
phallic • *adj* fallisk
phantom • *n* fantom
pharaoh • *n* farao
pharmacist • *n* apoteker, farmaceut, farmakonom
pharmacy • *n* apotek *(n)*
pheasant • *n* fasan
phenylalanine • *n* fenylalanin
philanthropist • *n* filantrop
philatelic • *adj* filatelistisk
philatelist • *n* frimærkesamler, filatelist
philately • *n* filateli
philology • *n* filologi
philosophy • *n* filosofi
phlegmatic • *adj* flegmatisk
phobia • *n* fobi
phoenix • *n* føniks
phone • *v* ringe • *n* telefon
phoneme • *n* fonem *(n)*
phonetics • *n* fonetik
phonology • *n* fonologi
phosphoric • *adj* fosforholdig, fosforlignende
phosphorous • *adj* fosforholdig, fosforlignende, fosforsyrlig
phosphorus • *n* fosfor *(n)*
photo • *n* foto, fotografi *(n)*, billede *(n)*
photocopier • *n* fotokopimaskine
photocopy • *v* fotokopiere • *n* fotokopi
photogenic • *adj* fotogen
photograph • *v* fotografere • *n* fotografi *(n)*
photography • *n* fotografi
photosynthesis • *n* fotosyntese
phyllo • *n* filo
phylum • *n* række
physical • *adj* fysisk
pianist • *n* pianist
piano • *n* klaver *(n)*
piccolo • *n* piccolofløjte
pick • *v* plukke
pickpocket • *n* lommetyv
picture • *n* billede *(n)*, foto *(n)*, fotografi *(n)*
picturesque • *adj* pittoresk, malerisk
pie • *n* tærte
piece • *n* stykke *(n)*, brik
pier • *n* mole
pig • *n* svin *(n)*, gris
pigeon • *n* due
piglet • *n* pattegris

pigsty • *n* svinesti
pike • *n* pike, gedde
pilgrim • *n* pilgrim
pill • *n* pille, tablet
pillory • *v* sætte i gabestokken • *n* gabestok
pillow • *n* pude
pilot • *n* pilot
pilsner • *n* pilsner
pimp • *n* alfons
pimple • *n* filipens
pin • *n* knappenål
pinch • *v* knibe, nappe, nive, klemme, hugge, negle, nuppe, snuppe, tage • *n* knib *(n)*, nap *(n)*, niv *(n)*, drys *(n)*
pine • *n* fyr, grantræ
pineapple • *n* ananas
pink • *n* lyserød • *adj* lyserød
pious • *adj* ydmyg, from
pipe • *n* rør *(n)*
piracy • *n* pirateri *(n)*, sørøveri *(n)*, kapring, piratkopiering
piranha • *n* piratfisk
pirate • *n* sørøver, pirat
pirouette • *n* piruet
piss • *n* pis
pistachio • *n* pistacie
pitchfork • *n* høtyv, fork
pitfall • *n* faldgrube, fælde
pixel • *n* pixel
pizza • *n* pizza
pizzeria • *n* pizzeria *(n)*
place • *n* sted
placenta • *n* moderkage
plague • *n* pest, plage, pestilens
plain • *adj* ensfarvet • *n* slette
plane • *n* plan, plan *(n)*, høvl, flyver, platan • *adj* plan • *v* høvle
planet • *n* planet
plant • *v* så, plante, placere • *n* plante, vækst
plantain • *n* vejbred
plaster • *v* pudse, kalke, gipse, klistre, overklistre • *n* salve, puds *(n)*, gips
plate • *n* tallerken
platelet • *n* blodplade
plating • *n* pladning
platinum • *n* platin *(n)*
platoon • *n* deling
platypus • *n* næbdyr *(n)*
play • *n* leg, spil, stykke
player • *n* spiller, skuespiller, spillemand, musiker
playground • *n* legeplads, sandkasse, tumleplads
plaza • *n* torv *(n)*
pleasant • *adj* behagelig, rar

please • *adv* vær så venlig
pleonasm • *n* pleonasme, dobbeltkonfekt
pliers • *n* tang
plod • *v* traske
plop • *v* dryppe, plumpe • *n* dryp
plough • *v* pløje • *n* plov
pluck • *v* plukke
plum • *n* blomme, blommetræ, lækkerbisken • *adj* blommefarvet
plumage • *n* fjerdragt
plus • *conj* og, plus
plutonium • *n* plutonium *(n)*
poacher • *n* krybskytte
pocket • *n* lomme
pod • *n* bælg, kapsel
poem • *n* digt *(n)*
poet • *n* digter
poetry • *n* poesi, digtekunst, lyrik, digtning
poinsettia • *n* julestjerne
point • *v* pege • *n* tidspunkt *(n)*, pointe, punkt *(n)*, punktum *(n)*, point *(n)*, komma *(n)*
poison • *v* forgifte • *n* gift
poisoning • *n* forgiftning
poisonous • *adj* giftig
pokeweed • *n* kermesbær
pole • *n* pol
polecat • *n* ilder
polemic • *n* polemik
police • *n* politi *(n)*
policeman • *n* politimand *(m)*
policy • *n* politik
polish • *v* polere, blanke, pudse, glatte • *n* pudsecreme, politur, glans, glathed, elegance, forfinelse
polite • *adj* høflig
political • *adj* politisk
politician • *n* politiker
politics • *n* politik
pollution • *n* forurening
polonium • *n* polonium *(n)*
poltroon • *n* kryster, kujon
polyethylene • *n* polyætylen *(n)*
polygon • *n* polygon
polytheism • *n* polyteisme
polytheistic • *adj* polyteistisk
pomegranate • *n* granatæble *(n)*
pomelo • *n* pomelo, pompelmus
pond • *n* dam
pony • *n* pony
pooch • *n* hund
poodle • *n* puddel, puddelhund
poor • *adj* fattig, stakkels
pope • *n* pave
poplar • *n* poppel, poppeltræ *(n)*
poppy • *n* valmue

population • *n* befolkning
populism • *n* populisme
porbeagle • *n* sildehaj
porcelain • *n* porcelæn *(n)*, porcelæn
pork • *n* svinekød *(n)*
pornographer • *n* pornograf
pornographic • *adj* pornografisk
pornography • *n* pornografi
porous • *adj* porøs
porridge • *n* grød
port • *n* port, havn
portable • *adj* bærbar
portcullis • *n* faldgitter
portrait • *n* portræt *(n)*, kontrafej *(n)*
positive • *adj* positiv
posse • *n* bande *(n)*
possess • *v* besidde, eje, besætte
possibility • *n* mulighed
possible • *adj* mulig
post • *n* stolpe, målstolpe, post
postage • *n* porto
postcard • *n* brevkort *(n)*, postkort *(n)*
postmark • *v* afstemple • *n* poststempel
postmodernism • *n* postmodernisme
postpone • *v* udsætte
pot • *n* potte, krukke, pot, græs
potassium • *n* kalium *(n)*
potato • *n* kartoffel
potentate • *n* potentat
pothole • *n* jættegryde
potpourri • *n* potpourri *(n)*
poultry • *n* fjerkræ *(n)*
pound • *n* pund *(n)*
pour • *v* hælde
powder • *n* pulver *(n)*
power • *n* magt
practice • *v* øve, træne, udøve • *n* praksis
pragmatic • *adj* pragmatisk
prairie • *n* præ014rie
praise • *v* rose
prance • *v* stejle, spankulere
prank • *n* spilopper
praseodymium • *n* praseodymium *(n)*
prattle • *v* plapre, pludre
prawn • *n* reje
praxis • *n* praksis
pray • *v* bede, tilbede
prayer • *n* bøn
preacher • *n* prædikant *(m)*
precious • *adj* dyrebar
precipitation • *n* nedbør
precise • *adj* præcis
preeminent • *adj* fremtrædende
prefer • *v* foretrække
prefix • *n* præfiks *(n)*
pregnancy • *n* graviditet, svangerskab
pregnant • *adj* gravid, højgravid

prelate • *n* Prælat
preparation • *n* forberedelse, præparation, tilberedning, præparat *(n)*
prepare • *v* berede, tilberede
preposition • *n* forholdsord *(n)*, præposition
prepuce • *n* forhud
prerequisite • *n* forudsætning
preservative • *n* konserveringsmiddel *(n)*
preserve • *n* naturreservat *(n)*
president • *n* præsident
presuppose • *v* forudsætte
pretend • *v* foregive
pretext • *n* påskud *(n)*
prettily • *adv* nydelig
previous • *adj* foregående, forrige
price • *v* prissætte, vurdere • *n* pris
prick • *n* prik *(n)*
pride • *n* stolthed
priest • *n* præst
priestess • *n* præstinde
primary • *adj* primær
prime • *adj* første, tidligste, førsteklasses,
primtal-, primær, hoved-, vigtigste • *v*
klargøre
prince • *n* prins, fyrste
princely • *adj* prinselig, fyrstelig
princess • *n* prinsesse
printer • *n* printer
priority • *n* prioritet
prism • *n* prisme *(n)*
prison • *n* fængsel, fængslet
prisoner • *n* fange
private • *n* menig • *adj* privat
prize • *n* præmie
probably • *adv* antageligvis
problem • *n* problem *(n)*
procrastinate • *v* udsætte, udskyde,
forhale, forsinke
procurement • *n* indkøbsafdeling, indkøb *(n)*, fremskaffelse
procyonid • *n* halvbjørn
prodigy • *n* vidunder
production • *n* produktion
profession • *n* erhverv, fag *(n)*
progeny • *n* afkom *(n)*
program • *n* program
project • *n* projekt
prolific • *adj* frugtbar, produktiv
promethium • *n* promethium *(n)*
promiscuous • *adj* promiskuøs
promise • *n* løfte *(n)*
promotion • *n* reklame, støtte
prong • *n* spids, tand, gren
pronoun • *n* pronomen, stedord
pronounce • *v* udtale
pronunciation • *n* udtale

proof • *n* bevis
proofreader • *n* korrekturlæser
propeller • *n* propel
propensity • *n* tilbøjelighed
property • *n* ejendom, besiddelse, ejendomsret, egenskab
prophecy • *n* profeti, spådom
prophet • *n* profet, spåmand *(m)*, spåkvinde *(f)*
propose • *v* foreslå, fri
proposition • *n* forslag *(n)*
propriety • *n* rigtighed, ordentlighed, sømmelighed
prosaic • *adj* prosaisk
proscenium • *n* proscenium *(n)*
prose • *n* prosa
prosody • *n* prosodi
prostate • *n* blærehalskirtel
prostitution • *n* prostitution
protactinium • *n* protactinium *(n)*
protect • *v* beskytte
protectorate • *n* protektorat *(n)*
protein • *n* protein *(n)*
protist • *n* protist
proton • *n* proton
proverb • *n* ordsprog *(n)*
province • *n* provins
provisional • *n* provisorie • *adj* provisorisk
provost • *n* provst
proximity • *n* nærhed
proxy • *n* fuldmægtig *(m)*
prude • *n* sippe, snerpe
prudery • *n* sippethed, snerperi *(n)*
prudish • *adj* sippet, snerpet
prune • *n* sveske
psalm • *n* salme
psittacosis • *n* psittacosis, ornithosis, papegøjesyge
psychology • *n* psykologi
psychometry • *n* psykometri, genstandslæsning
psychosomatic • *adj* psykosomatisk
psychotherapist • *n* psykoterapeut
ptarmigan • *n* fjeldrype
pub • *n* kro
puberty • *n* pubertet
pubis • *n* skamben *(n)*, kønsben *(n)*
public • *adj* offentlig
pudding • *n* blodbudding, budding
puddle • *n* pyt, pæl
puffin • *n* lunde, søpapegøje
pull • *v* trække
pulpit • *n* prædikestol
pulsar • *n* pulsar
puma • *n* puma
pumice • *n* pimpsten
pump • *n* pumpe
pumpkin • *n* græskar, græskarplante
pun • *n* ordspil *(n)*
punctuation • *n* tegnsætning
punish • *v* straffe
punishment • *n* straf
puny • *adj* sølle
pupil • *n* elev, pupil
puppet • *n* marionet
puppy • *n* hvalp
purgatory • *n* skærsild
purple • *adj* lilla
purpose • *n* mål, mening, intention, grund
pus • *n* pus *(n)*, materie
pusher • *n* pusher
pussy • *n* mis, missekat, kusse, fisse, tissekone, tøsedreng
putt • *v* putte
pygmy • *n* pygmæ
pyramid • *n* pyramide
pyre • *n* ild
python • *n* pyton

Q

qua • *adv* qua, i egenskab af, eks. han førte ordet qua formand
quack • *v* rappe • *n* rap *(n)*, kvaksalver
quacksalver • *n* kvaksalver
quadruped • *n* firbenet dyr
quadruple • *adj* firedobbelt
quagmire • *n* sump, dynd *(n)*, hængedynd *(n)*
quail • *n* vagtel
qualification • *n* kvalifikation
quality • *n* kvalitet
quantify • *v* kvantificere
quarantine • *n* karantæne
quark • *n* kvark
quarrel • *v* skændes • *n* skænderi *(n)*, uenighed
quarry • *n* stenbrud
quart • *n* kvart, fjerdedel gallon
quarter • *n* fjerdedel, kvart, kvartal *(n)*, kvarter *(n)*
quarterfinal • *n* kvartfinale
quartermaster • *n* kvartermester

quartile • *n* kvartil
quasar • *n* kvasar
quay • *n* kaj
queen • *v* dronning, udnævne, krone • *n* dronning, dame, bøsse
query • *n* spørgsmål
question • *n* spørgsmål
questionable • *adj* tvivlsom
queue • *v* stille, kø, danne • *n* kø, venteliste, stak
quick • *adj* hurtig, kvik
quickly • *adv* hurtig, hurtigt
quicksand • *n* kviksand
quicksilver • *n* kviksølv *(n)*

quiet • *n* stilhed, ro • *adj* stille, tyst, rolig
quill • *n* fjerpen
quillwort • *n* brasenføde
quilt • *n* vattæppe *(n)*
quince • *n* kvæde
quinine • *n* kinin
quiver • *n* kogger, pilekogger • *v* dirre, sitre, bævre
quiz • *n* quiz
quota • *n* kvote
quotation • *n* citation, citering
quotient • *n* kvotient

R

rabbi • *n* rabbiner
rabbit • *n* kanin
raccoon • *n* vaskebjørn
race • *n* løb *(n)*
racism • *n* racisme
racket • *n* ketsjer
radio • *n* radiofoni, radio
radioactive • *adj* radioaktiv
radioactivity • *n* radioaktivitet
radish • *n* radise
radius • *n* radius
radon • *n* radon *(n)*
raft • *n* flåde
rage • *v* rase • *n* raseri *(n)*, galskab
ragout • *n* ragout
raid • *n* razzia
rail • *n* skinne
railway • *n* jernbane
rain • *v* regne • *n* regn
rainbow • *n* regnbue
raindrop • *n* regndråbe
raisin • *n* rosin
rake • *n* rive, libertiner
ram • *n* vædder *(m)*, stenbukken, stempel, stødslæde
rampart • *n* volden
ramrod • *n* ladestok
rancid • *adj* harsk
rand • *n* rand
random • *adj* tilfældig, overflødig, ligegyldig
ransom • *n* løsesum
rape • *v* voldtage • *n* voldtægt
rare • *adj* rød, sjælden
raspberry • *n* hindbær, hindbær *(n)*
ratify • *v* ratificere
rational • *adj* rationel
rationality • *n* rationalitet

rattle • *n* rangle, rasle
rattlesnake • *n* klapperslange
raven • *n* ravn
ravine • *n* ravine
raw • *adj* rå
razor • *n* kniv, barberkniv
razorbill • *n* alk
reaction • *n* reaktion
read • *v* læse
reader • *n* læser
realism • *n* realismen
realist • *n* realist
realistic • *adj* realistisk
reality • *n* virkelighed, realitet
realm • *n* sfære, rige *(n)*
realtor • *n* ejendomsmægler
reason • *v* ræsonnere, overveje, slutte • *n* fornuft
rebel • *v* rebel
rebus • *n* rebus
recalcitrant • *adj* genstridig, stædig
receipt • *n* kvittering
receive • *v* få
receiver • *n* modtager
recent • *adj* frisk, nylig
receptive • *adj* modtagelig
recessive • *adj* recessiv
rechargeable • *adj* genopladelig
recipient • *n* modtager
reciprocal • *adj* reciprok
recitation • *n* recitation
recite • *v* recitere
recoil • *n* rekyl
recollect • *v* erindre
recommend • *v* anbefale
reconciliation • *n* forsoning
record • *n* optegnelse, dokument, plade, grammofonplade, post, rekord

recorder • *n* blokfløjte
rectangle • *n* rektangel
recycling • *n* genanvendelse, genbrug *(n)*
red • *adj* rød
redheaded • *adj* rødhåret
redundant • *adj* overflødig
reel • *v* rulle, spole, vinde, vakle, rave, slingre • *n* reel, tromle, rulle, hjul *(n)*, trisse
refer • *v* henvise, referere
referee • *v* dømme • *n* dommer
referendum • *n* folkeafstemning
referral • *n* henvisning
refine • *v* raffinere, rense, forbedre, forfine
refinement • *n* raffinement *(n)*
refrain • *n* refræn *(n)*
refrigerator • *n* køleskab *(n)*
regards • *n* hilsen
regent • *n* regent
region • *n* region
registration • *n* registrering
regret • *v* angre, fortryde
regular • *adj* regelmæssig, almindelig, normal, fast
regulation • *n* forordning
reign • *n* regeringstid
reindeer • *n* ren, rensdyr *(n)*
reject • *v* afvise
rejoice • *v* juble
related • *adj* relaterede, beslægtet
relation • *n* slægtning, familiemedlem *(n)*
relationship • *n* forhold *(n)*
relative • *n* pårørende, beslægtet, frænde • *adj* relativ
relatively • *adv* relativt
relax • *v* falde til ro, slappe af
release • *n* version, udgave
reliable • *adj* pålidelig
relief • *n* lettelse, relief
religious • *adj* religiøs
relish • *v* nyde • *n* nydelse
remainder • *n* rest
remaining • *adj* resterende, tilbageværende
remedy • *v* afhjælpe
remember • *v* huske, erindre
reminder • *n* påmindelse
remnant • *n* rest
remorse • *n* skyldfølelse, anger
rendezvous • *n* rendezvous *(n)*
renegade • *n* lovløs
rent • *v* leje, leje ud • *n* leje, husleje
repeat • *v* gentage, repetere
repentant • *adj* angrende
repercussion • *n* efterfølge
replace • *v* erstatte

reply • *v* svare, besvare, genmæle • *n* svar *(n)*, besvarelse
reproach • *v* bebrejde • *n* bebrejdelse
reproduction • *n* reproduktion
reptile • *n* krybdyr *(n)*
republic • *n* republik
reputation • *n* anseelse
request • *v* anmode • *n* ansøgning
requiem • *n* rekviem *(n)*
requisition • *v* rekvirere
resemblance • *n* lighed, sammenligning, sandsynlighed
resemble • *v* ligne, minde om
reserved • *adj* reserveret
residence • *n* bopæl
resident • *n* bosiddende
resignation • *n* fratræden
resource • *n* resurse, ressource
respectively • *adv* henholdsvis
resplendent • *adj* strålende
responsibility • *n* ansvar *(n)*
responsible • *adj* ansvarlig, ansvarsbevidst, ansvarsfuld, pålidelig
rest • *n* hvile, ro • *v* hvile
restaurant • *n* restaurant
restlessness • *n* rastløshed
restricted • *adj* afgrænset, begrænset
restrictive • *adj* restriktive
result • *n* resultat *(n)*
retail • *n* detailhandel, detailsalg *(n)*
retarded • *adj* retarderet, udviklingshæmmet
retch • *v* gylpe
reticulum • *n* netmave
retort • *n* replik, retort, destillerkolbe
retroactive • *adj* tilbagevirkende, retroaktiv
reveal • *v* afsløre
reveille • *n* reveille
revelation • *n* åbenbaring
revenant • *n* genganger
revenge • *n* hævn
revenue • *n* skatteindtægt, indtægt
revers • *n* revers
reviewer • *n* recensent *(m)*
revise • *v* revidere, repetere
revolt • *n* oprør *(n)*, opstand
revolution • *n* revolution
revolutionary • *adj* revolutionær
revue • *n* revy
rhenium • *n* rhenium *(n)*
rhetoric • *n* retorik, velformuleret, kancellistil
rhetorical • *adj* retorisk
rhinoceros • *n* næsehorn *(n)*
rhodium • *n* rhodium *(n)*
rhombus • *n* rombe, rhombe

rhubarb • *n* rabarber
rhythm • *n* rytme, mønster *(n)*
rib • *n* ribben
ribbon • *n* bånd *(n)*
rice • *n* ris *(n)*, ris
rich • *adj* rig
rickets • *n* rakitis, engelsk syge
ride • *v* ride, køre • *n* ridt *(n)*
rifle • *n* riffel
right • *n* ret, rettighed, højre, side • *adj* ret, lige, retvinklet, rigtig, korrekt, højre, konservativ, højre- • *v* rette, korrigere
right-handed • *n* højrehåndet
rigorous • *adj* intens
rim • *n* rand, indfatning, fælg
ring • *n* ring • *v* ringe
ringmaster • *n* sprechstallmeister
risk • *v* risikere • *n* risiko
rite • *n* rite, ritus
ritual • *n* ritual *(n)*
river • *n* flod, å
road • *n* gade, vej
roar • *v* brøle • *n* brøl *(n)*
rob • *v* røve, bestjæle, berøve, stjæle, tyvstjæle, begå røveri
robber • *n* røver
robe • *n* dameselskabskjole, skrud
robin • *n* rødhals, vandredrossel
rocket • *n* rucola, sennepskål
rococo • *n* rokoko • *adj* rokoko-
rod • *n* stang, stav, spanskrør, ris, stavbakterie
rodent • *n* gnaver
roe • *n* rogn
romantic • *n* romantiker
romanticist • *n* romantiker
roof • *n* tag *(n)*
rook • *n* råge, tårn *(n)*
room • *n* rum *(n)*, soveværelse
rooster • *n* hane
root • *n* rod, rod *(n)*
rope • *n* tov *(n)*
rosary • *n* bedekrans
rose • *n* rose
rosemary • *n* rosmarin

rot • *v* rådne
rotten • *adj* rådden
roundabout • *n* rundkørsel, karrusel, omkørsel
row • *n* række, rad, spektakel *(n)*, tumult, optøjer *(n)*, ballade, strid, skænderi *(n)*, slagsmål *(n)* • *v* ro, skændes, skælde ud
rowan • *n* almindelig røn, røn, rønnebærtræ *(n)*
rowanberry • *n* rønnebær
rowing • *n* ro, roning
royal • *adj* royal, kongelig
rubber • *n* gummi *(n)*
rubbish • *n* vrøvl
rubidium • *n* rubidium *(n)*
ruble • *n* rubel
ruby • *n* rubin
rudder • *n* ror *(n)*, haleror *(n)*, sideror *(n)*
rude • *adj* uhøflig, uforskammet, vulgær, sjofel, fræk, grov
rudimentary • *adj* elementær, simpel, fundamental, basal
rue • *n* rude
ruffled • *adj* kruset
rug • *n* måtte, tæppe *(n)*
ruin • *v* ødelæg • *n* ruin
rule • *n* regel
ruler • *n* lineal
rum • *n* rom
ruminant • *n* drøvtygger • *adj* drøvtyggende
ruminate • *v* drøvtygge, tygge drøv
run • *v* løbe, trille, rulle • *n* løb *(n)*, rute
rune • *n* rune
runner • *n* løber
rural • *adj* tyndtbefolket, rural
rusk • *n* tvebak, krydder, skorpe
rut • *n* vane *(n)*, trummerum *(n)*
rutabaga • *n* kålroe
ruthenium • *n* ruthenium *(n)*
rutherfordium • *n* rutherfordium *(n)*
ruthless • *adj* skånselløs, skånselsløs
rye • *n* rug

S

sable • *n* zobel
sack • *v* fyre • *n* sæk, sækfuld
sacrament • *n* sakramente
sacrifice • *v* ofre • *n* offer *(n)*
sacristy • *n* sakristi *(n)*
sad • *adj* trist
sadism • *n* sadisme

sadist • *n* sadist
sadistic • *adj* sadistisk
sadness • *n* sorg
safeguard • *v* beskytte, sikre • *n* beskyttelse, værn *(n)*
safety • *n* sikkerhed, sikring
saffron • *n* safran *(n)*

saga • n saga
sail • n sejl (n), sejltur • v sejle, flyve, komme, bruse
sailboat • n kutter
sailor • n matros
saint • v kanonisere • n helgen
salad • n salat
salami • n salami
salient • adj bemærkelsesværdig, prominent
saliva • n spyt (n)
salmon • n laks
salt • v salte, krydre • n salt (n), søulk • adj salt, saltholdig
salvation • n frelse
samarium • n samarium (n)
same • adj samme • pron samme
samovar • n samovar
samurai • n samurai
sand • n sand (n), sandstrand, strand
sandal • n sandal
sandbag • n sandsæk
sandbank • n sandbanke
sandbox • n sandkasse
sandstone • n sandsten
sandwich • n sandwich, amagermad
sandy • adj sandet, sandfarvet
sanitary • adj sanitær
sapient • adj intelligent, vis
sapper • n sappør
sapphire • n safir
sarcasm • n sarkasme
sarcophagus • n sarkofag
sash • n skærf (n)
satellite • n drabant, satellit
satire • n satire
satirical • adj satirisk
satirist • n satiriker
satisfied • adj tilfreds
satyr • n satyr
sauce • n sovs
saucepan • n kasserolle
saucer • n underkop, tallerken
sauerkraut • n surkål
sauna • n sauna
sausage • n pølse
savanna • n savanne
save • v redde, gemme, spare, opspare • n redning
saw • n sav
sawdust • n savsmuld (n)
sawmill • n savværk
say • v sige, fortælle
scab • n skab (n)
scabbard • n skede
scabies • n fnat
scaffold • n stillads (n), skafot (n)

scallion • n forårsløg
scalpel • n operationskniv
scam • n bondefanger
scandal • n skandale
scandalous • adj skandaløs
scandium • n skandium
scapegoat • n syndebuk
scar • n ar (n)
scarecrow • n fugleskræmsel (n)
scarf • n halstørklæde (n)
scene • n scene, optrin
schistosomiasis • n schistosomiasis
schizophrenia • n skizofreni
schnapps • n snaps
scholarship • n stipendium
scholasticism • n skolastik
school • n stime, skole
schooner • n skonnert
sciatica • n iskias
science • n videnskab, videnskabelighed, viden
scientist • n videnskabsmand
scimitar • n krumsabel
scissors • n saks
sclerosis • n sklerose, sclerose
scold • v skælde ud
scooter • n løbehjul, scooter
score • v score • n score, snes, partitur (n)
scorpion • n skorpion
scourge • v plage • n svøbe
scratch • n ridse
scrawny • adj mager
scream • n skrig (n)
screen • n skærm
screw • n skrue
script • n manuskript (n)
scrotum • n skrotum
scrum • n klynge
scrupulous • adj omhyggelig, samvittighedsfuld
scrutinize • v granske
sculpin • n ulk
scupper • n lænseport, spygat (n)
scurvy • n skørbug
scythe • n le
sea • n hav (n), sø
seagoing • adj havgående, søgående
seal • n sæl
seam • n søm, sutur
seaman • n sømand
seaplane • n vandfly
search • v søge, lede
seashell • n konkylie
seasickness • n søsyge
season • n årstid, sæson
seasoning • n krydre, smage til
seawater • n havvand (n)

seaweed • *n* tang
second • *n* sekundavare, sekund *(n)*, sekund, øjeblik, sekundant, støtte • *adj* anden, næst-, nummer to • *v* støtte, sekundere, bakke op
secondary • *adj* sekundær
secret • *adj* hemmelig
secretariat • *n* sekretariat
secretive • *adj* hemmelighedsfuld
sect • *n* sekt
section • *n* afsnit *(n)*
security • *n* sikkerhed
sedge • *n* star
seduce • *v* forføre
see • *v* se, forstå
seed • *n* frø *(n)*
seek • *v* søge
seem • *v* synes
seismologist • *n* seismolog
seize • *v* gribe
seizure • *n* beslaglæggelse, anfald *(n)*
seldom • *adv* sjælden
selenium • *n* selen *(n)*
self-determination • *n* selvbestemmelse
self-educated • *adj* selvlært
self-esteem • *n* selvværd
self-help • *n* selvhjælp
selfish • *adj* selvisk, egoistisk
sell • *v* sælge
semantics • *n* semantik, betydningslære
semen • *n* sæd
semester • *n* semester
semicolon • *n* semikolon *(n)*
semifinal • *n* semifinale
semiotics • *n* semiotik
semitone • *n* halvtone
semivowel • *n* halvvokal
senate • *n* senat
send • *v* sende
sender • *n* afsender
seniority • *n* anciennitet
sense • *n* fornemmelse
sensitive • *adj* følsom
sent • *v* sendte, sendt
sentence • *n* sætning
separate • *v* adskille
sequence • *n* rækkefølge, sekvens, tonerække, følge
seraph • *n* seraf
serf • *n* livegen
serfdom • *n* livegenskab *(n)*
sergeant • *n* sergent
series • *n* tv-serie, tv-program, række
serious • *adj* alvorlig
seriousness • *n* alvor
serotonin • *n* serotonin
serpent • *n* slange

serve • *v* tjene
sesame • *n* sesam
set • *v* sætte, stille, placere, fastsætte, indstille, forsænke, indfatte, dække, præsentere, lægge op til, konstruere, opstille, størkne, gå ned • *n* sætning, anlæg *(n)*, apparat *(n)*, samling, aggregat *(n)*, samlesæt *(n)*, mængde, gruppe, sætstykke *(n)*, scenario *(n)*, dekoration, opstilling, sæt *(n)* • *adj* klar, færdig, fastsat, bestemt, fast, opsat
seven • *n* syvtal *(n)*, syver
seventh • *adj* syvende
seventieth • *adj* halvfjerdsindstyvende
severe • *adj* hård, stærk, voldsom, streng
sex • *v* kønsbestemme, bolle, samleje, kneppe • *n* sex, kønsliv, seksualliv, seksuel omgang, samleje, erotik, køn
sextant • *n* sekstant
sexy • *adj* sexet
shack • *v* sove hos • *n* skur, hytte
shade • *n* skygge
shadow • *n* skygge
shag • *n* skarv *(m)*, topskarv
shake • *v* ryste, chokere, ryste af sig, rokke, give hånd på • *n* rysten, rusk *(n)*, milkshake
shallow • *adj* flad, lav, lavvandet, overfladisk, åndsforladt
shaman • *n* shaman
shamanism • *n* shamanisme
shame • *n* skam
shampoo • *n* shampoo
shanghai • *v* shanghaje
shard • *n* skår *(n)*
share • *v* dele, uddele • *n* del, aktie
shareholder • *n* aktionær, aktieejer
shark • *n* haj
sharp • *adj* skarp, spids
sharpshooter • *n* skarpskytte
shave • *n* barbering
shawl • *n* sjal *(n)*
she • *pron* hun
sheaf • *n* knippe *(n)*
sheath • *n* skede
sheathe • *v* stikke i skede
shed • *n* skur *(n)*
sheepish • *adj* fåret, flov
sheet • *n* ark *(n)*
shelduck • *n* gravand
shelf • *n* hylde
shellfish • *n* skaldyr *(n)*
shepherd • *n* fårehyrde, hyrde
shield • *n* skjold *(n)*, skjold, -skjold • *v* beskytte
shin • *n* skinneben *(n)*
shine • *v* skinne, lyse, stråle, glimte,

glimre, brillere, pudse, polere, blanke •
n skin (n), glans, brillans
ship • n skib
shirt • n bluse, skjorte, trøje
shit • n lort • v skide
shock • n chok (n)
shoe • v sko, beslå • n sko
shoehorn • n skohorn (n)
shoelace • n snørebånd (n)
shoemaker • n skomager
shoot • v skyde
shop • v handle, shoppe • n butik
shore • n bred
short • v kortslutte • n kortslutning • adj
kort, lav
shorts • n shorts
shot • n skud, kugle, hagl
shotgun • n haglbøsse
should • v skulle, burde
shoulder • n skulder, rabat
shout • v råbe, skrige • n råb (n), skrig (n)
shovel • n skovl
shower • n bruser, brusebad
shrew • n spidsmus, rappenskralde
shrewd • adj klog, fiffig, snu, listig
shrimp • n reje
shroud • n vant
shrug • v trække på skuldrene • n skuldertræk (n)
shuffle • v blande, slentre
shut • v lukke
shy • v kaste, smide • n kast
sibilant • n sibilant
sibling • n bror, søster, søskende
sick • n syg, syge • adj syg
sickle • n segl
sieve • n si, sigte
sigh • v sukke • n suk (n)
sight • n seværdighed, sigte (n)
sign • n tegn (n)
signal • n signal (n)
signature • n underskrift
silage • n ensilage
silence • n tavshed, stilhed
silencer • n lyddæmper, lydpotte
silicon • n silicium (n)
silicone • n silikone
silk • n silke
silkworm • n silkeorm
silly • adj dum, fjollet
silver • n sølv, sølvmønt • adj sølvfarvet
silverfish • n sølvfisk, sølvkræ (n)
silverware • n sølvtøj (n)
silverweed • n gåsepotentil
similar • adj lignende
similarity • n lighed
simile • n sammenligning, lignelse

simony • n simoni
simplified • adj forenklet
simplify • v forenkle
simultaneously • adv samtidigt
sin • n synd, synder
since • conj siden • prep siden
sine • n sinus
sinecure • n sinecure (n)
sinful • adj syndig
sing • v synge
singer • n sanger, sangerinde
singular • n ental
sink • n vask, køkkenvask
sinless • adj syndeløs, syndefri
sinner • n synder
sip • v sippe, nippe • n sip (n), nip (n),
slurk
sir • n herre
siskin • n grønirisk
sister • n søster, nonne, afdelingssygeplejerske
sister-in-law • n svigerinde
sit • v sidde
six • n sekstal (n)
sixth • n sjettedel • adj sjette
sixtieth • adj tressende, tresindstyvende
size • n størrelse
skald • n skjald
skein • n fed (n), dukke
skeleton • n skelet (n)
skeptical • adj skeptisk
skepticism • n skepticisme
skew • adj skæv
ski • n ski
skill • n færdighed
skim • v slå smut, rikochettere, skimme
skin • v skrabe, flå • n hud, skræl, skind
(n)
skinflint • n fedtsyl
skirt • n nederdel, skørt (n)
skua • n kjove
skull • n kranie (n), kranium (n)
sky • n himmel
skylark • n sanglærke
skylight • n tagvindue
skyscraper • n skyskraber
slander • v bagtale • n bagvaskelse
slang • n slang (n)
slapdash • adj forhastet • adv jasket
slash • n skråstreg
slaughter • v slagte
slave • v slave • n slave, slavinde, træl,
trælkone
slavery • n slaveri (n)
sleazy • adj skummel, lyssky
sledge • n slæde, kælk
sleep • v sove • n søvn

sleeper • *n* svelle
sleepy • *adj* søvnig
sleet • *n* slud *(n)*
sleeve • *n* ærme *(n)*, muffe
slim • *adj* slank, tynd
slippery • *adj* glat
slob • *n* sjuske, sjuskedorte
sloe • *n* slåen
slog • *v* ase, okse, traske
sloop • *n* slup
slot • *n* liste, lamel, sprække, revne, rille, kærv, spor
sloth • *n* dovenskab, dovendyr *(n)*
slough • *n* ham
slow • *adj* langsom
slowly • *adv* langsomt
slum • *n* slumkvarter, slum
slurp • *v* slubre
slut • *n* tøjte, mær
small • *adj* lille, liden
smallholder • *n* husmand
smallholding • *n* husmandssted *(n)*, husmandsbrug *(n)*
smallpox • *n* kopper
smart • *adj* smart, klog
smashing • *adj* fed
smell • *v* lugte, dufte, stinke • *n* lugt, lugtesans
smile • *v* smile • *n* smil *(n)*
smith • *n* smed
smoke • *v* ryge, røge • *n* røg, smøg
smoker • *n* ryger
smoking • *n* rygning
smooth • *v* glatte, udglatte • *adj* glat
snail • *n* snegl, med, skal
snake • *v* sno, slange • *n* slange
snapdragon • *n* løvemund
sneeze • *v* nyse • *n* nys *(n)*
snitch • *v* stikke, sladre • *n* tyv, tyveknægt, sladrehank, stikker, forræder
snob • *n* snob
snore • *v* snorke
snorkel • *v* snorkle • *n* snorkel
snot • *n* snot *(n)*
snout • *n* tryne
snow • *v* sne • *n* sne, kokain, snefald *(n)*
snow-blind • *adj* sneblind
snowball • *n* snebold
snowdrift • *n* snefane, snedrive
snowflake • *n* snefnug, hvidblomme
snowman • *n* snemand
snowmobile • *n* snescooter
so • *adv* sådan • *conj* så
soap • *n* sæbe
soapwort • *n* sæbeurt
sober • *adj* ædru, ædruelig, sober
soccer • *n* fodbold

socialism • *n* socialisme
society • *n* samfund *(n)*
sock • *n* sok
sodium • *n* natrium *(n)*
sofa • *n* sofa
soften • *v* blødgøre, blødgøres
softly • *adv* blidt
software • *n* software, programmel
soil • *n* jord, muldjord, grund • *v* tilsøle, svine, besudle
sojourn • *v* opholde sig • *n* ophold *(n)*, opholdssted *(n)*
solace • *n* trøst
solder • *v* lodde • *n* loddemetal *(n)*
soldier • *n* soldat
sole • *n* søtunge
solemn • *adj* højtidelig
solid • *n* fast, stof *(n)* • *adj* fast, solid, massiv, kompakt, tæt, grundig, grundfæstet
solidarity • *n* solidaritet
solitude • *n* ensomhed
solstice • *n* solhverv *(n)*
solvency • *n* solvens
solvent • *n* opløsningsmiddel
somebody • *pron* nogen
someday • *adv* en dag
something • *pron* noget
sometimes • *adv* somme tider, af og til, undertiden, stundom
somewhere • *adv* nogensteds, nogetsteds
somnambulism • *n* søvngængeri *(n)*
son • *n* søn, adoptivsøn
son-in-law • *n* svigersøn
sonata • *n* sonate
song • *n* sang, vise, slik
songbird • *n* sangfugl, sanglærke
sonnet • *n* sonet
soon • *adv* snart
soothing • *adj* lindrende, beroligende
sorbet • *n* sorbet
sore • *adj* øm
sorghum • *n* durra
sorrow • *n* sorg, smerte
sorry • *adj* ked af, sørgelig • *interj* undskyld, beklager
sort • *n* slags, sort, sortering • *v* sortere, løse
soul • *n* sjæl
sound • *adj* sund, rask, solid, sikker, pålidelig, fornuftig • *v* lyde, lade, dykke, lodde, sondere, pejle, prøve • *n* lyd, sund *(n)*, sonde
sour • *adj* sur
source • *n* kilde, udspring *(n)*
sourdough • *n* surdej • *adj* surdejs-
south • *n* syd
south-southeast • *n* sydsydøst

south-southwest • *n* sydsydvest
southeast • *n* sydøst
southwest • *n* sydvest
sow • *n* so
space • *n* rum, rummet, plads, mellem-rum, rum *(n)*
spaceship • *n* rumskib *(n)*
spacetime • *n* rumtid
spade • *n* spade, spar
spam • *n* spam
spark • *n* gnist
sparkler • *n* stjernekaster
sparrow • *n* spurv
spasm • *n* krampe
spat • *n* gamache
spatula • *n* palet, paletkniv, spatel
speak • *v* tale, snakke
speaker • *n* taler, højttaler
spear • *n* spyd *(n)*
species • *n* art
specimen • *n* eksemplar *(n)*
spectacles • *n* brille
speculate • *v* spekulere, gætte
speechless • *adj* mundlam, målløs
speed • *n* hastighed, hurtighed, fart • *v* køre hurtigt, køre for hurtigt
speedboat • *n* speedbåd
spell • *v* stave
spelt • *n* spelt
sperm • *n* sæd
spermatozoon • *n* sædcelle, spermatozo
sphere • *n* sfære, kugle
spherical • *adj* sfærisk
sphinx • *n* sfinks
spice • *n* krydderi
spider • *n* edderkop
spike • *n* spiger, nagle, spids, pig, aks *(n)*, pigsko, top
spill • *v* spilde
spinach • *n* spinat
spine • *n* rygsøjle, rygrad, ryg
spiral • *n* spiral
spire • *n* spir
spirit • *n* ånd, sjæl, liv *(n)*, mod *(n)*, kraft, spiritus, sprit, alkohol
spirits • *n* likør, spiritus
spiritual • *adj* åndelig
spit • *n* spid *(n)*, tange, spyt *(n)* • *v* spytte
spleen • *n* milt
spoiler • *n* spoiler
spoke • *n* ege
spokesman • *n* talsmand
spokesperson • *n* talsperson
spokeswoman • *n* talskvinde
sponge • *n* svamp
spoon • *n* ske
spoonbill • *n* skestork

spoonerism • *n* bakke snagvendt
spoonful • *n* skefuld
sporadic • *adj* sporadisk
sport • *n* sport
spouse • *n* ægtefælle
sprain • *v* forstuve • *n* forstuvning
spread • *v* fordele, sprede, strø, smøre, udbrede, brede • *n* spredning, udbredelse, opredning, opdækning, festmåltid, smørepålæg *(n)*, spændvidde, omfang *(n)*
spreader • *n* salingshorn
spring • *v* springe, hoppe • *n* forår *(n)*, vår, kilde, fjeder
springlike • *adj* forårsagtig
spruce • *n* gran, gran-
spur • *n* spore
spurge • *n* vortemælk
sputnik • *n* sputnik
squadron • *n* eskadrille
squalor • *n* snusk, smuds
square • *n* kvadrat *(n)*, torv *(n)* • *adj* kvadratisk
squat • *v* besætte
squeegee • *n* svaber
squeeze • *v* presse, trykke, klemme, knuge, mase • *n* klemme, trangt sted *(n)*, knus *(n)*
squid • *n* blæksprutte
squirrel • *n* egern *(n)*
stable • *v* stalde • *n* stald • *adj* stabil
stadium • *n* stadion *(n)*
staff • *n* stav, stang, stab, personale *(n)*
stage • *v* opføre • *n* stadie *(n)*, scene
stain • *n* plet
stair • *n* trappe
staircase • *n* trappe
stairs • *n* trappe
stake • *n* interessent
stallion • *n* hingst, hanhest, avlshingst
stamp • *v* trampe, stampe, stanse, udstanse, præge, stemple, frankere, frimærke • *n* stampen, stempel, præg
stand • *v* stå, rejse, stille, klare, holde, udholde, udstå, sætte • *n* standpunkt, tribune, estrade, vidneskranke, bevoksning, stade, stand, holdeplads
standard-bearer • *n* fanebærer
standby • *n* beredskab
stanza • *n* strofer
star • *n* stjerne
starboard • *n* styrbord
starch • *n* stivelse
stardom • *n* stjernestatus
stare • *v* glo, stirre
starfish • *n* søstjerne
stark • *adj* stærk
starling • *n* stær

starter • *n* forret
starvation • *n* sult, hunger
state • *v* erklære • *n* stat, delstat, tilstand
stately • *adj* anselig, prægtig, statelig
station • *n* station, tv-station
statistics • *n* statistik
statue • *n* statue
staysail • *n* stangsejl
steal • *v* stjæle
steam • *v* dampe • *n* damp
steamboat • *n* dampskib *(n)*, damper
steamer • *n* dampskib *(n)*
steaming • *adj* dampende
steamship • *n* dampskib *(n)*
steel • *n* stål *(n)*
steelyard • *n* bismer
steer • *n* stud *(m)* • *v* styre
stem • *n* stævn
step • *n* trit *(n)*, trin, trinbræt *(n)*, skridt *(n)*, fodspor *(n)*, gang
stepdaughter • *n* steddatter
stepfather • *n* stedfar
stepmother • *n* stedmor
steppe • *n* steppe
stereo • *n* stereoanlæg *(n)*
sterile • *adj* steril
stern • *n* agterstævn, agterende
stick • *n* pind, kvist, kæp, stav, stok, stang, gearstang
still • *adv* stadig
stingray • *n* pilrokke
stingy • *adj* fedtet, nærig, smålig
stinkhorn • *n* stinksvamp
stirrup • *n* stigbøjle
stitch • *n* maske
stochastic • *adj* stokastisk
stockfish • *n* tørfisk
stockholder • *n* aktionær, aktieejer
stole • *n* stola
stolen • *adj* stjålen, stjålet
stomach • *n* bug
stomachache • *n* mavepine
stone • *n* sten *(m)*
stony • *adj* stenet
stool • *n* afføring
stop • *v* stoppe, standse • *n* stoppested
storage • *n* lager
store • *v* lagre, beholde
stork • *n* stork
storm • *n* storm, stormvejr *(n)*
story • *n* historie
strait • *n* stræde *(n)*
strand • *n* strand
strange • *adj* underlig
stranger • *n* fremmed
strangle • *v* kvæle
stratosphere • *n* stratosfære

straw • *n* halm, strå
strawberry • *n* jordbær, jordbærplante • *adj* jordbærfarvet, jordbær
street • *n* gade *(n)*
streetlight • *n* gadelygte
stress • *v* stresse • *n* stress *(n)*
stretcher • *n* båre, løber
strike • *n* strejke
string • *v* trække på snor, opstrenge, strenge • *n* streng, serie, strygerne
stroke • *n* ae, apopleksi, slagtilfælde
strong • *adj* stærk, uregelmæssig
stronghold • *n* borg
strontium • *n* strontium
strop • *v* stryge
struggle • *v* kæmpe • *n* kamp
strut • *v* stoltsere, spankulere • *n* stiver
stubborn • *adj* stædig
stubbornness • *n* stædighed
stud • *n* avlshingst, avlstyr, tyr, knop, dup, ørestikke
student • *n* studerende
study • *v* studere, lære
stuffed • *adj* udstoppet, fyldt, farseret, stopmæt
stumble • *v* snuble, fejle, begå fejl • *n* snublen, fejl, fejltrin *(n)*
stupid • *adj* dum
sturgeon • *n* stør
sty • *n* sti
subcutaneous • *adj* subkutan
subject • *n* grundled *(n)*, subjekt *(n)*, emne *(n)*, tema *(n)*, fag *(n)*, borger
sublease • *v* fremleje • *n* fremleje
sublime • *v* sublimere • *adj* sublim
submarine • *n* ubåd
submit • *v* aflevere
subordinate • *adj* underordnet
subpoena • *n* stævning *(f)*
subscribe • *v* abonnere
subscription • *n* abonnement *(n)*
subset • *n* delmængde
subsidiary • *adj* subsidiær
substance • *n* substans, masse, hovedindhold, formue
substitute • *v* erstatte, substituere, udskifte • *n* erstatning, substitut, surrogat *(n)*, udskifter
subtitle • *n* undertekst
subtropical • *adj* subtropisk
subtropics • *n* subtroper
suburb • *n* forstad
success • *n* succes
succubus • *n* succubus
suck • *v* suge
sucrose • *n* sukrose, saccharose
sudden • *adj* brat, pludselig

suddenly • *adv* pludseligt
suffer • *v* lide
suffice • *v* holde
suffocate • *v* kvæles, kvæle
sugar • *v* søde, indsukre • *n* sukker *(n)*, skat, sukker
suggest • *v* forslå
suggestion • *n* forslag *(n)*
suicide • *n* selvmord *(n)*, selvmorder
suit • *n* kulør
sulfur • *v* svovle • *n* svovl *(n)*
sulk • *v* surmule
sullen • *adj* vrangvillig, mut, mørk, dyster, treven
sultan • *n* sultan
sultry • *adj* lummer, trykkende, sanselig, sensuel
summary • *n* resume *(n)*, resumé *(n)*
summer • *n* sommer
summit • *n* top, bjergtop, topmøde *(n)*
sun • *n* sol
sunbather • *n* solbader
sundew • *n* soldug
sundial • *n* solur *(n)*
sunflower • *n* solsikke
sunglasses • *n* solbriller
sunrise • *n* solopgang
sunset • *n* solnedgang
sunshine • *n* solskin *(n)*
super • *adj* super
superfluous • *adj* overflødig
superlative • *n* superlativ
supermarket • *n* supermarked *(n)*
superstition • *n* overtro
supper • *n* aftensmad
supply • *v* levere, skaffe, yde, afhjælpe, erstatte, vikariere • *n* udbud *(n)*, forsyning, leverance, forsynings-, føde-, forråd *(n)*
support • *v* støtte
surcharge • *n* overpris, overtryk
surface • *n* overflade *(n)*
surname • *n* efternavn *(n)*, familienavn *(n)*, slægtsnavn *(n)*
surprise • *v* overraske • *n* overraskelse
surprised • *adj* overrasket
surrealism • *n* surrealismen
surreptitiously • *adv* hemmeligt
surrogate • *n* substitut, surrogat *(n)*
surround • *v* omringe

surroundings • *n* omgivelse
surveillance • *n* overvågning
survive • *v* overleve
sushi • *n* sushi
suspect • *v* suspekt
sustainable • *adj* bæredygtig
swallow • *n* svale, landsvale
swamp • *n* mose
swan • *n* svane
swarm • *n* sværm
swastika • *n* svastika, hagekors *(n)*
swear • *v* sværge
sweat • *n* sved • *v* svede
sweater • *n* sweater
swede • *n* kålroe
sweet • *n* konfekt, bolsje, slik • *adj* sød, sødet, usaltet, fersk, sødlig, frisk, melodisk, behagelig, blid, venlig, ren • *adv* sødt, let
sweeten • *v* søde
sweetness • *n* sødme
swell • *v* svulme, erigere • *n* dønning
swift • *adj* hurtig
swim • *v* svømme • *n* svømmetur
swimsuit • *n* badedragt
switchblade • *n* springkniv
sword • *n* sværd
swordfish • *n* sværdfisk
swordtail • *n* sværddrager
sycophant • *n* spytslikker
sycophantic • *adj* slesk
syllable • *n* stavelse
syllogism • *n* syllogisme
symbiosis • *n* symbiose
symbol • *n* symbol *(n)*
symbolically • *adv* symbolsk
symbolize • *v* symbolisere
symmetrical • *adj* symmetrisk
symphony • *n* symfoni
synagogue • *n* synagoge
synchronize • *v* synkronisere
synchronous • *adj* synkron
syndicate • *n* syndikat
syndrome • *n* syndrom *(n)*
synonym • *n* synonym *(n)*
synthesizer • *n* synthesizer
syphilis • *n* syfilis
syrup • *n* sirup
system • *n* system *(n)*

T

table • *n* bord *(n)*, tabel
tablecloth • *n* dug
tablespoon • *n* spiseske, grydeske, spiseskefuld
tachometer • *n* omdrejningstæller
tackle • *n* talje, tackling, takling
tadpole • *n* haletudse
taffeta • *n* taft *(n)*
taiga • *n* nåleskov
tail • *n* hale
tailback • *n* bilkø
tailor • *n* skrædder, skrædderske
take • *v* tage
talcum • *n* talkum *(n)*
talent • *n* talent *(n)*
talented • *adj* begavet, talentfuld
talk • *v* tale, snakke, fortælle • *n* samtale, drøftelse, snak, foredrag *(n)*, forelæsning
talkative • *adj* snaksom
talkativeness • *n* snaksomhed
tall • *adj* høj
tallow • *n* talg
talus • *n* ur
tame • *v* tæmme • *adj* tam
tamper • *v* snyde
tampon • *n* tampon
tan • *v* brun • *n* solbrændt
tandem • *n* tandem, tandemcykel
tangerine • *n* mandarin
tank • *n* tank, beholder, kampvogn
tanker • *n* tankskib *(n)*, tanker, tankbil, tankvogn
tanner • *n* garver
tannin • *n* tannin
tantalum • *n* tantal
tape • *n* bånd
taper • *n* kærte, vokslys *(n)*
tapir • *n* tapir
tar • *n* tjære
target • *v* sigte efter, rette mod • *n* mål, skydeskive
tarragon • *n* estragon
tarsier • *n* spøgelsesabe
tartan • *n* tartan *(n)*
task • *n* opgave
tassel • *n* kvast
tattoo • *n* tatovering
tawny • *adj* gulbrun, gyldenbrun
tax • *v* beskatte • *n* skat
taxi • *v* taxie • *n* taxa, taxi, vogn, hyrevogn
tea • *n* te, the
teach • *v* undervise, lære
teacher • *n* lærer *(m)*, lærerinde *(f)*
teak • *n* teaktræ
teakettle • *n* vandkoger
teapot • *n* tepotte, tekande

tear • *v* flå, rive, revne • *n* flænge, rift, tåre
tease • *v* drille • *n* drillepind
technetium • *n* technetium
technician • *n* tekniker
technique • *n* teknik
technology • *n* teknologi
tedious • *adj* kedelig, trættende, triviel
telegram • *n* telegram
telegraph • *n* telegraf
telephone • *v* telefonere, ringe • *n* telefon
telescope • *n* teleskop *(n)*
television • *n* tv *(n)*, fjernsyn *(n)*
telltale • *n* sladrehank, sladderhank • *adj* afslørende, røbende
tellurium • *n* tellur
temper • *n* temperament *(n)*, gemyt *(n)*, natur, sind *(n)*
temperature • *n* temperatur
template • *n* skabelon
temple • *n* tempel, tinding *(m)*
temporal • *adj* verdslig
temporary • *n* vikar • *adj* midlertidig
temptation • *n* fristelse
ten • *n* tital *(n)*, tier
tench • *n* suder
tendentious • *adj* tendentiøs
tender • *adj* øm, mør • *n* forsyningsskib, tender
tendon • *n* sene
tennis • *n* tennis
tenor • *n* tenor, tone, mening, hovedindhold *(n)*, indhold *(n)*
tenosynovitis • *n* seneskedehindebetændelse
tent • *n* telt *(n)*
tenth • *n* tier, tiendedel • *adj* tiende
tepid • *adj* lunken
terbium • *n* terbium
terminal • *n* terminal
termite • *n* termitter
tern • *n* terne
terrace • *n* terrasse
terrible • *adj* frygtelig
territory • *n* territorium *(n)*
terrorism • *n* terrorisme
terrorist • *n* terrorist
tertiary • *adj* tertiær
testament • *n* testamente
testosterone • *n* testosteron *(n)*
tetrameter • *n* tetrameter
text • *n* tekst
textbook • *n* lærebog • *adj* sædvanlig
thallium • *n* thallium
than • *prep* end
thankfulness • *n* taknemmelighed, taknemlighed

thankless • *adj* utaknemmelig
thanks • *n* tak • *interj* tak
that • *pron* det, som
the • *art* -en, -et *(n)*, -ne, den, det *(n)*, de
theater • *n* teater *(n)*
theft • *n* tyveri *(n)*
theism • *n* teisme
thence • *adv* deraf følger, deden
theology • *n* Religionsvidenskab
theosophy • *n* teosofi
therapist • *n* terapeut
therapy • *n* terapi, behandling
there • *adv* der, did, derhen
therefore • *adv* derfor
therewith • *adv* dermed
thermodynamics • *n* varmelære
thermosphere • *n* termosfære
thermostat • *n* termostat
thesaurus • *n* begrebsordbog, saggruppe-ordbog, tesaurus, synonymordbog
thesis • *n* tesis, tese, afhandling, disputats
theta • *n* theta *(n)*
they • *pron* de
thick • *adj* tyk • *adv* tykt
thicket • *n* krat *(n)*, buskads *(n)*
thief • *n* tyv, tyveknægt
thigh • *n* lår *(n)*
thimble • *n* fingerbøl *(n)*, kovs
thin • *v* fortynde
thing • *n* ting
think • *v* tænke, reflektere, mene, tro, synes, antage
third • *n* tredjedel, terts • *adj* tredje
thirdly • *adv* for det tredje
thirst • *v* tørste • *n* tørst
thirsty • *adj* tørstig
thirteenth • *adj* trettende
thirtieth • *adj* tredivte
this • *pron* dette
thistle • *n* tidsel
thither • *adv* did, derhen
thorium • *n* thorium
thorn • *n* torn
thorp • *n* torp
thou • *pron* du
though • *adv* dog • *conj* dog
thought • *n* tanke, tankevirksomhed
thousandth • *adj* tusinde
thread • *n* tråd
threatened • *adj* truet *(n)*
three • *n* tre
three-dimensional • *adj* tredimensional
threshold • *n* tærskel, dørtærskel, tærskelværdi, bundgrænse
thrice • *adv* tre gang
thrips • *n* thrips

thrive • *v* trives
throat • *n* hals, svælg
throne • *n* trone
through • *prep* gennem, igennem, på grund af
throw • *v* kaste
throw-in • *n* indkast *(n)*
thrush • *n* drossel
thud • *n* bump
thulium • *n* thulium
thumb • *n* tommelfinger, tommeltot
thumbnail • *n* tommelfingernegl, skitse, frimærke *(n)*
thunder • *n* torden
thunderstorm • *n* tordenvejr *(n)*
thus • *adv* dennelunde, således
ticket • *n* billet, bøde
tickle • *v* kilde
tide • *n* tidevand *(n)*
tie • *v* binde
tier • *n* lag
tiger • *n* tiger
tigress • *n* huntiger
tile • *n* tegl
till • *prep* indtil
time • *v* tage tid, time, tidsindstille • *n* tid, afsoningstid, klokken, gang
timid • *adj* frygtsom
tin • *n* tin
tinfoil • *n* stanniol *(n)*, sølvpapir *(n)*
tinnitus • *n* tinnitus
tired • *adj* træt
tissue • *n* stof, serviet, lommetørklæde, toiletpapir, væv *(n)*
tit • *n* brystvorte, bryst *(n)*, pat
titanium • *n* titan
tithe • *n* tiende
to • *prep* til
toad • *n* tudse, padde
toast • *n* ristet brød *(n)*, skål
tobacco • *n* tobak
today • *n* i dag • *adv* i dag, i vore dage
toddler • *n* småbarn *(n)*
toe • *n* tå
together • *adv* sammen
toilet • *n* toilette *(n)*, påklædningsrum, garderobe, toilet *(n)*, badeværelse *(n)*, wc *(n)*, lokum *(n)*, toiletkumme
token • *n* tegn, mærke, minde, polet
tolerance • *n* tolerance
tollgate • *n* bom
tom • *n* hankat
tomato • *n* tomat
tomboy • *n* drengepige
tomorrow • *n* morgendag • *adv* i morgen
ton • *n* ton *(n)*
tone • *v* tone, forstærke, styrke, harmonis-

ere • *n* tone, klang, tonefald, farvetone, nuance, tonus, spændingstilstand

tongue • *n* tunge

tonight • *n* i aften, i nat • *adv* i aften, i nat

tonsil • *n* mandel

too • *adv* ligeså, for

tool • *v* bearbejde, udstyre, maskine • *n* instrument *(n)*, redskab *(n)*, værktøj *(n)*, pik *(n)*

tooth • *n* tand, tænder

toothbrush • *n* tandbørste

toothpaste • *n* tandpasta

top • *n* snurretop

topology • *n* topologi

topple • *v* vælte, styrte, omstyrte

torch • *n* fakkel

torment • *n* smerte

tornado • *n* tornado

tortoise • *n* skildpadde

torture • *v* tortere, torturere • *n* tortur

totem • *n* totem

touch • *v* røre, berøre, bevæge

tourism • *n* turisme

tourist • *n* turist

tourniquet • *n* årepresse

towel • *n* håndklæde *(n)*

tower • *n* tårn *(n)*

town • *n* by

townsman • *n* borger *(m)*

toxic • *adj* giftig

toxicological • *adj* toksokologisk

toxicologist • *n* toksikolog

toy • *n* legetøj *(n)*

tractor • *n* traktor

trade • *n* handel, byttehandel

trademark • *n* varemærke

tradition • *n* tradition, overlevering

traditional • *adj* traditionel

traditionally • *adv* traditionelt

traffic • *n* trafik, færdsel

tragedy • *n* tragedie

trail • *v* følge • *n* spor

train • *v* øve, træne • *n* tog *(n)*, optog *(n)*, række, kæde, slæb *(n)*

traitor • *n* forræder

tram • *n* sporvogn

tramp • *n* vagabund

trampoline • *n* trampolin

tranquil • *adj* rolig, stille

tranquillity • *n* stilhed, ro

transaction • *n* forretning, overenskomst, transaktion

transfer • *v* overføre, forflytte, overdrage, stige om, skifte • *n* forflyttelse, overflytning, transport, flytning

transit • *n* passage

translate • *v* oversætte

translation • *n* oversættelse

translator • *n* oversætter, tolk, interpreter

transliteration • *n* translitteration

transparent • *adj* transparent, gennemsigtig, klar, gennemskuelig, åbenbar, oplagt

transplant • *v* omplante, udplante, transplantere • *n* transplantation, transplantat *(n)*

transport • *v* transportere, deportere • *n* transport

transsexual • *adj* transseksuel

transvestite • *n* transvestit

trapdoor • *n* lem, luge, faldlem

trapezoid • *n* trapez *(n)*

trash • *n* affald *(n)*, affaldscontainer, skrammel

traverse • *v* at traversere

trawler • *n* trawler

tray • *n* bakke

tread • *v* træde

treason • *n* forræderi

treatise • *n* afhandling

treble • *v* tredoble

tree • *n* træ *(n)*

trefoil • *n* trekløver

triangle • *n* trekant, triangel

triangular • *adj* trekantet

tribe • *n* stamme

tributary • *n* biflod

trichotillomania • *n* trikotillomani

trigger • *n* udløser

trimaran • *n* trimaran

trip • *n* rejse

triumph • *n* triumf, sejrsceremoni, triumftog *(n)* • *v* triumfere, sejre

troll • *n* trold, troll

trombone • *n* basun

trope • *n* skabelon

tropopause • *n* tropopause

troposphere • *n* troposfære

troublemaker • *n* fredsforstyrrer

trough • *n* trug, kar, rende, tagrende, bølgedal, lavtryksudløber

trout • *n* ørred

truck • *v* køre, en, lastbil • *n* lastbil, truck

trudge • *v* traske

true • *adj* sand

trump • *n* trumf

trumpet • *v* trompetere, spille, trompet, forkynde, udbasunere • *n* trompet, trompetist, trompetstød

trumpeter • *n* trompetist, trompeter

trunk • *n* snabel

truss • *v* binde op • *n* brokbind *(n)*

trust • *n* tillid, tiltro

truth • *n* sandhed

try • *v* forsøge, prøve, afprøve, teste
tsar • *n* zar
tuber • *n* knold
tuberculosis • *n* tuberkulose
tugboat • *n* slæbebåd
tulip • *n* tulipan
tumult • *n* tumult, tummel, oprør *(n)*
tumulus • *n* gravhøj
tuna • *n* tun
tundra • *n* tundra
tuneful • *adj* melodiøs
tungsten • *n* wolfram
tunnel • *n* tunnel
turban • *n* turban
turbulence • *n* turbulens
turkey • *n* kalkun, fjols *(n)*
turmeric • *n* gurkemeje
turn • *v* dreje, vende, blive, forvandle, vende sig mod, sur • *n* drejning, bøjning, omdrejning, snoning, omgang, tur, dobbeltslag *(n)*, anfald *(n)*, ildebefindende *(n)*, tilbøjelighed
turnip • *n* majroe

turnover • *n* omsætning
turnstile • *n* drejekors
turquoise • *n* turkis • *adj* turkis
turtle • *n* skildpadde
tusk • *n* stødtand
tuxedo • *n* smoking
tweet • *n* pip *(n)*, kvidder *(n)*
twelfth • *adj* tolvte
twentieth • *adj* tyvende
twenty-one • *n* enogtyve
twilight • *n* tusmørke *(n)*, skumring, gry *(n)*, daggry
twin • *n* tvilling
twine • *n* snor, sejlgarn
two • *n* total *(n)*
type • *n* type
typewriter • *n* skrivemaskine
typhoon • *n* tyfon
typhus • *n* tyfus
typical • *adj* typisk
tyrant • *n* tyran
tyre • *n* dæk

U

ubiquitous • *adj* allestedsnærværende
udder • *n* yver *(n)*
ugly • *adj* grim
ultimatum • *n* ultimatum *(n)*
ultraviolet • *adj* ultraviolet
umbrella • *n* paraply
umlaut • *n* omlyd
unanimous • *adj* enstemmig, enig
unauthorized • *adj* uautoriseret
unavoidable • *adj* uundgåelig
unborn • *adj* ufødt
unbreakable • *adj* ubrydelig
uncertainty • *n* usikkerhed
uncle • *n* onkel, farbror, morbror
unconscious • *adj* bevidstløs
underage • *adj* mindreårig
underdeveloped • *adj* underudviklet
undernourishment • *n* underernæring
understand • *v* forstå, fatte, begribe, mene, opfatte, indse, underforstå
understanding • *n* forståelse, forstand, aftale • *adj* forstående
undertaker • *n* bedemand
underwear • *n* undertøj *(n)*
underworld • *n* underverden
undisturbed • *adj* uforstyrret
undoing • *n* undergang
unearth • *v* grave
unemployed • *n* da • *adj* arbejdsløs

unemployment • *n* arbejdsløshed
unequivocal • *adj* utvivlsom
unfold • *v* folde ud
unfortunate • *adj* uheldig, ulykkelig
unfortunately • *adv* uheldigvis, desværre
unheard-of • *adj* uhørt, uerhørt
unicorn • *n* enhjørning
unicycle • *n* unicykel, ethjulet cykel
unidentified • *adj* uidentificeret
uniformity • *n* ensartethed
uninterested • *adj* uinteresseret
union • *n* union
unit • *n* enhed
unity • *n* enhed
universe • *n* univers *(n)*
university • *n* universitet
unknown • *adj* ubekendt, ukendt
unleaded • *adj* blyfri
unless • *conj* medmindre, undtagen
unlucky • *adj* unheldig
unmarried • *adj* ugift
unnatural • *adj* unaturlig
unnecessary • *adj* unødvendig
unobtrusive • *adj* beskeden, tilbageholdende, stilfærdig
unofficial • *adj* uofficiel
unorthodox • *adj* uortodoks
unpardonable • *adj* utilgivelig
unpasteurized • *adj* upasteuriseret

unperturbed • *adj* uforstyrret
unpretentious • *adj* uhøjtidelig
unprofessional • *adj* uprofessionel
unreliable • *adj* upålidelig
unreported • *adj* urapporteret
unrest • *n* uro
unspoken • *adj* usagt
until • *prep* indtil
untrue • *adj* usand
untruth • *n* usandhed
unworthy • *adj* uværdig
up • *v* forøge, forfremme • *adj* oppe, med forsiden opad, med • *adv* opad, itu, i stykker, op • *prep* op, i, op ad
up-to-date • *adj* ajour, up to date
upset • *adj* oprørt
upsilon • *n* ypsilon *(n)*

uranium • *n* uran
uremia • *n* uræmi
urinal • *n* urinal *(n)*, urinale *(n)*
urine • *n* urin
use • *v* bruge
useful • *adj* nyttig
useless • *adj* ubrugelig
user • *n* bruger, konsument, misbruger, udbytter
usually • *adv* som regel, sædvanligvis
usurer • *n* ågerkarl
usury • *n* åger
utopia • *n* utopi
utter • *adj* fuldkommen, komplet • *v* ytre, udtrykke, udstøde
uvula • *n* drøbel

V

vacant • *adj* ledig
vacation • *v* tage, holde • *n* ferie, fratrædelse, fraflytning
vacuum • *v* støvsuge • *n* vakuum *(n)*
vagabond • *n* vagabond, landevejsridder, landstryger, stodder
vagina • *n* vagina, skede
valkyrie • *n* valkyrie
valley • *n* dal
valuable • *adj* værdifuld
value • *v* vurdere, værdsætte, skatte • *n* værdi, værd *(n)*, valør
valve • *n* ventil
vampire • *n* vampyr
van • *n* kassevogn, varevogn
vanadium • *n* vanadium
vandalism • *n* vandalisme
vanilla • *n* vanilje
vanish • *v* forsvinde
vapor • *n* damp
various • *adj* forskellige
varnish • *n* fernis, lak *(n)*
vase • *n* vase
vassal • *n* vasal
vast • *adj* enorm
vector • *n* vektor
vegan • *n* veganer
vegetable • *n* grøntsag, grønsag
vegetarian • *n* vegetar, planteæder
vegetarianism • *n* vegetarisme
vehicle • *n* køretøj
veil • *v* dække, sløre, skjule • *n* dække *(n)*, slør *(n)*
vein • *n* vene
velocity • *n* hastighed

velvet • *n* fløjl *(n)*
vendor • *n* sælger, leverandør
veneer • *v* finere • *n* finer
vengeance • *n* hævn
vengeful • *adj* hævngerrig
venom • *n* gift *(m)*
ventricle • *n* hjertekammer, ventrikel
veranda • *n* veranda
verb • *n* udsagnsord *(n)*, verbum *(n)*
verbatim • *adv* ordret, ord for ord, ord til andet
verdigris • *n* ir
verily • *adv* sandelig
vermin • *n* skadedyr *(n)*
vernacular • *n* national sprog *(n)*, daglig tale
verse • *n* vers *(n)*, strofe
vertebrate • *n* hvirveldyr *(n)*
vertical • *adj* lodret
very • *adv* meget, særlig
vessel • *n* fartøj *(n)*
vestibule • *n* vestibule
vestige • *n* spor *(n)*, antydning
vestigial • *adj* rudimentær
veteran • *n* veteran • *adj* erfaren, veteran
veterinarian • *n* dyrlæge
veto • *n* veto
viaduct • *n* viadukt
viaticum • *n* viaticum
vibraphone • *n* vibrafon
vice • *n* last, dårlig vane
vicinity • *n* nærhed, nabolag *(n)*, omegn
victim • *n* offer *(n)*, slagteoffer *(n)*
victory • *n* sejr
view • *n* udsigt, syn

vigilance • *n* årvågenhed
village • *n* landsby, by
villain • *n* skurk, slyngel
vindictive • *adj* hævngerrig
vinegar • *n* eddike
vineyard • *n* vingård
viola • *n* bratsch
violent • *adj* voldsom, voldelig, kraftig, heftig
violin • *n* violin
violinist • *n* violinist
virgin • *n* jomfru, mø
virtual • *adj* virtuel
virtue • *n* dyd
virtuoso • *n* virtuos
virus • *n* virus
visa • *n* visum
viscous • *adj* viskøs
vise • *n* skruestik, skruetvinge
visible • *adj* synlig
visit • *v* besøge • *n* besøg *(n)*
vista • *n* udsigt, vue *(n)*
visual • *adj* visuel
vitalism • *n* vitalisme
vitamin • *n* vitamin *(n)*
vixen • *n* hunræv
vizier • *n* vesir

vocabulary • *n* ordforråd
vocational • *adj* erhvers-
vodka • *n* vodka
voice • *v* udtryk, udtrykke, udtale, stemt, stemme • *n* stemme, røst, stemning, lyd, gennemslagskraft, vilje, form
voiced • *adj* stemt
voiceless • *adj* ustemt
void • *n* tomrum *(n)*
volcano • *n* vulkan
vole • *n* studsmus
volt • *n* volt
voluble • *adj* veltalende, snakkesalig
volunteer • *n* frivillig
voluptuous • *adj* sanselig, vellystig, frodig, yppig
vomit • *v* brække sig, kaste op • *n* bræk *(n)*, opkast *(n)*
vote • *v* stemme • *n* afstemning
voter • *n* vælger
vowel • *n* vokal
vulgar • *adj* vulgær, obskøn, uanstændig, simpel, ordinær, gemen
vulnerable • *adj* sårbar
vulture • *n* grib
vulva • *n* vulva, tissekone

W

wage • *n* løn
wail • *n* hyl *(n)*, jammer, klageråb *(n)*
waist • *n* talje, hvepsetalje
waistcoat • *n* vest
wait • *v* vente
waiter • *n* tjener
waitress • *n* servitrice
wake • *v* vågne, vække
walk • *v* gå, gå fri, vandre, gå tur med • *n* gåtur, vandretur, gang, gangart, fodsti
walkie-talkie • *n* walkie-talkie
wall • *n* mur, væg, vejrandøje
wallet • *n* tegnebog
wallflower • *n* hjørneklap
wallpaper • *n* tapet *(n)*
walnut • *n* valnøddetræ *(n)*, valnød
walrus • *n* hvalros
want • *v* ville, kræve
war • *n* krig *(n)*
warbler • *n* sanger, skovsanger
wardrobe • *n* garderobe, garderobeskab *(n)*, klædeskab *(n)*
warehouse • *n* lager *(n)*
warhead • *n* sprænghoved *(n)*
warlock • *n* heksemester, troldkarl, trold-

mand, magiker
warm • *adj* varm, lun • *v* varme, opvarme, holde, varm, interessere
warn • *v* advare
warning • *n* advarsel • *interj* advarsel
warranty • *n* garanti
warrior • *n* kriger
warship • *n* krigsskib *(n)*
wart • *n* vorte
warthog • *n* vortesvinet *(n)*
wartime • *n* krigstid
wary • *adj* varsom, forsigtig, på vagt
wash • *v* vaske
washcloth • *n* vaskeklud
wasp • *n* hveps, gedehams
waspish • *adj* giftig, hvas, skarp
watch • *n* armbåndsur *(n)*, vagt • *v* se, holde øje med, iagttage, se efter, vogte på
watchmaker • *n* urmager
watercress • *n* tykskulpet Brøndkarse
waterfall • *n* vandfald *(n)*
watermark • *n* vandmærke *(n)*
watermelon • *n* vandmelon
waterproof • *v* imprægnere • *adj* vandfast, vandtæt, imprægneret

watt • *n* watt *(n)*
wave • *v* vifte, vaje, vinke
wavelength • *n* bølgelængde
wax • *v* vokse • *n* voks
waxwing • *n* silkehale
way • *n* vej, måde, facon
we • *pron* vi
weak • *adj* svag
weakling • *n* svækling
weakness • *n* svaghed
wealth • *n* rigdom, velstand, formue
weapon • *n* våben *(n)*
wear • *v* have, på
weasel • *n* brud
weather • *n* vejr *(n)*, luv
weathercock • *n* vejrhane
weave • *v* væve, spinde
wedding • *n* bryllup *(n)*, vielse
wedge • *n* kile
weed • *n* ukrudt, hash, tjald *(n)*
week • *n* uge
weekday • *n* almindelig ugedag
weekend • *n* weekend
weekly • *adv* ugentlig
weep • *v* græde
weigh • *v* veje
weight • *n* vægt, masse
weird • *adj* mærkelig, besynderlig, ejendommelig
welcome • *v* byde velkommen • *n* byde velkommen • *adj* velkommen • *interj* velkommen
welder • *n* svejser, svejseapparat *(n)*, svejsemaskine
welfare • *n* lykke, velfærd, forsorg
well • *interj* tja • *n* brønd
well-preserved • *adj* velbevaret
werewolf • *n* varulv
west • *n* vest
western • *adj* vestlig
wet • *adj* våd
wether • *n* bede
whale • *n* hval
wharf • *n* kaj
what • *pron* hvad
whatchamacallit • *n* dingenot, dimsedut, dippedut
whatever • *pron* hvad som helst, ligegyldigt
wheat • *n* hvede
wheel • *n* hjul *(n)*
wheelbarrow • *n* trillebør
wheelchair • *n* rullestol, kørestol
wheeze • *v* hvæse • *n* hvæs *(n)*
whelk • *n* konk
whelp • *n* hvalp
when • *n* hvornår • *adv* hvornår • *conj* hvornår, når, da • *pron* hvornår
whence • *adv* hvorfra, hvoraf, hveden
whenever • *adv* når som helst, hver gang
where • *adv* hvor • *conj* hvor • *pron* hvor
whereas • *conj* hvorimod, eftersom
wherefore • *conj* hvorfor
whereupon • *conj* hvorefter, hvorpå
wherever • *adv* hvor, hvor i alverden • *conj* hvor, hvor end
whether • *conj* om
whey • *n* valle
while • *conj* mens, medens
whine • *v* hvine • *n* hvin *(n)*
whip • *v* piske • *n* pisk
whisk • *v* piske • *n* piskeris *(n)*, dusk, visk
whisker • *n* knurhår, hårsbredde
whiskey • *n* whisky
whisper • *v* hviske • *n* hvisken
whistle • *v* fløjte, hvisle • *n* fløjte, fløjt *(n)*
white • *n* hvid • *adj* hvid
whither • *adv* hvorhen
whitish • *adj* hvidlig
who • *pron* hvem, som
whole • *n* hele *(n)*, helhed • *adj* hel
whom • *pron* hvem, hvilken
whore • *n* luder, prostitueret, hore, skøge, hor
whose • *pron* hvis
why • *adv* hvorfor
wick • *n* væge
wide • *adj* bred, vid
widow • *n* enke
widower • *n* enkemand
wife • *n* hustru, kone, frue
wig • *n* paryk
wight • *n* væsen *(n)*, menneske *(n)*, vætte
wild • *adj* vild
will • *n* vilje, testamente *(n)*
willow • *n* pil, piletræ *(n)*
wilt • *v* visne
wily • *adj* snu
wind • *v* blæse, sno, vikle, trække op • *n* vind, luftstrøm, fjert, prut
windmill • *n* vindmølle
window • *n* vindue *(n)*, rude, tidsrum *(n)*, interval *(n)*
windowpane • *n* rude
windowsill • *n* vindueskarm
windshield • *n* forrude
wine • *n* vin
wing • *n* vinge, flyvinge
wink • *v* blinke
winner • *n* vinder
winter • *n* vinter
wipe • *v* tørre, slette
wire • *n* tråd

wireless • *adj* trådløs
wisdom • *n* visdom
wisent • *n* visent, europæisk bison
wish • *v* ønske • *n* ønske
wistful • *adj* længselsfuld, vemodig
witch • *n* heks
witch-hunt • *n* heksejagt
witchcraft • *n* hekseri *(n)*, heksekunst, trolddom
with • *prep* med
wither • *v* visne
within • *prep* uden
without • *prep* uden
witness • *n* vidne *(n)*
wittiness • *n* vittighed
wizard • *n* troldmand
woad • *n* vajd
wok • *n* wok
wolf • *n* ulv
wolverine • *n* jærv
woman • *n* kvinde
womb • *n* livmoder
wonder • *n* vidunder *(n)*, under *(n)*, mirakel *(n)*, vidunder-, fundere, spekulere, tænke
wonderful • *adj* vidunderlig
wont • *n* vane
woo • *v* kurtisere
woodlouse • *n* bænkebider
woodpecker • *n* spætte
woodruff • *n* skovmærke
woodwind • *n* træblæser

woof • *n* vov, vuf
wool • *n* uld
word • *n* ord *(n)*
work • *n* arbejde *(n)*, arbejdsplads, værk *(n)*, forsvarsværk *(n)* • *v* arbejde, bane sig vej, brodere, betjene, anvende, gære, udnytte, bearbejde, forarbejde, drive, udvirke, få til at ske, sætte i arbejde, få til at arbejde, virke, gå, fungere
worker • *n* arbejder
workplace • *n* arbejdsplads
world • *n* menneskehed, verden
worm • *n* orm
wormwood • *n* malurt
worse • *adj* værre
worst • *adj* værst
wort • *n* urt
worthless • *adj* værdiløs
wound • *v* såre • *n* skade, sår *(n)*
wrath • *n* vrede
wreath • *n* krans
wren • *n* gærdesmutte
wrench • *n* skruenøgle
wring • *v* vride
wrinkle • *v* krølle
wrist • *n* håndled *(n)*
wristwatch • *n* armbåndsur *(n)*
write • *v* skrive, digte, forfatte
writer • *n* forfatter
wrong • *adj* forkert

X

xenon • *n* xenon *(n)*
xenophobia • *n* xenofobi
xylography • *n* xylografi

xylophone • *n* xylofon

Y

yacht • *n* yacht
yak • *n* yak, yakokse
yam • *n* yams
yard • *n* gård
yarn • *n* garn *(n)*, garn
yarrow • *n* røllike
yawn • *v* gabe • *n* gab *(n)*
year • *n* år
yearbook • *n* årbog, blå bog
yearly • *adj* årlig
yeast • *n* gær
yellow • *v* gulne • *n* gul • *adj* gul

yes • *n* ja
yesterday • *adv* i går
yesteryear • *n* i fjor
yew • *n* taks, takstræ *(n)*, takstræ
yodel • *v* jodle
yogurt • *n* jogurt
yoke • *n* åg
yolk • *n* æggeblomme
you • *pron* jer, dig, Dem, I, du, De, man, en
young • *adj* ung
ytterbium • *n* ytterbium

yttrium • *n* yttrium
yum • *adj* mums

yurt • *n* jurte

Z

zebra • *n* zebra
zeitgeist • *n* tidsånd
zero • *v* nulstille • *n* nul *(n)*, ingenting,
nulpunkt *(n)*, nulværdi • *adj* nul, ingen
zinc • *n* zink *(n)*
zirconium • *n* zirkonium

zither • *n* citer
zodiac • *n* zodiak, dyrekreds
zombie • *n* zombie
zone • *n* zone

DANISH-ENGLISH

A

å • *n* river
abaca • *n* abaca
abacus • *n* abacus
abasi • *n* abasia
abbed • *n* abbot
abbedi • *n* abbey
abbedisse • *n* abbess
abdicere • *v* abdicate
abdicering • *n* abdication
abdikation • *n* abdication
abe • *n* ape, monkey
abekat • *n* monkey, nigger
åben • *adj* naked
åbenbar • *adj* obvious, transparent
åbenbaring • *n* revelation
åbenbart • *adv* apparently
abnorm • *adj* abnormal
abonnement • *n* subscription
abonnere • *v* subscribe
aboriginer • *n* aborigine
abort • *n* abortion
abrikos • *n* apricot
abrikosfarvet • *adj* apricot
abrikostræ • *n* apricot
absint • *n* absinthe
absolut • *adv* absolutely
abstrakt • *n* abstract
absurd • *adj* absurd, nonsensical
absurditet • *n* absurd
acceleration • *n* acceleration
accelerere • *v* accelerate
accent • *n* accent
acceptabel • *adj* palatable
acceptere • *v* allow
actinium • *n* actinium
addere • *v* add
addict • *n* addict
adgangskode • *n* password
adjektiv • *adj* adjectival • *n* adjective
administrator • *n* administrator
admiral • *n* admiral
admittans • *n* admittance
adoptivsøn • *n* son
adressat • *n* addressee
adresse • *n* address
adskille • *v* separate
advare • *v* caution, warn
advarsel • *n* caution, caveat, warning • *interj* warning
adverbium • *n* adverb
advokat • *n* lawyer
ae • *n* stroke
æble • *n* apple
æblemost • *n* cider

æde • *v* eat, gorge
ædelgran • *n* fir
ædelse • *n* food
ædelsten • *n* gem
ædru • *adj* sober
ædruelig • *adj* sober
æg • *n* egg
ægcelle • *n* ovum
ægge • *v* egg
æggeblomme • *n* yolk
æggehvide • *n* albumen
æggelikør • *n* eggnog
æggeskal • *n* eggshell
æggestok • *n* ovary
ægte • *adj* genuine
ægtefælle • *n* spouse
ægtemand • *n* husband
ægteskab • *n* marriage
æh • *interj* huh
ækvator • *n* equator
ækvivalent • *n* equivalent
ælling • *n* duckling
ælte • *v* knead • *n* mud
ændre • *v* change
ændring • *n* amendment, change
ær • *n* maple
æra • *n* era
ærbar • *adj* modest
ærbødighed • *n* deference
ære • *n* honor
ærefrygt • *n* awe
ærinde • *n* errand
ærkebiskop • *n* archbishop
ærkeengel • *n* archangel
ærlig • *adj* honest
ærlighed • *n* honesty
ærme • *n* sleeve
aerodrom • *n* aerodrome
aerodynamik • *n* aerodynamics
aerodynamisk • *adj* aerodynamic
aerologi • *n* aerology
ært • *n* pea
æsel • *n* ass, donkey
æselhingst • *n* jack
æske • *v* box • *n* box
æstetik • *n* aesthetic, aesthetics
æstetisk • *adj* aesthetic
æt • *n* family
ætiologi • *n* aetiology
af • *prep* by, of
afasi • *n* aphasia
afbarke • *v* bark
afbestille • *v* cancel
afbestilling • *n* cancel

afbildning • *n* depiction, map
afbøde • *v* cushion
afbrænding • *n* burn
afbrudt • *adj* intermittent
afbryde • *v* interrupt
afdelingssygeplejerske • *n* sister
affald • *n* garbage, junk, trash
affaldscontainer • *n* trash
affatte • *v* couch
affiks • *n* affix
afføde • *v* beget
afføring • *n* feces, stool
affyre • *v* fire
afgang • *n* departure
afgøre • *v* decide
afgørelse • *n* decision
afgørende • *adj* crucial, decisive
afgrænset • *adj* restricted
afgrænsning • *n* demarcation
afgrøde • *n* crop
afgrund • *n* abyss
afgud • *n* god
afgudsdyrkelse • *n* idolatry
afhænge • *v* depend
afhandling • *n* thesis, treatise
afhjælpe • *v* remedy, supply
afholdende • *adj* abstemious
afkom • *n* progeny
aflagt • *n* hand-me-down
afleve • *v* submit
aflevere • *v* deliver
aflive • *v* destroy
afløb • *n* drain
aflyd • *n* ablaut
aflyse • *v* cancel
aflysning • *n* cancel
aforisme • *n* aphorism
afpresning • *n* blackmail, extortion
afpresse • *v* blackmail
afprøve • *v* try
afpudse • *v* dress
afrette • *v* dress
afrodisiakum • *n* aphrodisiac
afsender • *n* sender
afskærmning • *n* guard
afskaffe • *v* abrogate, disband
afsked • *n* leave
afskedige • *v* can, fire
afskrabe • *v* abrade
afsky • *n* abhorrence, disgust • *v* loathe
afskyelig • *adj* heinous
afskyelighed • *n* abomination
afskygning • *n* hue
afsløre • *v* explode, reveal
afslørende • *adj* telltale
afslutning • *n* closure, end
afsnit • *n* episode, section

afsoningstid • *n* time
afstand • *n* distance
afstemning • *n* ballot, vote
afstemple • *v* postmark
aftagende • *adj* down
aftagning • *n* cut
aftale • *n* agreement, understanding
aften • *n* evening, night
aftenmad • *n* dinner
aftensmad • *n* supper
aftenvagt • *n* babysitter
afvente • *v* await
afvigelse • *n* departure, deviation, error, inflection
afvikle • *v* execute
afvise • *v* reject
åg • *n* yoke
agent • *n* agent, factor
åger • *n* usury
ager • *n* field
agere • *v* act
agerhøne • *n* partridge
ågerkarl • *n* usurer
agern • *n* acorn
agernet • *n* glans
aggregat • *n* set
aggression • *n* aggression
aggressiv • *adj* aggressive
agnostiker • *n* agnostic
agorafobia • *n* agoraphobia
agronom • *n* agronomist
agronomi • *n* agronomy
agterende • *n* stern
agterstævn • *n* stern
agurk • *n* cucumber
ahorn • *n* maple
airconditioneret • *adj* air-conditioned
ajour • *adj* up-to-date
ak • *interj* alas
akademiker • *n* academic, graduate
akavet • *adj* awkward
akeleje • *n* columbine
akkompagnatør • *n* accompanist
akkord • *n* chord
akkordeon • *n* accordion
akkumulere • *v* accumulate
akkusativ • *n* accusative
akrobat • *n* acrobat
akrobatik • *n* acrobatics
akronym • *n* acronym
akrylisk • *adj* acrylic
aks • *n* ear, spike
akt • *n* act
aktie • *n* equity, share
aktieejer • *n* shareholder, stockholder
aktionær • *n* shareholder, stockholder
aktiv • *adj* active • *n* asset

aktivist • *n* activist
aktivt • *adj* fierce
aktuel • *adj* current
akupunktur • *n* acupuncture
akustisk • *adj* acoustic
akvarium • *n* aquarium
akvavit • *n* aquavit
ål • *n* eel
alabast • *n* alabaster
alanin • *n* alanine
alarmerende • *adv* alarmingly
albatros • *n* albatross
albino • *n* albino
albue • *v* elbow • *n* elbow
albueskæl • *n* limpet
album • *n* book
aldeles • *adv* all
alder • *n* age
alderdom • *n* age
aldrig • *adv* never
ålefisk • *n* eel
ålekrage • *n* cormorant
alen • *n* ell
alf • *n* fairy
alfa • *n* alpha
alfabet • *n* alphabet
alfabetisk • *adj* alphabetic
alfanumerisk • *adj* alphanumeric
alfons • *n* pimp
alge • *n* alga
algebra • *n* algebra
algoritme • *n* algorithm
alibi • *n* alibi
alk • *n* razorbill
alkalisk • *adj* alkaline
alkalitet • *n* alkalinity
alkohol • *n* alcohol, drink, spirit
alkoholiker • *n* alcoholic
alkoholisme • *n* alcoholism
alkove • *n* alcove
alkymist • *n* alchemist
alle • *pron* everyone
allé • *n* avenue
allehånde • *n* allspice
allerede • *adv* already
allestedsnærværende • *adj* ubiquitous
alliance • *n* alliance
alligator • *n* alligator
allike • *n* jackdaw
allitteration • *n* alliteration
allokering • *n* allocation
almægtig • *adj* almighty
almanak • *n* almanac
almen • *adj* general
almindelig • *adj* common, general, normal, regular
alpaka • *n* alpaca

alrune • *n* mandrake
alt • *n* all • *pron* everything
altæder • *n* omnivore
altan • *n* balcony
alter • *n* altar
alternativ • *adj* alternative
altid • *adv* always
altmuligmand • *n* factotum
altruistisk • *adj* altruistic
alvidende • *adj* omniscient
alvor • *n* seriousness
alvorlig • *adj* serious
amagermad • *n* sandwich
amatør • *n* amateur
ambassade • *n* embassy
ambassadør • *n* ambassador
ambitiøs • *adj* ambitious
ambolt • *n* anvil
ambra • *n* ambergris
ambrosia • *n* ambrosia
ambulance • *n* ambulance
amen • *adv* amen
americium • *n* americium
amfibium • *n* amphibian
amfiteater • *n* amphitheater
ammunition • *n* ammunition
amnesi • *n* amnesia
amnesti • *n* amnesty
amorf • *adj* amorphous
amt • *n* county
amylase • *n* amylase
anabolisme • *n* anabolism
anæstesi • *n* anesthesia
anagram • *n* anagram
anakronistisk • *adj* dated
analfabet • *n* illiterate
analgetikum • *n* analgesic
analyse • *n* analysis
ananas • *n* pineapple
anarki • *n* anarchy
anarkisme • *n* anarchism
anatomi • *n* anatomy
anatomisk • *adv* anatomically
anbefale • *v* encourage, recommend
anciennitet • *n* seniority
and • *n* duck
ånd • *n* ghost, spirit
ånde • *v* breathe
åndelig • *adj* spiritual
andemad • *n* duckweed
anden • *adj* second
anderledes • *adj* different • *adv* otherwise
andetsteds • *adv* elsewhere
andre • *adj* other
andrik • *n* drake
android • *adj* android
androide • *n* android

åndsforladt • *adj* inane, shallow
åndssvag • *adj* dumb
anemone • *n* anemone
anerkendelse • *n* approval
anfald • *n* seizure, turn
anflyvning • *n* approach
angående • *prep* about
anger • *n* remorse
angivelig • *adv* allegedly
angiver • *n* betrayer
angre • *v* regret
angreb • *n* attack, charge
angrende • *adj* repentant
angribe • *v* attack
angriber • *n* attacker
angst • *n* anxiety, fear
ångstrøm • *n* angstrom
anholde • *v* arrest
anholdelse • *n* arrest
anime • *n* anime
anis • *n* anise
ankel • *n* ankle
anker • *n* anchor
ankerkat • *n* cat
anklage • *n* accusation, charge • *v* denounce
ankomme • *v* arrive
ankomst • *n* advent, arrival
anlæg • *n* factory, garden, set
anledning • *n* occasion
anmode • *v* request
annektion • *n* annexation
annihilere • *v* annihilate
annoncere • *v* advertise
annullation • *n* annulment
annullere • *v* cancel
annullering • *n* annulment, cancel, cancellation
anonym • *adj* anonymous
anonymitet • *n* anonymity
anopi • *n* anopia
anopsi • *n* anopia
anoreksi • *n* anorexia
anormal • *adj* abnormal • *adv* abnormally
ansætte • *v* employ, hire
ansat • *n* employee
anseelse • *n* reputation
anselig • *adj* stately
ansigt • *n* countenance, face
ansigtstræk • *n* feature
ansigtsudtryk • *n* face
ansjos • *n* anchovy
ansøger • *n* applicant
ansøgning • *n* request
anstændig • *adj* modest
ansvar • *n* responsibility
ansvarlig • *adj* responsible

ansvarsbevidst • *adj* responsible
ansvarsfuld • *adj* responsible
antænde • *v* light
antage • *v* assume, think
antageligvis • *adv* probably
antagelse • *n* assumption
antaget • *adj* alleged
antal • *n* amount
antenne • *n* aerial
antepenultimær • *adj* antepenultimate
antibiotisk • *adj* antibiotic
antidepressiv • *n* antidepressant
antilope • *n* antelope
antimon • *n* antimony
antiobiotikum • *n* antibiotic
antioxidant • *n* antioxidant
antologi • *n* anthology
antonym • *n* antonym
antonymi • *n* antonymy
antracit • *n* anthracite
antropologi • *n* anthropology
antropologisk • *adj* anthropological
antropomorf • *adj* anthropomorphic
antydning • *n* vestige
anus • *n* anus
anvende • *v* work
aorist • *n* aorist
aorta • *n* aorta
aparte • *adj* fond
apati • *n* apathy
apnø • *n* apnea
apokope • *n* apocope
apologet • *n* apologist
apopleksi • *n* stroke
aposiopese • *n* aposiopesis
apostrof • *n* apostrophe
apostrofe • *n* apostrophe
apotek • *n* pharmacy
apoteker • *n* pharmacist
apparat • *n* apparatus, set
appelsin • *interj* cheese • *n* orange
appelsintræ • *n* orange
appendiks • *n* appendix
appetit • *n* appetite
apropos • *adv* apropos • *prep* apropos
apsis • *n* apse
ar • *n* are, scar
år • *n* year
ara • *n* macaw
arbejde • *n* occupation, work • *v* work
arbejder • *n* laborer, worker
arbejdsgiver • *n* employer
arbejdsløs • *adj* unemployed
arbejdsløshed • *n* unemployment
arbejdsmæssig • *adj* occupational
arbejdsmand • *n* laborer
arbejdsom • *adj* diligent, industrious

arbejdsplads • *n* work, workplace
arbitrær • *adj* arbitrary
årbog • *n* yearbook
åre • *n* oar
areal • *n* area
årepresse • *n* tourniquet
argon • *n* argon
argumentere • *v* argue
århundred • *n* century
århundrede • *n* century
arie • *n* air, aria
aristokrati • *n* aristocracy
ark • *n* sheet
arkæolog • *n* archaeologist
arkæologi • *n* archaeology
arkaisk • *adj* archaic
arkaisme • *n* archaism
arkitekt • *n* architect
arkitektur • *n* architecture
arkiv • *n* archive
arkivalie • *n* file
arkivere • *v* archive, file
årlig • *adj* annual, yearly • *adv* annually
årligt • *adv* annually
arm • *n* arm
armbånd • *n* bracelet
armbåndsur • *n* watch, wristwatch
armbrøst • *n* crossbow
arme • *n* army
armhule • *n* armpit
armstol • *n* armchair
aroma • *n* aroma
arrangere • *v* arrange
arrestere • *v* arrest
arrogance • *n* arrogance
arrogant • *adj* arrogant
arsen • *n* arsenic
årstid • *n* season
art • *n* kind, species
årti • *n* decade
artikel • *n* article
artiskok • *n* artichoke
årvågenhed • *n* vigilance
arvelig • *adj* hereditary, inheritable
arvestykke • *n* heirloom
arving • *n* heir, heiress
ase • *v* slog
aseksualitet • *n* asexuality
asie • *n* gherkin
aske • *n* ash
askebæger • *n* ashtray
asp • *n* aspen
asparges • *n* asparagus
aspartam • *n* aspartame
aspekt • *n* dimension
aspetræ • *n* aspen
astat • *n* astatine

asterisk • *n* asterisk
asteroide • *n* asteroid
astma • *n* asthma
astrofysik • *n* astrophysics
astrolog • *n* astrologer
astrologi • *n* astrology
astronaut • *n* astronaut
astronom • *n* astronomer
asyl • *n* asylum
asymmetrisk • *adj* asymmetrical
atavistisk • *adj* atavistic
atlas • *n* atlas
atlet • *n* athlete
atlingand • *n* garganey
atmosfære • *n* atmosphere
atol • *n* atoll
atom • *n* atom
atonal • *adj* atonal
atrium • *n* atrium
atrofi • *n* atrophy
attende • *adj* eighteenth
attendedel • *n* eighteenth
attener • *n* eighteenth
attentat • *n* assassination
attentatmand • *n* assassin
attitude • *n* attitude
attrå • *v* desire
attribut • *n* attribute
atypisk • *adj* atypical
aubergine • *n* eggplant
audiologi • *n* audiology
aura • *n* aura
autenticitet • *n* authenticity
autentificere • *v* authenticate
autentisk • *adj* authentic
autisme • *n* autism
autistisk • *adj* autistic
autodidakt • *n* autodidact • *adj* autodidactic
autodidaktisk • *adj* autodidactic
autograf • *n* autograph
autokrat • *n* autocrat
automat • *n* kiosk
automatik • *adj* automatic
automatisk • *adv* automatically
automobil • *n* car
autonomi • *n* autonomy
autopsi • *n* autopsy
autorisation • *n* authorization
av • *interj* ouch
avantgarde • *n* avant-garde
avenue • *n* avenue
avis • *n* newspaper
avispapir • *n* newspaper
avle • *v* beget
avlshingst • *n* stallion, stud
avlstyr • *n* stud

avocado • *n* avocado
avokado • *n* avocado

azalea • *n* azalea

B

baby • *n* baby
babysitning • *n* babysitting
babysitting • *n* babysitting
baccarat • *n* baccarat
bachelor • *n* bachelor
backgammon • *n* backgammon
bad • *n* bathe
båd • *n* boat
bade • *v* bath
både • *conj* both
badedragt • *n* swimsuit
bådehus • *n* boathouse
badekåbe • *n* bathrobe
badekar • *n* bath, bathtub
bådeskur • *n* boathouse
badeværelse • *n* bathroom, toilet
badland • *n* badlands
badminton • *n* badminton
bægerglas • *n* beaker
bæk • *n* burn
bækken • *n* pelvis
bælg • *n* pod
bælte • *n* belt
bænk • *n* bench
bænkebider • *n* woodlouse
bær • *n* berry
bærbar • *adj* portable
bære • *v* carry
bæredygtig • *adj* sustainable
bærepose • *n* bag
bæst • *n* brute
bæver • *n* beaver
bævre • *v* quiver
bag • *prep* behind
bag- • *adj* hinder
bagage • *n* luggage
bagbord • *n* larboard
bagdel • *n* backside, behind
bage • *v* bake
bagefter • *prep* after, behind • *adv* afterwards, behind
bagel • *n* bagel
bager • *n* baker
bageri • *n* bakery
bagest • *adj* hinder
bagi • *adv* aback
bagklogskab • *n* hindsight
bagkrop • *n* abdomen
bagning • *n* baking
bagside • *n* back, backside, behind

bagtale • *v* libel, slander
bagud • *adv* behind
bagværk • *n* pastry
bagvaske • *v* libel
bagvaskelse • *n* slander
bajonet • *n* bayonet
bak • *adv* aback
bakke • *n* hill, tray
baklava • *n* baklava
bakterie • *n* bacteria
bakteriofag • *n* bacteriophage
bakteriologi • *n* bacteriology
bal • *n* ball
bål • *n* fire
balalajka • *n* balalaika
balde • *n* buttock, cheek
balder • *n* can
balkon • *n* balcony
ballade • *n* fight, row
ballast • *n* ballast
balle • *n* buttock
ballet • *n* ballet
ballon • *n* balloon
balsam • *n* balsam
balsamin • *n* balsam
balsamisk • *adj* balmy
balustrade • *n* balustrade
bambus • *n* bamboo
banal • *adj* light
banan • *n* banana
bånd • *n* fret, ribbon, tape
band • *n* band
bandage • *n* bandage
bande • *n* cushion, posse
bandy • *n* bandy
bane • *n* bane, course, down, field • *v* clear
bang • *interj* bang
bange • *adj* afraid, frightened
bangebuks • *n* chicken, coward
banjo • *n* banjo
bank • *n* bank
banke • *n* bank • *v* clobber, drum
bankerot • *adj* bankrupt • *n* bankruptcy
banket • *n* banquet
bankfilial • *n* bank
banner • *n* banner
bannerreklame • *n* banner
bar • *n* bar • *adj* bare, naked
barbecue • *n* barbecue

barbering • *n* shave
barberkniv • *n* razor
bare • *conj* once
båre • *n* stretcher
barfodet • *adv* barefoot, barefooted
barfred • *n* keep
barium • *n* barium
bark • *n* bark
barmhjertighed • *n* mercy
barn • *n* child, kid
barndom • *n* childhood
barndomstid • *n* childhood
barnebarn • *n* grandchild
barnepige • *n* babysitter
barneplejerske • *n* nurse
barnlig • *adj* juvenile
barnløs • *adj* childless
baronesse • *n* baroness
barrier • *n* barrier
barrikade • *n* barricade
barsle • *v* deliver
baryton • *n* baritone
basal • *adj* basic, rudimentary
basalt • *n* basalt
basar • *n* bazaar
baseball • *n* baseball
baseret • *v* based • *adj* based
basilikum • *n* basil
basis • *n* backbone, basis
basisk • *adj* basic
basketball • *n* basketball
bassin • *n* basin
bastard • *n* bastard
basun • *n* trombone
batik • *n* batik
batteri • *n* bank, battery
bauxit • *n* bauxite
bavian • *n* baboon
bearbejde • *v* tool, work
bebo • *v* dwell
beboelig • *adj* livable
bebrejde • *v* blame, reproach
bebrejdelse • *n* reproach
bed • *n* bed, patch
bede • *v* ask, pray • *n* beet, wether
bedekrans • *n* rosary
bedemand • *n* undertaker
bedrage • *v* cheat, deceive
bedre • *adj* better • *adv* better
bedrift • *n* achievement, enterprise
bedst • *adj* best
bedste • *n* choice
bedstefar • *n* grandfather
bedstemor • *n* grandmother
beduin • *n* bedouin
befæste • *v* fortify
befolkning • *n* population

befri • *v* deliver, free, liberate
begå • *v* commit, perpetrate
begær • *n* concupiscence, desire, lust • *v* lust
begære • *v* desire, lust
begavet • *adj* talented
begivenhed • *n* event, incident, occasion
begrænse • *v* border, constrain, curtail
begrænset • *adj* bound, restricted
begrænsning • *n* limitation
begrave • *v* bury, earth
begravelse • *n* funeral, grave
begravelses- • *adj* funeral
begreb • *n* concept
begrebsordbog • *n* thesaurus
begribe • *v* fathom, grasp, perceive, understand
begribelig • *adj* fathomable
begynde • *v* begin, commence
begynder • *n* neophyte
behagelig • *adj* pleasant, sweet
behagelighed • *n* comfort
behandle • *v* dress
behandling • *n* therapy
behåret • *adj* hairy
beherske • *v* govern
beholde • *v* store
beholder • *n* tank
behov • *n* need, occasion
behøve • *v* need
beige • *n* beige
bejae • *v* affirm
bekæmpe • *v* fight
bekende • *v* confess
bekendt • *adj* familiar • *n* friend
bekendtgøre • *v* cry, denounce
beklæde • *v* dress
beklædning • *n* dress
beklager • *interj* sorry
bekostning • *n* condition
bekræfte • *v* confirm
bekvemmelighed • *n* comfort
Bekymring • *n* concern
belægge • *v* flag
belærende • *adj* didactic
belastning • *n* burden
belejlig • *adj* opportune
belejre • *v* besiege
beløb • *n* amount
beløbe • *v* amount
belyse • *v* light
belyst • *adj* light
bemærke • *v* notice, observe
bemærkelsesværdig • *adj* salient
ben • *n* bone, leg
benævnelse • *n* designation
benzin • *n* gasoline

berede • *v* prepare
beredskab • *n* standby
beregne • *v* figure
beretning • *n* history
berettende • *adj* narrative
beriberi • *n* beriberi
berkelium • *n* berkelium
berliner • *n* doughnut
berolige • *v* calm
beroligende • *adj* soothing
berømmelse • *n* fame
berøre • *v* touch
berøve • *v* rob
bersærk • *n* berserk
beruset • *adj* drunken, inebriated, intoxicated
berygtet • *adj* infamous, notorious
beryl • *n* beryl
beryllium • *n* beryllium
besætte • *v* possess, squat
besættelse • *n* obsession, occupation
besejre • *v* conquer, defeat
besidde • *v* possess
besiddelse • *n* property
beskadige • *v* damage
beskadigelse • *n* damage
beskæftigelse • *n* occupation
beskære • *v* cut
beskatte • *v* tax
besked • *n* message
beskeden • *adj* modest, unobtrusive
beskidt • *adj* dirty
beskrive • *v* describe
beskrivelse • *n* description
beskylde • *v* denounce
beskyldning • *n* accusation
beskytte • *v* protect, safeguard, shield
beskyttelse • *n* safeguard
beslå • *v* shoe
beslægtet • *adj* related • *n* relative
beslaglæggelse • *n* seizure
beslagsmed • *n* farrier
beslutning • *n* decision
beslutsom • *adj* decisive
beslutsomhed • *n* decision
beslutte • *v* decide
besøg • *n* visit
besøge • *v* visit
bespotte • *v* blaspheme
bestanddel • *n* component
bestemme • *v* govern
bestemt • *adj* explicit, set
bestialsk • *adj* bestial
bestik • *n* cutlery
bestikke • *v* bribe
bestikkelse • *n* bribe
bestjæle • *v* rob

bestyrer • *n* manager
bestyrtelse • *n* consternation
besudle • *v* soil
besvær • *n* difficulty, hassle
besvare • *v* reply
besvarelse • *n* reply
besvime • *v* faint
besvimelse • *n* faint
besynderlig • *adj* curious, funny, weird
beta • *n* beta
betændelse • *n* inflammation
betagende • *adj* fascinating
betale • *v* foot, pay
betaling • *n* pay
betalingsmiddel • *n* money
betegnelse • *n* designation
betingning • *n* conditioning
betjene • *v* work
beton • *n* concrete • *adj* concrete
betoning • *n* accent
betragte • *v* observe
betryggende • *adv* adequately
betyde • *v* mean
betydning • *n* meaning
betydningslære • *n* semantics
beundrer • *n* admirer
beundringsværdig • *adj* admirable
bevæge • *v* move, touch
bevægelse • *n* motion, move, movement
bevæggrund • *n* motive
bevågenhed • *n* attention
bevaring • *n* conservation
bevidst • *adj* deliberate • *adv* deliberately
bevidsthed • *n* consciousness
bevidstløs • *adj* unconscious
bevis • *n* evidence, proof
bevise • *v* evidence
bevogte • *v* guard
bevoksning • *n* stand
bh • *n* bra
bi • *n* bee
biavler • *n* beekeeper
bibetydning • *n* connotation
bibliografi • *n* bibliography
bibliotek • *n* library
bibliotekar • *n* librarian
bid • *n* bite, morsel
bide • *v* bite
bidende • *adj* bitter
bidirektional • *adj* bidirectional
bidrage • *v* contribute
bidragsyder • *n* contributor
bidragyder • *n* contributor
bidsel • *n* bridle
bifag • *n* minor
biflod • *n* tributary
bigami • *n* bigamy

bikini • *n* bikini
bikube • *n* beehive
bil • *n* car
bilag • *n* annex
bilist • *n* motorist
bilkø • *n* tailback
billard • *n* billiards
bille • *n* beetle
billede • *n* image, photo, picture
billet • *n* ticket
billetpris • *n* fare
billige • *v* countenance
billighedsret • *n* equity
billigt • *adv* cheaply
binær • *adj* binary
bind • *n* book
binde • *v* bind, tie
bindeled • *n* nexus
bindeord • *n* conjunction
bindestreg • *n* hyphen
bingospil • *n* bingo
bio • *n* cinema
biograf • *n* cinema, movie
biografi • *n* biography
biokemi • *n* biochemistry
biokemiker • *n* biochemist
biologi • *n* biology
biologisk • *adj* biological
biomedicin • *n* biomedicine
biomedicinsk • *adj* biomedical
biopsi • *n* biopsy
biord • *n* adverb
biotisk • *adj* biotic
bipolær • *adj* bipolar
bipolar • *adj* bipolar
birk • *n* birch
bisamrotte • *n* muskrat
biskop • *n* bishop
bismer • *n* steelyard
bison • *n* buffalo
bisp • *n* bishop
bistå • *v* aid
bistættelse • *n* funeral
bistand • *n* aid
bistro • *n* bistro
bitter • *n* bitter • *adj* bitter
bivoks • *n* beeswax
bivuak • *n* bivouac
bizar • *adj* bizarre
bjæffe • *v* bark
bjælke • *n* beam
bjerg • *n* mountain
bjergskred • *n* landslide
bjergtop • *n* summit
bjørn • *n* bear
blå • *n* blue • *adj* blue
blåbær • *n* bilberry, blueberry

blad • *n* leaf
bladgrønt • *n* chlorophyll
blæk • *n* ink
blæksprutte • *n* cuttlefish, octopus, squid
blænde • *v* blind, glare
blære • *n* bladder, blister
blærehalskirtel • *n* prostate
blæse • *v* blow, wind
blaffer • *n* hitchhiker
blåhals • *n* bluethroat
blåklokke • *n* harebell
blande • *v* mix, shuffle
blandet • *adj* miscellaneous
blanding • *n* composition, mix
blandt • *prep* among
blank • *adj* blank
blanke • *v* polish, shine
blanket • *n* form
blanko- • *n* blank
blåøjet • *adj* blue-eyed
blasfemi • *n* blasphemy
blasfemisk • *adj* blasphemous
ble • *n* diaper
bleg • *adj* light, pale, pallid
blege • *v* bleach
blegemiddel • *n* bleach
blegt • *adj* pale
blender • *n* blender, mixer
blid • *adj* sweet
blidt • *adv* softly
blind • *adj* blind
blindtarm • *n* appendix
blindtarmsbetændelse • *n* appendicitis
blink • *n* lure
blinke • *v* flash, wink
blive • *v* be, become, fall, get, go, turn
blod • *n* blood
blodbad • *n* bloodbath
blodbudding • *n* pudding
bløde • *v* bleed
blødgøre • *v* soften
blødgøres • *v* soften
blodhund • *n* bloodhound
blodig • *adj* bloody, gory
blodigle • *n* leech
blodmangel • *n* anemia
blodplade • *n* platelet
blodprøve • *n* blood
blodskam • *n* incest
blodtørst • *n* bloodlust
blodtørstig • *adj* bloodthirsty
blodurt • *n* bloodroot
blokade • *n* blockade
blokere • *v* block
blokfløjte • *n* recorder
blomkål • *n* cauliflower
blomme • *n* plum

blommefarvet • *adj* plum
blommetræ • *n* plum
blomst • *n* flower
blomsterbed • *n* flowerbed
blomstre • *v* flower
blomstrende • *adj* colorful
blomstringstid • *n* heyday
blond • *adj* fair
blondine • *n* blond
blotte • *v* flash
blottet • *adj* naked
blufærdig • *adj* modest
bluse • *n* shirt
blusse • *v* flame
bly • *n* lead
blyant • *n* pencil
blyfri • *adj* unleaded
blyglans • *n* galena
bo • *v* dwell, live
boble • *n* bubble
bøddel • *n* executioner
bøde • *n* ticket
bodybuilder • *n* bodybuilder
bodybuilding • *n* bodybuilding
bøffel • *n* buffalo
bøg • *n* beech
bog • *n* book
bogbinder • *n* bookbinder
bogbus • *n* bookmobile
bøgetræ • *n* beech
bogfinke • *n* chaffinch
boghandel • *n* bookshop
bogholder • *n* accountant, bookkeeper
boghvede • *n* buckwheat
bogorm • *n* bookworm
bogreol • *n* bookcase
bogstav • *n* letter
boheme • *n* bohemian
bøhmand • *n* bogeyman
bøje • *v* bow, compare, inflect • *n* buoy
bøjle • *n* hanger
bøjle-bh • *n* bra
bøjning • *n* turn
boks • *n* box
bokse • *v* box
boksning • *n* boxing
bold • *n* ball
bølge • *n* outbreak
bølgedal • *n* trough
bølgelængde • *n* wavelength
bølle • *n* bully
bolle • *n* bun • *v* fuck, sex
bolsje • *n* sweet
bolster • *n* bolster
bolværk • *n* bulwark
bom • *n* tollgate
bombe • *v* bomb • *n* bomb

bomuld • *n* cotton • *adj* cotton
bøn • *n* prayer
bonde • *n* farmer, pawn, peasant
bondefanger • *n* scam
boner • *n* boner
bønfalde • *v* beseech, implore
bønne • *n* bean
bønner • *n* bean
boomerang • *n* boomerang
bopæl • *n* residence
bor • *n* boron, drill
bord • *n* table
bordel • *n* brothel
bore • *v* bore, drill
borg • *n* castle, stronghold
borger • *n* citizen, subject, townsman
borgerskab • *n* citizenship
borgmester • *n* mayor
borgtårn • *n* keep
børn • *n* child
børnehave • *n* kindergarten
børnehjem • *n* orphanage
borsjtj • *n* borscht
børste • *n* bristle, brush • *v* brush
børstehår • *n* bristle
bortføre • *v* abduct
bortgang • *n* departure
bortlede • *v* drain
bosiddende • *n* resident
bøsning • *n* box
bøsse • *n* fairy, gay, queen
botanik • *n* botany
botaniker • *n* botanist
botanisere • *v* botanize
botanisk • *adj* botanical
botulisme • *n* botulism
bouillon • *n* bouillon
bouquet • *n* bouquet
bov • *n* bow
bøvl • *n* hassle
bøvs • *n* burp
bøvse • *v* burp
boykot • *n* boycott
boykotte • *v* boycott
bræ • *n* glacier
bræge • *v* baa
bræk • *n* vomit
brækjern • *n* crowbar
brænde • *v* burn
brændemærke • *v* brand • *n* brand
brændenælde • *n* nettle
brændevin • *n* aquavit
brændstof • *n* fuel
brændt • *v* burned
brag • *n* bang, crash, detonation
brage • *v* bang
brak • *adj* brackish

brakvand • *adj* brackish
branche • *n* business
brand • *n* fire
brandmand • *n* jellyfish
brandmur • *n* firewall
brandsår • *n* burn
bras • *n* junk
brasen • *n* bream
brasenføde • *n* quillwort
brat • *adj* abrupt, sudden
bratsch • *n* viola
bravo • *interj* bravo
bred • *n* bank, coast, shore • *adj* deep,
wide
bredbånd • *n* broadband
brede • *v* spread
bregne • *n* fern
brems • *n* botfly
bremse • *v* arrest • *n* botfly, brake
brev • *n* letter
breviar • *n* breviary
brevkort • *n* postcard
bridge • *n* bridge
brik • *n* counter, piece
briks • *n* couch
brillans • *n* shine
brille • *n* spectacles
brillere • *v* shine
bringe • *v* bring
brint • *n* hydrogen
brise • *n* breeze
bro • *n* bridge
broccoli • *n* broccoli
broche • *n* brooch
brochure • *n* brochure
brød • *n* bread
broder • *n* brethren, brother
brodere • *v* work
broderskab • *n* brotherhood
brødflov • *adj* peckish
brødfrugt • *n* jackfruit
brødfrugttræ • *n* jackfruit
brøk • *n* fraction
brok • *n* hernia
brokbind • *n* truss
brøkdel • *n* fraction
brøl • *n* bellow, roar
brøle • *v* bellow, moo, roar
brom • *n* bromine
brombær • *n* blackberry
brønd • *n* well
bronkitis • *n* bronchitis
bronze • *n* bronze • *adj* bronze
bronzefarvet • *adj* bronze
bronzere • *v* bronze
bror • *n* brother, sibling
brosme • *n* cusk

brosten • *n* cobblestone
brud • *n* bride, weasel
brudepige • *n* bridesmaid
brudgom • *n* bridegroom
bruge • *v* use
bruger • *n* user
brun • *n* brown • *adj* brown • *v* tan
brune • *v* brown
brunette • *n* brunette
brunkul • *n* lignite
bruse • *v* fizzle, sail
brusebad • *n* shower
brusen • *n* fizzle
bruser • *n* shower
brusk • *n* cartilage, gristle
brutal • *adj* brutish
brygge • *v* brew
brygger • *n* brewer
bryggeri • *n* brewery
bryllup • *n* marriage, wedding
bryllupsrejse • *n* honeymoon
brysk • *adj* brusque
bryst • *n* breast, tit
brystholder • *n* bra
brystvorte • *n* nipple, tit
bud • *n* bid, message, messenger, offer
budding • *n* pudding
budget • *n* budget
budskab • *n* message
bue • *n* arc, arch, bow • *v* bow
bueskydning • *n* archery
bueskytte • *n* archer
bug • *n* abdomen, stomach
bughule • *n* abdomen
bugspytkirtel • *n* pancreas
bugt • *n* bay, gulf
buk • *n* bow, box, goat
buket • *n* bouquet
bukke • *v* bow
bukkehorn • *n* fenugreek
buks • *n* pants
buksbom • *n* box
bukser • *n* pants
bulldozer • *n* bulldozer
bullet • *n* bullet
bulmeurt • *n* henbane
bump • *n* thud
bund • *n* bottom
bundgrænse • *n* threshold
bungalow • *n* bungalow
bur • *n* cage
burde • *v* ought, should
bureau • *n* office
bureaukrat • *n* bureaucrat
bureaukrati • *n* bureaucracy
bureaukratisk • *adj* bureaucratic
burette • *n* burette

burre • *n* burdock
bus • *n* bus
busk • *n* bush
buskads • *n* thicket
bussemand • *n* bogeyman, booger
buste • *n* bust
butik • *n* shop
by • *n* city, town, village
byg • *n* barley

bygge • *v* build, construct, craft
byggeri • *n* building
bygning • *n* building
bynke • *n* mugwort
byrde • *n* burden
bytte • *n* kill
byttehandel • *n* barter, trade

C

cabriolet • *n* cabriolet, convertible
calcium • *n* calcium
californium • *n* californium
caliper • *n* caliper
camouflere • *v* camouflage
campingvogn • *n* caravan
cannabis • *n* cannabis
carbon • *n* carbon
carcinogen • *n* carcinogen
ceder • *n* cedar
cedertræ • *n* cedar
cedrat • *n* citron
celle • *n* cell
cello • *n* cello
cellofan • *n* cellophane
cellulose • *n* cellulose
cembalist • *n* harpsichordist
cembalo • *n* harpsichord
cement • *n* cement
cementere • *v* cement
centrifuge • *n* centrifuge
centrifugere • *v* centrifuge
centrum • *n* center, gold
cerebral • *adj* cerebral
ceremoni • *n* ceremony
cerium • *n* cerium
champagne • *n* champagne
champion • *n* champion
charm • *n* charm
charme • *n* charm
charmere • *v* charm
chassis • *n* chassis
chatte • *v* chat
chauffør • *n* driver
chauvinisme • *n* chauvinism
check • *n* cheque
chef • *n* manager
chikane • *n* harassment
chikanere • *v* hassle
chili • *n* chili, pepper
chille • *v* chill
chimpanse • *n* chimpanzee
chinchilla • *n* chinchilla

chintz • *n* chintz
chips • *n* chip
chok • *n* shock
chokere • *v* shake
chokolade • *n* chocolate, cocoa
chutney • *n* chutney
ciffer • *n* digit, figure
cigar • *n* cigar
cigaret • *n* cigarette
cirka • *adv* about • *prep* about, circa
cirkel • *n* circle
cirkulær • *adj* circular
cirkus • *n* circus
citation • *n* citation, quotation
citer • *n* zither
citering • *n* citation, quotation
citron • *n* lemon
citrongul • *adj* lemon
citronsommerfugl • *n* brimstone
civil • *adj* civil
civilisation • *n* civilization
civilisering • *n* civilization
clairvoyance • *n* clairvoyance
clairvoyant • *adj* clairvoyant
clipse • *v* clip
cognac • *n* cognac
cola • *n* cola
collie • *n* collie
computer • *n* computer
cool • *adj* cool
cowboy • *n* cowboy
crash • *n* crash
crashe • *v* crash
crawl • *n* crawl
creme • *v* cream • *n* cream
cremefarvet • *adj* cream
cup • *n* cup
curium • *n* curium
cyanid • *n* cyanide
cykel • *n* bicycle
cykle • *v* cycle • *n* cycling
cyklist • *n* cyclist
cyklus • *n* cycle

cylinder • *n* cylinder
cylindrisk • *adj* cylindrical
cyste • *n* cyst

cystein • *n* cysteine

D

då • *n* doe
da • *conj* as, when • *n* unemployed
dåb • *n* baptism
dåd • *n* act, deed
daddel • *n* date
dadel • *n* criticism
dadle • *v* blame
dådyr • *n* fawn
dådyrfarvet • *adj* fawn
dæk • *n* deck, tyre
dække • *v* cover, set, veil • *n* veil
dæmning • *n* dam
dæmon • *n* demon, fiend
dag • *n* day
dagblad • *n* newspaper
dagbog • *n* diary
daggry • *v* dawn • *n* dawn, twilight
daglig • *adj* daily
dagligmærke • *n* definitive
dagligsprog • *adj* colloquial
dagligt • *adv* daily
dal • *n* dale, valley
dam • *n* draughts, pond
damask • *n* damask
dame • *n* queen
dameselskabskjole • *n* robe
damp • *n* steam, vapor
dampe • *v* steam
dampende • *adj* steaming
damper • *n* steamboat
dampskib • *n* steamboat, steamer, steamship
Danish • *n* coif
danne • *v* queue
dans • *n* dance
danse • *v* dance
danser • *n* dancer
danserinde • *n* dancer
dårlig • *adj* bad, evil
dårskab • *n* foible
dåse • *n* box, can
data • *n* data
databank • *n* database
database • *n* database
datamat • *n* computer
date • *n* date
datere • *v* date
dateret • *adj* dated
datering • *n* date

datja • *n* dacha
dato • *n* date
datter • *n* daughter
datterdatter • *n* granddaughter
dattersøn • *n* grandson
dav • *interj* hello, hi
david • *n* davit
De • *pron* you
de • *art* the • *pron* they
debat • *n* debate
debut • *n* debut
decimal • *n* decimal
deden • *adv* thence
defækere • *v* defecate
definition • *n* definition
deisme • *n* deism
dej • *n* dough
dejlig • *adj* lovely
dekade • *n* decade
dekantere • *v* decant
dekoration • *n* set
del • *n* choice, part, share
dele • *v* share
delelig • *adj* divisible
delfin • *n* dolphin
delikat • *adj* delicious
deling • *n* platoon
delmængde • *n* subset
delstat • *n* state
delta • *n* delta
deltage • *v* participate
Dem • *pron* you
demarkationslinje • *n* demarcation
demens • *n* dementia
demokrati • *n* democracy
demonstration • *n* demonstration
demonstrere • *v* demonstrate
demoralisere • *v* demoralize
den • *adj* one • *art* the
dennelunde • *adv* thus
dens • *pron* its
deoxyribose • *n* deoxyribose
depeche • *n* baton
deportere • *v* transport
deprimeret • *adj* down
der • *adv* there
derfor • *adv* hence, therefore
derhen • *adv* there, thither
dermed • *adv* therewith

dersom • *conj* if
desintegrere • *v* disintegrate
despekt • *n* disdain
despoti • *n* despotism
despotisk • *adj* despotic
dessert • *n* dessert
destillerkolbe • *n* retort
desværre • *adv* unfortunately
det • *pron* it, that • *adj* one • *art* the
detailhandel • *n* retail
detailsalg • *n* retail
detalje • *n* circumstance, detail
detaljer • *n* detail
detaljeret • *adj* elaborate
dets • *pron* its
dette • *pron* this
deviere • *v* deviate
diabetiker • *n* diabetic
diakon • *n* deacon
dialekt • *n* dialect
dialog • *n* dialogue
diamant • *n* diamond
diare • *n* diarrhea
diaré • *n* diarrhea
diarre • *n* diarrhea
diarré • *n* diarrhea
did • *adv* there, thither
didaktisk • *adj* didactic
diesel • *n* diesel
differens • *n* difference
differentiabel • *adj* differentiable
differentiering • *n* differentiation
difteri • *n* diphtheria
difteritis • *n* diphtheria
diftong • *n* diphthong
dig • *pron* you
dige • *n* dike
digt • *n* poem
digte • *v* write
digtekunst • *n* poetry
digter • *n* poet
digtning • *n* poetry
diktatur • *n* dictatorship
dild • *n* dill
dildo • *n* dildo
diller • *n* dick, penis
dimension • *n* dimension
diminutiv • *n* diminutive • *adj* diminutive
dimsedut • *n* whatchamacallit
dingenot • *n* whatchamacallit
diode • *n* diode
diplom • *n* diploma
diplomat • *n* diplomat
diplomati • *n* diplomacy
dippedut • *n* whatchamacallit
direkte • *adv* dead • *adj* live

dirigent • *n* conductor
dirigere • *v* direct
dirre • *v* quiver
disk • *n* counter
diskussion • *n* discussion
diskutere • *v* discuss
disputats • *n* thesis
dissekere • *v* dissect
distortion • *n* distortion
distrikt • *n* district
diverse • *adj* miscellaneous
diversitet • *n* diversity
djævel • *n* devil, fiend
djævlen • *n* devil
dø • *v* die
dobbeltkonfekt • *n* pleonasm
dobbeltslag • *n* turn
dobbelttydig • *adj* ambiguous
døbe • *v* baptize, name
dobra • *n* dobra
docerende • *adj* didactic
død • *adj* dead, flat • *adv* dead • *n* death, departure
døde • *n* dead, instant
dodekaeder • *n* dodecahedron
dødelig • *adj* mortal
dødelighed • *n* mortality
Døden • *n* death
dødshjælp • *n* euthanasia
dog • *adv* however, though • *conj* though
doge • *n* doge
dogme • *n* dogma
døgn • *n* day
doktor • *n* doctor
doktorere • *v* doctor
dokument • *n* document, record
dokumentarfilm • *n* documentary
dokumentation • *n* documentation
dolk • *n* dagger, dick
dollar • *n* dollar
domkirke • *n* cathedral
dømme • *v* find, referee
dommer • *n* judge, referee
dompap • *n* bullfinch
domstol • *n* court
donkraft • *n* jack
dønning • *n* swell
donut • *n* doughnut
dopamin • *n* dopamine
dør • *n* door
dørklokke • *n* doorbell
dørmåtte • *n* doormat
dørtærskel • *n* threshold
dørvogter • *n* bouncer
døv • *adj* deaf
doven • *adj* lazy
dovendyr • *n* sloth

dovenskab • *n* sloth
drab • *n* kill
drabant • *n* satellite
dræn • *n* drain
dræne • *v* drain
drage • *n* dragon, kite
drager • *n* beam
dragt • *n* dress
dramaturgisk • *adj* dramaturgic
draug • *n* ghost
dreje • *v* turn
drejekors • *n* turnstile
drejning • *n* turn
dreng • *n* boy
drengene • *n* boy
drengepige • *n* tomboy
dreven • *adj* astute
drik • *n* beverage
drikke • *v* drink
drikoffer • *n* libation
dril • *n* drill
drille • *v* tease
drillepind • *n* tease
drink • *n* drink
drivaksel • *n* crankshaft
drivbænk • *n* hotbed
drive • *v* drive, work
drivgods • *n* flotsam
drivhus • *n* greenhouse
drivrem • *n* belt
drøbel • *n* uvula
drøftelse • *n* deliberation, talk
drøm • *n* dream
dromedar • *n* dromedary
drømme • *v* dream
dronning • *v* queen • *n* queen
dronte • *n* dodo
drossel • *n* thrush
drøvtygge • *v* ruminate
drøvtyggende • *adj* ruminant
drøvtygger • *n* ruminant
drue • *n* grape
druesukker • *n* dextrose, glucose
drukken • *adj* intoxicated
dryp • *n* plop
dryppe • *v* drip, plop
drys • *n* pinch

du • *pron* thou, you
dualis • *n* dual
dublet • *n* doublet
due • *n* dove, pigeon
duehøg • *n* goshawk
duel • *n* duel
duellere • *v* duel
duft • *n* aroma, fragrance
dufte • *v* smell
dug • *n* dew, tablecloth
dukke • *n* doll, skein • *v* duck
dum • *adj* dull, dumb, foolish, silly, stupid
dumaen • *n* duma
dumpe • *v* fail
dun • *n* down
dunkel • *adj* ambiguous, dark
dup • *n* stud
durian • *n* durian
durra • *n* sorghum
dusin • *n* dozen
dusk • *n* whisk
dvæle • *v* dwell
dværg • *n* dwarf
dværgfalk • *n* merlin
dyb • *n* deep • *adj* deep, fast, hollow
dybsindig • *adj* deep
dybt • *adv* deep, fast
dybttænkende • *adj* deep
dyd • *n* virtue
dygtig • *adj* able, good
dykke • *v* duck, sound
dykker • *n* diver
dynamit • *n* dynamite
dynasti • *n* dynasty
dynd • *n* quagmire
dyr • *n* animal • *adj* dear, expensive
dyrebar • *adj* dear, precious
dyrekreds • *n* zodiac
dyrisk • *adj* animal, bestial, brutish
dyrkbar • *adj* arable
dyrke • *v* cultivate, farm, grow
dyrlæge • *n* veterinarian
dyse • *n* jet
dysprosium • *n* dysprosium
dyster • *adj* sullen

E

eagle • *n* eagle
ebbe • *n* ebb
ecclesiologi • *n* ecclesiology
ed • *n* oath
edderfugl • *n* eider

edderkop • *n* spider
eddike • *n* vinegar
ederdun • *n* eiderdown
ederdunsdyne • *n* eiderdown
efeu • *n* ivy

efter • *adv* after • *prep* after, behind, by, following
efterår • *n* autumn
efterfølge • *n* repercussion
efterfølger • *n* follower
eftergivende • *adj* fond
efterlade • *v* abandon
efterligne • *v* copy
efterligning • *n* imitation
eftermiddag • *n* afternoon
efternavn • *n* surname
efterretninger • *n* intelligence
efterretningstjeneste • *n* intelligence
eftersnakker • *n* follower
eftersom • *conj* as, whereas
efterspørgsel • *n* demand
eftertænksom • *adj* pensive
eg • *n* oak
ege • *n* spoke
egen • *adj* own
egenkapital • *n* equity
egenskab • *n* accident, chemistry, property
egentlig • *adv* actually • *adj* intrinsic
egern • *n* squirrel
egetræ • *n* oak
egnethed • *n* fitness
egoistisk • *adj* selfish
eidetisk • *adj* eidetic
einsteinium • *n* einsteinium
ej • *adv* not
ejakulation • *n* ejaculation
eje • *v* own, possess
ejefald • *n* genitive
ejekær • *adj* jealous
ejendom • *n* property
ejendommelig • *adj* weird
ejendomsmægler • *n* realtor
ejendomsret • *n* property
ejer • *n* owner
ejerlejlighed • *n* condominium
ekklesiologi • *n* ecclesiology
ekko • *n* echo
eklektiker • *n* eclectic
eklektisk • *adj* eclectic
ekliptika • *n* ecliptic
eksalteret • *adj* excited
eksamen • *n* examination
eksekvere • *v* execute
eksem • *n* eczema
eksempel • *n* example
eksemplar • *n* copy, specimen
ekshibitionist • *n* exhibitionist
eksistens • *n* existence
eksistere • *v* exist
eksludere • *v* exclude
eksorbitant • *adj* exorbitant

eksotisk • *adj* ethnic, fond
ekspedient • *n* clerk
ekspeditrice • *n* clerk
eksplicit • *adj* explicit
eksplodere • *v* explode
eksplorere • *v* explore
eksplosion • *n* detonation
eksponent • *n* exponent
ekstensiv • *adj* extensive
ekstra • *adj* extra
ekstraordinær • *adj* extraordinary
ekstrem • *adj* extreme
ektoplasma • *n* ectoplasm
el • *n* alder, electricity
elefant • *n* elephant
elefanthue • *n* balaclava
elegance • *n* polish
elegant • *adj* elegant
elegi • *n* elegy
elektricitet • *n* electricity
elektriker • *n* electrician
elektromagnetisk • *adj* electromagnetic
elektromagnetisme • *n* electromagnetism
elektron • *n* electron
elektronik • *n* electronics
element • *n* element
elementær • *adj* basic, elementary, rudimentary
elementar- • *adj* elementary
elementarpartikel • *n* particle
elementer • *n* element
elendighed • *n* misery
elev • *n* pupil
elevator • *n* lift
elevatorstol • *n* car
elfenben • *n* ivory
elg • *n* moose
eliksir • *n* elixir
elite • *n* choice
eller • *conj* or
ellers • *adv* else, otherwise
ellevte • *adj* eleventh
ellevtedel • *n* eleventh
elm • *n* elm
elmetræ • *n* elm
elsdyr • *n* moose
elske • *v* neck
elskede • *n* darling, love
elsker • *n* lover
elskerinde • *n* lover
elskværdig • *adj* amiable
elskværdighed • *n* kindness
emalje • *n* enamel
emboli • *n* embolism
emigrere • *v* emigrate
emission • *n* emission

emmer • *n* emmer
emne • *n* subject
empati • *n* empathy
empirisk • *adj* empirical
emu • *n* emu
en • *art* an • *v* concrete, truck • *adj* one • *pron* one, you
én • *n* one • *pron* one
encyklopædi • *n* encyclopedia
end • *prep* than
ende • *n* end
endegyldig • *adj* final
endelig • *adj* final
endetarmsåbning • *n* anus
endogami • *n* endogamy
endollarseddel • *n* one
endoskopi • *n* endoscopy
ene • *n* juniper • *adj* one
enebær • *n* juniper
ener • *n* one
energi • *n* energy
eneste • *adj* one, only
enfoldig • *adj* naive
eng • *n* meadow
engang • *adv* once
engel • *n* angel
englærke • *n* meadowlark
engobe • *n* engobe
engsnarre • *n* corncrake
enhed • *n* unit, unity
enhjørning • *n* unicorn
enig • *adj* unanimous
enighed • *n* agreement
enke • *n* widow
enkekejserinde • *n* empress
enkelhed • *n* easiness
enkemand • *n* widower
enogtyve • *n* twenty-one
enøjet • *adj* one-eyed
enorm • *adj* huge, vast
ensartethed • *n* uniformity
ensbetydende • *v* amount
ensfarvet • *adj* plain
ensformig • *adj* level, monotonous
ensilage • *n* silage
ensom • *adj* lonely
ensomhed • *n* loneliness, solitude
enstemmig • *adj* unanimous
enstonig • *adj* monotonous
ental • *n* singular
entomolog • *n* entomologist
entomologi • *n* entomology
entusiast • *n* enthusiast, fiend
enzym • *n* enzyme
epicykel • *n* epicycle
epilepsi • *n* epilepsy
epileptiker • *n* epileptic

epileptisk • *adj* epileptic
episk • *adj* epic
epitel • *n* epithelium
epoke • *n* age
er • *v* is
erbium • *n* erbium
erektion • *n* erection
erfare • *v* experience, learn
erfaren • *adj* veteran
erfaring • *n* experience
erhvers- • *adj* vocational
erhverv • *n* occupation, profession
erigere • *v* swell
erindre • *v* recollect, remember
erkendelse • *n* cognition
erklære • *v* state
ernæring • *n* nutrition
ernæring- • *adj* nutritional
ernæringmæssig • *adj* nutritional
erobre • *v* conquer
erotik • *n* eroticism, sex
erotisk • *adj* erotic
erstatning • *n* substitute
erstatte • *v* replace, substitute, supply
es • *n* ace
eskadrille • *n* squadron
esoterisk • *adj* esoteric, occult
esp • *n* aspen
espetræ • *n* aspen
espingol • *n* blunderbuss
espresso • *n* espresso
essay • *n* composition
esse • *n* forge
essens • *n* essence
estimat • *n* estimate
estimere • *v* estimate
estrade • *n* stand
estragon • *n* tarragon
et • *art* an • *n* one • *adj* one
etablering • *n* establishment
etage • *n* level
etape • *n* leg
etik • *n* ethics
etikette • *n* etiquette
etnisk • *adj* ethnic
etologi • *n* ethology
ettal • *n* one
etymologi • *n* etymology
eufemisme • *n* euphemism
eufori • *n* euphoria
euforisk • *adj* euphoric
europium • *n* europium
evakuere • *v* evacuate
evangelium • *n* gospel
evident • *adv* clearly
evig • *n* perdition • *adj* perennial
evighed • *n* eternity

evne • *n* ability
evolution • *n* evolution

F

få • *v* get, have, receive
fabel • *n* fable
fabelagtig • *adj* fabulous • *adv* fabulously
fable • *v* fable
fabrik • *n* factory
fabrikant • *n* maker
fabrikat • *n* make
fabriksbygning • *n* factory
fabulere • *v* fable
facade • *n* face
facet • *n* facet
facettere • *v* facet
facilitere • *v* facilitate
facon • *n* way
fadder • *n* godfather, godparent
fader • *n* father
fæ • *n* mug
fædreland • *n* fatherland
fægtning • *n* fencing
fælde • *n* pitfall
fælg • *n* rim
fælled • *n* common
fælles • *adj* common, mutual
fælleskøn • *adj* common
fællesmængde • *n* intersection
fænge • *v* kindle
fængsel • *n* prison
fængsle • *v* imprison, incarcerate
fængslende • *adj* fascinating
fængslet • *n* prison
færdig • *adj* set
færdighed • *n* skill
færdsel • *n* traffic
færge • *n* ferry
fæstning • *n* fortress
fætter • *n* cousin, dude
fag • *n* profession, subject
faggrænse • *n* demarcation
fagot • *n* bassoon
fagottist • *n* bassoonist
fajance • *n* faience
fakir • *n* fakir
fakkel • *n* torch
faktor • *n* factor
faktorisere • *v* factor
faktotum • *n* factotum
faktum • *n* fact
falanks • *n* phalanx
falbyde • *v* hawk
fald • *n* fall, halyard

falde • *v* drop, fall
faldgitter • *n* portcullis
faldgrube • *n* pitfall
faldlem • *n* trapdoor
faldskærm • *n* parachute
falk • *n* falcon, kestrel
fallisk • *adj* phallic
fallit • *adj* bankrupt • *n* bankruptcy
falme • *v* fade
falsk • *adj* false
fåmandsvælde • *n* oligarchy
familie • *n* family
familie- • *n* family
familiemedlem • *n* relation
familienavn • *n* surname
famle • *v* finger
fanden • *n* devil
fane • *n* flag
fanebærer • *n* standard-bearer
fange • *v* catch • *n* prisoner
fangekælder • *n* dungeon
fangenskab • *n* imprisonment
fantasi • *n* fiction
fantasi- • *adj* imaginary
fantastisk • *adj* fabulous, fantastic
fantom • *n* phantom
far • *n* father
farao • *n* pharaoh
farbror • *n* uncle
fare • *n* danger, peril • *v* farrow
fårehyrde • *n* shepherd
fåret • *adj* sheepish
farlig • *adj* dangerous, perilous
farmaceut • *n* pharmacist
farmakonom • *n* pharmacist
fars • *n* forcemeat
farseret • *adj* stuffed
fart • *n* speed
fartøj • *n* bark, craft, vessel
farve • *v* color, dye • *n* color, hue
farve- • *adj* color
farvefast • *adj* fast
farvel • *interj* bye, farewell, goodbye • *n* farewell
farveløs • *adj* blank
farverig • *adj* colorful, gay
farvet • *n* colored • *adj* colored
farvetone • *n* color, hue, tone
fasan • *n* pheasant
fascinerende • *adj* fascinating

fascisme • *n* fascism
fascist • *n* fascist
fast • *v* concrete • *adj* fast, regular, set, solid • *adv* fast • *n* solid
faste • *v* fast
faster • *n* aunt
fasthed • *n* character
fastland • *n* mainland
fastsætte • *v* set
fastsat • *adj* set
fatte • *v* fathom, understand
fattig • *adj* poor
favn • *n* fathom
fe • *n* fairy
feature • *n* feature
feber • *n* fever
febersyg • *adj* febrile
febril • *adj* febrile
fed • *adj* bold, fat, obese, smashing • *n* clove, skein
fedme • *n* obesity
fedt • *n* fat • *interj* great
fedtet • *adj* stingy
fedtsyl • *n* skinflint
fejebakke • *n* dustpan
fejhed • *n* cowardice
fejl • *n* error, mistake, stumble
fejle • *v* err, fail, stumble
fejlernæret • *adj* malnourished
fejlernæring • *n* malnutrition
fejlfri • *adj* faultless
fejlslutning • *n* fallacy
fejltagelse • *n* error, gaffe
fejltrin • *n* stumble
fejre • *v* celebrate
fejring • *n* celebration
fellatio • *n* fellatio
felt • *n* field
feltråb • *n* password
feminin • *adj* feminine
femininum • *n* feminine
feminisme • *n* feminism
femkant • *n* pentagon
femmer • *n* five
femtal • *n* five
femte • *n* fifth • *adj* fifth
femtende • *adj* fifteenth
fender • *n* fender
fennikel • *n* fennel
fenylalanin • *n* phenylalanine
ferie • *n* holiday, vacation
fermentere • *v* ferment
fermentering • *n* fermentation
fermium • *n* fermium
fernis • *n* varnish
fersk • *adj* fresh, sweet
fersken • *n* peach

ferskentræ • *n* peach
fertilitet • *n* fertility
fest • *n* celebration, party
feste • *v* celebrate
festival • *n* festival
festlig • *adj* festive
festmåltid • *n* feast, spread
fiasko • *n* failure, fiasco
fiffig • *adj* shrewd
figen • *n* fig
figentræ • *n* fig
figur • *n* character, figure
fikse • *v* mend
fiktion • *n* fiction
fil • *n* file
filantrop • *n* philanthropist
filateli • *n* philately
filatelist • *n* philatelist
filatelistisk • *adj* philatelic
filial • *n* branch
filigran • *n* filigree
filipens • *n* pimple
film • *n* film, movie
filme • *v* film
filo • *n* phyllo
filologi • *n* philology
filosofi • *n* philosophy
filt • *n* felt
filte • *v* felt
filthat • *n* felt
fin • *adj* bully, good
finale • *n* final, finale
financiel • *adj* fiscal
finans- • *adj* fiscal
finansiel • *adj* financial
finansiere • *v* finance
finde • *v* find
finer • *n* veneer
finere • *v* veneer
finger • *n* finger
fingeraftryk • *n* fingerprint
fingerbøl • *n* foxglove, thimble
fingerere • *v* finger
fingerfærdighed • *n* dexterity
fingernegl • *n* fingernail
fingerpeg • *n* clue
fingersætning • *v* finger
fingerspids • *n* fingertip
finish • *n* finish
finke • *n* finch
finne • *n* fin
finskytte • *n* marksman
fint • *interj* bully • *adj* cool
fipskæg • *n* goatee
firben • *n* lizard
firedobbelt • *adj* quadruple
firsindstyvende • *adj* eightieth

firtal • *n* four
fis • *n* fart, flatulence
fise • *v* fart
fisk • *n* fish
fiskal • *adj* fiscal
fiske • *v* fish • *adj* fishing
fiskeagtig • *adj* fishy
fiskehandler • *n* fishmonger
fiskekrog • *n* fishhook
fiskemand • *n* fishmonger
fiskeørn • *n* osprey
fisker • *n* fisherman
fiskeri • *n* fishing
fisse • *n* cunt, pussy
fjært • *n* fart, flatulence
fjærte • *v* fart
fjæs • *n* mug
fjeder • *n* spring
fjeldrype • *n* ptarmigan
fjende • *n* enemy
fjendtlig • *adj* enemy
fjendtlighed • *n* hostility
fjer • *n* feather
fjerde • *adj* fourth
fjerdedel • *n* quarter
fjerdedelsnode • *n* crotchet
fjerdragt • *n* coat, plumage
fjerkræ • *n* poultry
fjern • *adj* distant, far
fjerne • *v* erase
fjernsyn • *n* television
fjerpen • *n* quill
fjert • *n* wind
fjollet • *adj* silly
fjols • *n* fool, nincompoop, nit, turkey
fjord • *n* fjord
fjortende • *adj* fourteenth
flå • *v* skin, tear
flad • *adj* flat, shallow
flåde • *n* fleet, raft
flade • *n* face, facet, flat
flademål • *n* area
fladfisk • *n* flatfish
flænge • *n* tear
flæsk • *n* bacon
flag • *n* flag
flage • *v* flag
flagermus • *n* bat
flaggivning • *n* flag
flagskib • *n* flagship
flagstang • *n* flagpole
flamboyant • *adj* flamboyant
flamingo • *n* flamingo
flamme • *v* flame • *n* flame, light
flammekaster • *n* flamethrower
flange • *n* flange
flanke • *n* flank

flankere • *v* flank
flaske • *n* bottle
flegmatisk • *adj* phlegmatic
fleksibel • *adj* flexible
flerårig • *adj* perennial
flere • *adj* multiple
flersproget • *adj* multilingual
flertydig • *adj* ambiguous
fletning • *n* braid
flint • *n* flint
flise • *v* flag • *n* flag
flitig • *adj* industrious
flittig • *adj* diligent
flod • *n* flow, river
fløde • *n* cream • *adj* light
flodhest • *n* hippopotamus
fløjl • *n* corduroy, velvet
fløjlsblomst • *n* marigold
fløjt • *n* whistle
fløjte • *n* flute, whistle • *v* whistle
flok • *n* flock, herd
flokkes • *v* cluster
flot • *adj* flash
flov • *adj* sheepish
flue • *n* fly
fluesvamp • *n* amanita
fluktuation • *n* fluctuation
fluor • *n* fluorine
flusmiddel • *n* flux
flux • *n* flux
fly • *n* aircraft, airplane • *v* flee
flydende • *adj* fluent, fluid, liquid • *adv* fluently
flygte • *v* flee
flygtig • *adj* fugitive
flygtning • *n* fugitive
flynder • *n* flounder
flyselskab • *n* airline
flystyrt • *n* crash
flytning • *n* move, transfer
flytte • *v* move
flyve • *v* sail
flyvemaskine • *n* aircraft, airplane
flyvende • *v* flying
flyver • *n* plane
flyvinge • *n* wing
flyvning • *n* flight
fnat • *n* scabies
fnys • *n* grunt
fnyse • *v* grunt
fobi • *n* phobia
fod • *n* foot
fodbold • *n* football, soccer
fodboldspil • *n* football
fødder • *n* foot
føde • *n* food
føde- • *n* supply

foder • *n* feed, fodder
føderation • *n* federation
fødevare • *n* foodstuff
fodpleje • *n* pedicure
fodre • *v* feed
fødselsdag • *n* birthday
fødselshjælper • *n* midwife
fodspor • *n* footprint, step
fodsti • *n* walk
fodtøj • *n* footwear
fodtusse • *n* grunt
føjelig • *adj* ductile, flexible
fokus • *n* focus
fokusere • *v* focus
føl • *n* foal
føle • *v* feel, lust
fole • *v* foal
følehorn • *n* feeler
følelse • *n* emotion, feeling
føler • *n* feeler
føletråd • *n* feeler
følfod • *n* coltsfoot
følge • *v* follow, observe, trail • *n* following, sequence
følgende • *adj* following
følgesvend • *n* follower
foliering • *n* foliation
folk • *n* people
folkeafstemning • *n* referendum
folkedrab • *n* genocide
folkeskole- • *adj* elementary
folketælling • *n* census
folklore • *n* folklore
følsom • *adj* sensitive
føn • *n* foehn
fondue • *n* fondue
fonem • *n* phoneme
fonetik • *n* phonetics
føniks • *n* phoenix
fonologi • *n* phonology
for • *conj* for • *prep* for • *adv* too
før • *adv* before • *conj* before • *prep* before
forældelse • *n* obsolescence
forælder • *n* parent
forældet • *adj* dated, obsolete
foragt • *n* disdain
foran • *prep* before • *adv* fast
forandre • *v* change
forandring • *n* change, flux
foranledige • *v* occasion
forår • *n* spring
forarbejde • *v* work
forårsage • *v* cause, occasion
forårsagtig • *adj* springlike
forårsløg • *n* scallion
forbandelse • *n* curse, hex
forbandet • *adv* damn

forbavse • *v* astonish
forbavselse • *n* astonishment
forbedre • *n* amelioration • *v* mend, refine
forbedring • *n* amelioration, improvement
forberedelse • *n* preparation
forbi • *adv* by • *adj* over
forbier • *n* miss
forbinde • *v* bandage, link
forbindelse • *n* connection, contact, link, marriage, nexus
forbitret • *adj* bitter
forblive • *v* dwell
forbløffe • *v* astound
forblommet • *adj* ambiguous
forbøn • *n* intercession
forbrænding • *n* burn, combustion
forbrydelse • *n* crime
forbryder • *n* criminal, felon
forbudt • *adj* forbidden
forbund • *n* alliance
forbyde • *v* forbid
forceret • *adj* crash
fordampe • *v* evaporate
fordampning • *n* evaporation
fordel • *n* advantage
fordele • *v* spread
fordi • *conj* because, for
fordøje • *v* digest
fordømme • *v* condemn
fordømmelse • *n* perdition
fordømt • *v* damn
fordummende • *adj* dumb
foredrag • *n* talk
foregående • *adj* previous
foregive • *v* pretend
forekomme • *v* occur
forelæsning • *n* talk
forene • *v* combine
forening • *n* marriage
forenkle • *v* simplify
forenklet • *adj* simplified
foreslå • *v* move, offer, propose
foretagende • *n* enterprise
foretagsomhed • *n* enterprise
foretrække • *v* choose, prefer
forfader • *n* grandfather
forfægte • *v* champion
forfærdelig • *adv* dreadfully
forfalske • *v* doctor, forge
forfalsker • *n* forger
forfatning • *n* constitution
forfatte • *v* write
forfatter • *n* author, writer
forfine • *v* refine
forfinelse • *n* polish

forflytte • *v* transfer
forflyttelse • *n* transfer
forfølgelse • *n* chase
forfølger • *n* follower
forføre • *v* seduce
forfremme • *v* up
forfriskende • *adj* fresh
forgifte • *v* poison
forgiftning • *n* poisoning
forglemmigej • *n* forget-me-not
forhale • *v* procrastinate
forhastet • *adj* slapdash
forhekset • *adj* bewitched
forhindre • *v* abstain
forhold • *n* relationship
forholdsord • *n* preposition
forhud • *n* prepuce
fork • *n* fork, pitchfork
forkaste • *v* explode
forkert • *adj* wrong
forklæde • *n* apron
forklaring • *n* explanation
forknyt • *adj* despondent
forkølelse • *n* cold
forkorte • *v* abbreviate, abridge, cancel, curtail
forkortelse • *n* abbreviation
forkortet • *adj* abridged
forkrøblet • *adj* crippled
forkynde • *v* trumpet
forlade • *v* abandon, forgive
forlængelse • *n* extension
forlegenhed • *v* confuse
forløb • *n* course
forløse • *v* deliver
forlovet • *adj* engaged
form • *n* form, voice
formaldehyd • *n* formaldehyde
formand • *n* gaffer
forme • *v* form
formel • *adj* formal
formiddag • *n* forenoon
formindske • *adj* depleted
formode • *v* assume
formodning • *n* assumption
formue • *n* substance, wealth
formular • *n* form
fornærme • *v* heckle
fornærmelse • *n* insult
fornemmelse • *n* sense
fornøjet • *adj* cheerful
fornuft • *n* reason
fornuftig • *adj* sound
forøge • *v* up
forordning • *n* regulation
forråd • *n* hoard, supply
forråde • *v* betray

forræder • *n* betrayer, snitch, traitor
forræderi • *n* treason
forrest • *n* first
forret • *n* starter
forretning • *n* business, transaction
forretningsmand • *n* businessman
forrige • *adj* previous
forrude • *n* windshield
forsænke • *v* set
forseelse • *n* error
forsigtig • *adj* careful, cautious, circumspect, wary • *adv* carefully
forsigtighed • *n* caution
forsigtigt • *adv* gingerly
forsikring • *n* insurance
forsinke • *v* procrastinate
forsinket • *adv* behind
forskel • *n* difference
forskellig • *adj* different
forskellige • *adj* various
forslå • *v* suggest
forslag • *n* proposition, suggestion
forsøg • *n* attempt
forsøge • *v* attempt, essay, try
forsømme • *v* fail, neglect
forsømmelse • *n* neglect
forsømthed • *n* neglect
forsoning • *n* reconciliation
forsorg • *n* welfare
forspil • *n* foreplay
først • *n* first • *adv* first
forstå • *v* appreciate, conceive, dig, get, see, understand
forstad • *n* suburb
forståelse • *n* understanding
forstående • *adj* understanding
forstærke • *v* tone
forstærker • *n* amplifier
forstand • *n* understanding
første • *adj* first, prime
førsteklasses • *adj* champion, prime
forstene • *v* petrify
forstoppelse • *n* constipation
forstuve • *v* sprain
forstuvning • *n* sprain
forstyrrelse • *n* disorder, disturbance
forsvar • *n* apology, defender, defense, maintenance
forsvare • *v* champion, defend
forsvarer • *n* apologist, defender
forsvarsværk • *n* work
forsvinde • *v* disappear, vanish
forsvundet • *adj* lost
forsyning • *n* supply
forsynings- • *n* supply
forsyningsskib • *n* tender
forsyningstropper • *n* logistics

fortælle • *v* narrate, say, talk
fortællende • *adj* narrative
fortæller • *n* narrator
fortære • *v* eat
fortidig • *adj* archaic
fortjene • *v* deserve
fortjeneste • *n* desert
fortløbende • *adj* consecutive
fortøje • *v* moor
fortøjning • *n* mooring
fortov • *n* pavement
fortrin • *n* advantage
fortryde • *v* regret
fortynde • *v* thin
forud • *adv* before
forudsætning • *n* prerequisite
forudsætte • *v* presuppose
forudse • *v* anticipate, foresee
forudsigeligt • *adj* foreseeable
forum • *n* forum
forurene • *v* contaminate
forurening • *n* pollution
forvandle • *v* turn
forveksle • *v* confuse
forvirre • *v* buffalo, confuse
forvirrelse • *n* confusion
forvirret • *adj* confused
forvirring • *n* confusion
forvise • *v* abandon, expatriate
forvitre • *v* crumble
forvitring • *n* efflorescence
fosfor • *n* phosphorus
fosforholdig • *adj* phosphoric, phosphorous
fosforlignende • *adj* phosphoric, phosphorous
fosforsyrlig • *adj* phosphorous
fossil • *n* fossil • *adj* fossilized
foster • *n* fetus
foto • *n* photo, picture
fotogen • *adj* photogenic
fotografere • *v* photograph
fotografi • *n* photo, photograph, photography, picture
fotokopi • *n* photocopy
fotokopiere • *v* photocopy
fotokopimaskine • *n* photocopier
fotosyntese • *n* photosynthesis
fra • *prep* from
fræk • *adj* fresh, rude
frækhed • *n* cheek
frænde • *n* relative
fraflytning • *n* vacation
fragment • *n* fragment
frakke • *n* coat, paletot
francium • *n* francium
frankere • *v* stamp

fråseri • *n* gluttony
fratrædelse • *n* vacation
fratræden • *n* resignation
fravær • *n* absence
fraværende • *adj* absent
fred • *n* peace
fredelig • *adj* amicable, peaceable
fredsforstyrrer • *n* troublemaker
fredsommelig • *adj* peaceable
fredstid • *n* peacetime
fregat • *n* frigate
fregne • *n* freckle
frekvens • *n* frequency
frelse • *n* salvation
fremfusende • *adj* impetuous
fremkalde • *v* disgust, evoke
fremleje • *v* sublease • *n* sublease
fremmane • *v* evoke
fremmed • *adj* ethnic, foreign • *n* stranger
fremmede • *adj* foreign
fremmedgøre • *v* alienate
fremmedord • *n* loanword
fremover • *adv* henceforth
fremragende • *adj* banner
fremskaffelse • *n* procurement
fremstille • *v* make
fremtid • *n* future
fremtidig • *adj* future
fremtrædende • *adj* preeminent
fremtvinge • *v* force
freske • *n* fresco
fresko • *n* fresco
freskomaleri • *n* fresco
fri • *adj* clear, free • *v* propose
fribytter • *n* filibuster
fridag • *n* holiday
frigøre • *v* liberate
frihed • *n* freedom, leave, liberty
frikendelse • *n* acquittal
frimærke • *v* stamp • *n* thumbnail
frimærkesamler • *n* philatelist
frisk • *adj* fresh, new, recent, sweet
frisør • *n* hairdresser
fristed • *n* haven
fristelse • *n* temptation
fritænker • *n* freethinker
fritage • *v* free
fritaget • *n* exempt
fritstående • *adj* detached, freestanding
fritstille • *v* fire
fritte • *n* ferret
friværdi • *n* equity
frivillig • *n* volunteer
frø • *n* frog, seed
frodig • *adj* voluptuous
frøken • *n* miss
frokost • *v* lunch • *n* lunch

from • *adj* devout, pious
frossen • *adj* frozen
frost • *n* frost
frue • *n* wife
frugt • *n* fruit
frugtbar • *adj* fertile, fruitful, prolific
frugtbarhed • *n* fertility
frugtkød • *n* flesh
fruktose • *n* fructose
frustrerende • *adj* frustrating
frustreret • *adj* frustrated
frygt • *n* awe, fear
frygtelig • *adv* dreadfully • *adj* heinous, terrible
frygtsom • *adj* timid
fuchsia • *n* fuchsia
fugl • *n* bird
fuglehus • *n* aviary
fuglerede • *n* nest
fugleskræmsel • *n* scarecrow
fugleunge • *n* chick
fugtig • *adj* damp
fuld • *adj* drunk, drunken, full, inebriated, intoxicated
fuldende • *v* accomplish
fuldkommen • *adj* utter

fuldmægtig • *n* proxy
fuldskab • *n* drunkenness
fuldstændig • *adv* absolutely, all • *adj* full
fuldtonet • *adj* full
fund • *n* find
fundament • *n* backbone, foundation
fundamental • *adj* fundamental, rudimentary
fundere • *n* wonder
fungere • *v* function, work
fungibel • *adj* fungible
funklende • *adj* bright
funktion • *n* function
fyldestgørende • *adj* comprehensive
fyldig • *adj* ample
fyldt • *adj* full, stuffed
fyr • *n* bloke, boy, cat, dude, lighthouse, pine
fyre • *v* can, fire, sack
fyrretyvende • *adj* fortieth
fyrste • *n* prince
fyrstelig • *adj* princely
fyrtårn • *n* lighthouse
fyrværkeri • *n* firework, fireworks
fysisk • *adj* physical

G

gå • *v* go, walk, work
gab • *n* yawn
gabe • *v* gape, yawn
gabestok • *n* pillory
gåde • *n* conundrum
gade • *n* road, street
gadelygte • *n* lamppost, streetlight
gadget • *n* gadget
gadolinium • *n* gadolinium
gæld • *n* debt
gælle • *n* gill
gær • *n* yeast
gærdesmutte • *n* wren
gære • *v* ferment, work
gæring • *n* fermentation
gæst • *n* guest
gæste • *v* guest
gæstfrihed • *n* hospitality
gæt • *n* guess
gætte • *v* speculate
gaffel • *n* fork
gafle • *v* fork
gal • *adj* mad
galakse • *n* galaxy
galaktose • *n* galactose
galde • *n* bile

galeon • *n* galleon
galge • *n* gallows
gallium • *n* gallium
galoche • *n* galosh
galop • *n* gallop
galopere • *v* gallop
galskab • *n* insanity, madness, rage
galt • *n* boar
gamache • *n* gaiter, spat
gambit • *n* gambit
gammel • *adj* old
gammeldags • *adj* archaic, old-fashioned
gang • *n* course, march, step, time, walk
gangart • *n* walk
gangræn • *n* gangrene
garage • *n* garage
garant • *n* guarantee, guarantor
garantere • *v* guarantee
garanti • *n* caution, guarantee, warranty
gård • *n* farm, yard
garderobe • *n* toilet, wardrobe
garderobeskab • *n* wardrobe
gårdhave • *n* atrium, patio
gardin • *n* blind, curtain
gårdsplads • *n* courtyard
garn • *n* net, yarn

garnison • *n* garrison
gartner • *n* gardener
garver • *n* tanner
gas • *n* gas
gås • *n* goose
gase • *n* gander
gåsepotentil • *n* silverweed
gåtur • *n* walk
gave • *n* gift
gavnlig • *adj* beneficial
gearkasse • *n* gearbox
gearstang • *n* stick
gebyr • *n* fee
ged • *n* goat
gedde • *n* pike
gedehams • *n* hornet, wasp
gedekid • *n* kid
geek • *n* geek
gejser • *n* geyser
gelejde • *v* accompany
gemen • *adj* vulgar
gemme • *v* hide, save
gemmested • *n* hideout
gemse • *n* chamois
gemyt • *n* temper
genanvendelse • *n* recycling
genbrug • *n* recycling
gendarm • *n* gendarmerie
general • *n* general
generation • *n* age, generation
genere • *v* hassle
generel • *adj* general
genfærd • *n* ghost
genganger • *n* ghost, revenant
gengivelse • *n* definition
geni • *n* genius
genial • *adj* genial
genmæle • *v* reply
gennem • *prep* during, through
gennem- • *v* browse
gennemføre • *v* clear
gennemrode • *v* browse
gennemse • *v* browse
gennemsigtig • *adj* clear, transparent
gennemskuelig • *adj* transparent
gennemslagskraft • *n* voice
gennemsnit • *n* average
gennemsøge • *v* browse
gennemtænkt • *adj* deliberate
genom • *n* genome
genopladelig • *adj* rechargeable
genotype • *n* genotype
genre • *n* genre
gensidig • *adj* mutual
genstandslæsning • *n* psychometry
genstridig • *adj* recalcitrant
gentage • *v* repeat

genus • *n* genus
geodæsi • *n* geodesy
geofysik • *n* geophysics
geografi • *n* geography
geokemi • *n* geochemistry
geolog • *n* geologist
geomanti • *n* geomancy
geometri • *n* geometry
gepard • *n* cheetah
geranium • *n* geranium
germanium • *n* germanium
gerningsmand • *n* perpetrator
gerrig • *adj* miserly
gerundium • *n* gerund
gespenst • *n* ghost
gestalt • *n* gestalt
gestikulere • *v* gesticulate
geværhane • *n* hammer
geværild • *n* gunfire
gidsel • *n* hostage
gift • *adj* married • *n* poison, venom
giftermål • *n* marriage
giftig • *adj* poisonous, toxic, waspish
gigantisk • *adj* gigantic
ginseng • *n* ginseng
ginsengrod • *n* ginseng
gips • *n* gypsum, plaster
gipse • *v* plaster
giraf • *n* giraffe
give • *v* give
glad • *v* fond • *adj* gay, glad, happy
gladiator • *n* gladiator
glæde • *n* happiness
glane • *v* gawk
glans • *n* polish, shine
glansfuld • *adj* lustrous
glas • *n* glass
glasur • *n* icing
glasværk • *n* glassworks
glat • *adj* slippery, smooth
glathed • *n* polish
glatte • *v* polish, smooth
glemme • *v* forget
glemt • *adj* forgotten
glente • *n* kite
gletsjer • *n* glacier
glimre • *v* shine
glimt • *v* flash • *n* flash
glimte • *v* flash, shine
glo • *v* gawk, glare, stare
global • *adj* global
globus • *n* globe
glød • *n* ember
gløgg • *n* glogg
glorie • *n* halo
glosar • *n* glossary
glosarium • *n* glossary

glosebog • *n* glossary
gloseliste • *n* glossary
glossar • *n* glossary
glossarium • *n* glossary
glossehæfte • *n* glossary
glukose • *n* glucose
glycin • *n* glycine
gnaven • *adj* cranky
gnaver • *n* rodent
gnavesår • *n* chafe
gnejs • *n* gneiss
gnier • *n* miser
gnieragtig • *adj* miserly
gnist • *n* spark
gnu • *n* gnu
gø • *v* bark
god • *adj* clear, good
godbid • *n* confection, morsel
goddag • *interj* hi
gode • *n* good
gøde • *v* manure
godhed • *n* good, kindness
godkendelse • *n* approval
godnatsang • *n* lullaby
gødning • *n* dung, fertilizer, manure
gods • *n* cargo
godsejer • *n* lord
gødske • *v* manure
godt • *adj* good
godtgøre • *v* evidence
gøen • *n* bark
gøg • *n* cuckoo
golf • *n* golf
golfer • *n* golfer
golfspiller • *n* golfer
gongong • *n* gong
gonoré • *n* gonorrhea
gople • *n* jellyfish
gør-det-selv • *adj* do-it-yourself
gøre • *v* concrete, do, laugh, make
gøs • *n* jack
grå • *n* gray • *adj* gray
grå-bynke • *n* mugwort
gråand • *n* mallard
gråd • *n* cry
grad • *n* degree
gradvis • *adv* gradually
græde • *v* cry, weep
grænse • *v* border • *n* border, demarcation
grænsedragning • *n* demarcation
græs • *n* grass, pot
græshoppe • *n* grasshopper
græskar • *n* pumpkin
græskarplante • *n* pumpkin
græsplæne • *n* grass, lawn
grævling • *n* badger

graf • *n* graph
grafit • *n* graphite
grammatik • *n* grammar
grammofon • *n* gramophone
grammofonautomat • *n* jukebox
grammofonplade • *n* record
gran • *n* spruce
gran- • *n* spruce
granat • *n* grenade
granatæble • *n* pomegranate
gråne • *v* gray
granit • *n* granite
granske • *v* scrutinize
grantræ • *n* pine
grape • *n* grapefruit
grapefrugt • *n* grapefruit
gratis • *adv* gratis
gratulere • *v* congratulate
grav • *n* grave
gravand • *n* shelduck
grave • *v* delve, dig, unearth
gravemaskine • *n* excavator
graver • *n* gravedigger
gravhøj • *n* tumulus
gravid • *adj* pregnant
graviditet • *n* pregnancy
gravko • *n* excavator
gravsten • *n* gravestone, headstone
greb • *n* fork
gren • *n* bough, branch, dick, prong
greve • *n* count, earl
grevinde • *n* countess
grib • *n* vulture
gribe • *v* claw, grasp, seize
gribebræt • *n* fingerboard
grif • *n* griffin
grim • *adj* ugly
grimasse • *n* grimace
grimassere • *v* grimace
grin • *n* laughter
grine • *v* laugh
gris • *n* pig
gro • *v* grow
grød • *n* mash, porridge
grødomslag • *n* cataplasm
grøn • *n* green • *adj* green
grønirisk • *n* siskin
grønkål • *n* kale
grønkorn • *n* chloroplast
grønlandshval • *n* bowhead
grønsag • *n* vegetable
grøntsag • *n* vegetable
grotesk • *adj* grotesque
grotte • *n* grotto
grov • *adj* harsh, rude
grovæde • *v* devour
grubearbejder • *n* miner

grufuld • *adj* heinous
grumset • *adj* dirty
grund • *n* occasion, purpose, soil
grundfæstet • *adj* solid
grundig • *adj* solid
grundlæggelse • *n* foundation
grundlæggende • *adj* basic, fundamental
grundlag • *n* foundation
grundled • *n* subject
grundlov • *n* constitution
grundstof • *n* element
grundstykke • *n* lot
gruppe • *n* group, nexus, set
grus • *n* gravel
grusom • *adj* atrocious, cruel
grusomhed • *n* atrocity
gry • *n* twilight
grydeske • *n* tablespoon
grynt • *n* grunt
grynte • *v* grunt
guava • *n* guava
gud • *n* god
gudbarn • *n* godchild
guddatter • *n* goddaughter
guddommelig • *adj* divine
gudelig • *adj* godlike
gudfader • *n* godfather
gudfar • *n* godfather
gudinde • *n* goddess
gudløs • *adj* godless
gudmoder • *n* godmother
gudmor • *n* godmother
gudsøn • *n* godson

guide • *n* guide
guirlande • *n* festoon
guitar • *n* guitar
guitarist • *n* guitarist
gul • *n* amber, yellow • *adj* yellow
gulbrun • *adj* tawny
guld • *n* gold • *adj* gold
guldblomme • *n* arnica
guldfisk • *n* goldfish
guldlaks • *n* argentine
guldmedalje • *n* gold
guldmønt • *n* gold
guldsmed • *n* dragonfly, goldsmith, jeweler
gulerod • *n* carrot
gullasch • *n* goulash
gulne • *v* yellow
gulsot • *n* jaundice
gulv • *n* floor
gumle • *v* chew
gummi • *n* rubber
gurkemeje • *n* turmeric
guvernør • *n* governor
gyde • *n* alley
gylden • *adj* gold, golden
gyldenbrun • *adj* tawny
gylp • *n* fly
gylpe • *v* retch
gymnasium • *n* gymnasium
gymnastik • *n* gymnastics
gynækologi • *n* gynecology
gyroskop • *n* gyroscope

H

ha • *interj* ha, haha
håb • *n* hope
håbe • *v* hope
habil • *adj* able
habitat • *n* habitat
håbløs • *adj* hopeless
had • *n* hatred
hade • *v* hate
Hadefuld • *adj* hateful
hæhæ • *interj* haha
hæk • *n* hedge
hæl • *n* heel
hælde • *v* pour
hænde • *v* happen
hændelse • *n* event
hænge • *v* hang, hook
hængedynd • *n* quagmire
hængekøje • *n* hammock
hængelås • *n* padlock

hængsel • *n* hinge
hær • *n* army
hætte • *n* hood
hævdelse • *n* maintenance
hæve • *v* lift
hævn • *n* revenge, vengeance
hævngerrig • *adj* vengeful, vindictive
hafnium • *n* hafnium
hage • *n* chin, hook
hagekors • *n* swastika
hagiografi • *n* hagiography
hagl • *n* hail, shot
haglbøsse • *n* shotgun
haiku • *n* haiku
haj • *n* shark
hajj • *n* hajj
hakke • *n* chatter • *v* hesitate
hakkebræt • *n* dulcimer
hale • *n* tail

halefinne • *n* fin
haleror • *n* rudder
haletudse • *n* tadpole
halleluja • *interj* hallelujah
hallo • *interj* hello, hi
halm • *n* haulm, straw
halo • *n* halo
hals • *n* neck, throat
halshugge • *v* behead, decapitate
halshugning • *n* decapitation
halskæde • *n* necklace
halstørklæde • *n* scarf
halv • *adj* half
halvbjørn • *n* procyonid
halvdel • *n* half
halvfemsindstyvende • *adj* ninetieth
halvfjerdsindstyvende • *adj* seventieth
halvkugle • *n* hemisphere
halvmåne • *n* crescent, half-moon
halvø • *n* peninsula
halvtone • *n* semitone
halvtredser • *n* fifty
halvtredserne • *n* fifties
halvtredsindstyvende • *adj* fiftieth
halvtredsindstyvendedel • *n* fiftieth
halvvokal • *n* semivowel
ham • *n* slough
hamburger • *n* hamburger
hammer • *n* hammer
hammerhaj • *n* hammerhead
hamp • *n* cannabis, hemp
hamre • *v* hammer
hamster • *n* hamster
hamstre • *v* hoard
han • *n* bull, cock, instant • *pron* he
hånd • *n* hand
håndbold • *n* handball
handel • *n* commerce, market, trade
håndflade • *n* palm
håndfuld • *n* hand, handful
håndgemæng • *n* melee
håndjern • *n* handcuff, handcuffs, manacle
håndklæde • *n* towel
håndlæsning • *n* palmistry
håndlanger • *n* minion
håndlavet • *v* craft
handle • *v* act, shop
håndled • *n* wrist
handling • *n* act
håndmikser • *n* mixer
håndsbred • *n* handful
handske • *n* glove
håndskrift • *n* hand, handwriting, manuscript
håndtag • *n* handle
håndtryk • *n* handshake

handue • *n* dove
håndværk • *n* craft
håndværker • *n* craft
håne • *v* heckle
hane • *n* rooster
hanekam • *n* cockscomb
hanekylling • *n* cockerel
hangås • *n* gander
hanhest • *n* stallion
hankat • *n* tom
hankøn • *adj* masculine
hanrej • *n* cuckold
hans • *pron* his
hår • *n* hair
hårbørste • *n* hairbrush
hård • *adj* severe
hårdfør • *adj* hardy
hårdknude • *n* knot
hardware • *n* hardware
hare • *n* hare
harekilling • *n* leveret
hareskaar • *n* harelip
håret • *adj* hairy
harke • *v* hawk
harmonika • *n* accordion
harmonisere • *v* tone
harpe • *n* harp
harpun • *n* harpoon
hårsbredde • *n* whisker
harsk • *adj* rancid
harve • *n* harrow
hase • *n* hamstring
hash • *n* cannabis, hashish, weed
hashish • *n* hashish
hasselmus • *n* dormouse
hasselnød • *n* hazelnut
hastighed • *n* speed, velocity
hat • *n* hat
haubits • *n* howitzer
haussespekulant • *n* bull
haussist • *n* bull
hav • *n* sea
have • *n* garden • *v* have, wear
havearbejde • *v* garden
havegang • *n* path
havfrue • *n* mermaid
havgående • *adj* seagoing
havn • *n* haven, port
havre • *n* oat
havregryn • *n* oatmeal, oats
havvand • *n* seawater
heat • *n* heat
hedde • *v* hight
hede • *n* heat, moor
hede-melbærris • *n* bearberry
hedebølge • *n* heat
heden • *adv* hence

hedeslag • *n* heatstroke
hedning • *adj* ethnic
hedonisme • *n* hedonism
heftig • *adj* impetuous, violent
hej • *interj* hello, hi • *n* hey
hejre • *n* heron
heks • *n* hex, witch
heksejagt • *n* witch-hunt
heksekunst • *n* witchcraft
heksemester • *n* warlock
hekseri • *n* witchcraft
hel • *adj* whole
helårlig • *adj* perennial
held • *n* luck
heldig • *adj* fortunate, happy, lucky
hele • *n* whole
helgen • *n* hallow, saint
helhed • *n* whole
helikopter • *n* helicopter
helium • *n* helium
helleflynder • *n* halibut
hellere • *conj* before
hellig • *adj* holy
helligdag • *n* holiday
hellige • *v* hallow
helliggøre • *v* hallow
helt • *adv* flat • *n* hero
heltal • *n* integer
heltemod • *n* heroism
heltemodig • *adj* heroic
heltinde • *n* heroine
hemlock • *n* hemlock
hemmelig • *adj* secret
hemmelighedsfuld • *adj* dark, secretive
hemmeligt • *adv* surreptitiously
hende • *pron* her
hendes • *pron* hers
henholdsvis • *adv* respectively
henhøre • *v* belong
henkoge • *v* can
henrettelse • *n* execution
hensmuldre • *v* crumble
hente • *v* fetch
hentydning • *n* allusion, innuendo
henvejre • *v* dispel
henvise • *v* refer
henvisning • *n* referral
hepatitis • *n* hepatitis
her • *adv* here
heraldik • *n* heraldry
herhen • *adv* here, hither
herlig • *adj* delicious
hermafrodit • *n* hermaphrodite
hermafroditisk • *adj* hermaphrodite
hermelin • *n* ermine
heroin • *n* heroin
heroisk • *adj* heroic

herre • *v* lord • *n* lord, sir
herregård • *n* castle
herske • *v* govern
hersker • *n* lord
hertug • *n* duke
hertugdømme • *n* duchy
hertuginde • *n* duchess
hertz • *n* hertz
hest • *n* horse
hestekød • *n* horsemeat
hestekraft • *n* horsepower
hestevogn • *n* carriage
heteroseksuel • *n* heterosexual • *adj* heterosexual
hetman • *n* hetman
heureka • *interj* eureka
heuristik • *n* heuristic
heuristisk • *adj* heuristic
hexadecimal • *adj* hexadecimal
hid • *adv* hither
hidtil • *adv* hitherto
hierarki • *n* hierarchy
hierarkisk • *adj* hierarchical
hieroglyf • *n* hieroglyph
hik • *n* hiccup
hikke • *v* hiccup • *n* hiccup
hil • *v* hail
hilsen • *n* greeting, regards
himmel • *n* sky
himmelfart • *n* assumption
himmelsk • *adj* celestial
hind • *n* doe
hindbær • *n* raspberry
hindre • *v* hinder
hindring • *n* barrier
hingst • *n* horse, stallion
hirse • *n* millet
historie • *n* history, story
historisk • *adj* historical
hittebarn • *n* orphan
hjælp • *n* aid, assistance, benefit, help • *interj* help
hjælpe • *v* aid, help
hjælpeløs • *adj* feckless, helpless
hjælpemiddel • *n* aid
hjælper • *n* aid
hjælpsom • *adj* accommodating, helpful
hjelm • *n* helmet
hjem • *n* home • *adv* home
hjemad • *adv* home
hjemby • *n* hometown
hjemland • *n* home
hjemløs • *adj* homeless
hjemløshed • *n* homelessness
hjemme • *v* belong • *adv* home
hjemmearbejde • *n* homework
hjemsted • *n* homestead

hjemve • *n* homesickness
hjerne • *n* brain
hjernelap • *n* lobe
hjerte • *n* heart
hjertekammer • *n* ventricle
hjerteløs • *adj* heartless
hjerter • *n* heart, hearts
hjord • *n* herd
hjørne • *n* angle, nook
hjørneklap • *n* wallflower
hjort • *n* deer
hjul • *n* reel, wheel
hø • *n* hay
hob • *n* herd
hobby • *n* hobby
høflig • *adj* polite
hofte • *n* hip
hofteholder • *n* girdle
høg • *n* hawk
høj • *adj* high, loud, tall
højde • *n* level
højdedrag • *n* down
højgravid • *adj* pregnant
højre • *n* right • *adj* right
højre- • *adj* right
højrehåndet • *n* right-handed
højrøvet • *adj* arrogant
højtaler • *n* loudspeaker
højtidelig • *adj* solemn
højtideligholde • *v* celebrate
højttaler • *n* speaker
holde • *v* deliver, hold, stand, suffice, vacation, warm
holdeplads • *n* stand
holdepunkt • *n* clue
holdning • *n* attitude, carriage
holm • *n* island
holmium • *n* holmium
homo • *n* gay
homofobi • *n* homophobia
homogenitet • *n* homogeneity
homoseksualitet • *n* homosexuality
homoseksuel • *n* homosexual • *adj* homosexual
høne • *n* chicken, hen
honning • *n* honey
hook • *n* hook
hop • *n* jump, leap
hoppe • *n* horse, mare • *v* jump, leap, spring
hør • *n* flax, linen
hor • *n* whore
horde • *n* horde
hore • *n* whore
høre • *v* belong, hear
horehus • *n* brothel
hørfarvet • *adj* flaxen

hørfrø • *n* linseed
horisont • *n* horizon
horkarl • *n* adulterer
hormon • *n* hormone
horn • *n* crescent, horn
hornhinde • *n* cornea
horoskop • *n* horoscope
hortensia • *n* hydrangea
hospital • *n* hospital
høst • *n* autumn
høstak • *n* haystack
hoste • *v* cough • *n* cough
hot • *adj* hot
hotel • *n* hotel
høtyv • *n* fork, pitchfork
hov • *n* hoof
hoved • *n* head
hoved- • *adj* prime
hovedbrud • *n* conundrum
hovedgærde • *n* headboard
hovedindhold • *n* substance, tenor
hovedord • *n* noun
hovedpine • *n* headache
hovedpulsåre • *n* aorta
høvl • *n* plane
høvle • *v* plane
hud • *n* flesh, skin
hudfarve • *n* color
hudflette • *v* excoriate
hug • *n* cut
hugge • *v* pinch
hugorm • *n* adder
hugtand • *n* fang
hukommelse • *n* memory
hukommelsestab • *n* amnesia
hul • *n* hole • *adj* hollow
hule • *n* cave, den
hulens • *adv* damn • *interj* damn
human • *adj* human
humanisme • *n* humanism
humle • *n* hop
humlebi • *n* bumblebee
hummer • *n* den, lobster
hun • *n* cow • *pron* she
hun- • *adj* female
hund • *n* dog, hound, pooch
hundegalskab • *n* hydrophobia
hundeslæde • *n* dogsled
hundesnor • *n* leash
hundredåret • *adj* centenary
hundredårsdag • *n* centennial
hundue • *n* dove
hunger • *n* starvation
hungersnød • *n* famine
hunkøn • *adj* feminine
hunlig • *adj* female
hunløve • *n* lioness

hunræv • *n* vixen
hunsvane • *n* pen
huntiger • *n* tigress
hurtig • *adj* fast, quick, swift • *adv* quickly
hurtighed • *n* speed
hurtigt • *adv* quickly
hus • *n* house
husbåd • *n* houseboat
husbond • *n* husband
husfru • *n* housewife
husholdning • *n* economy
husholdningsarbejde • *n* housework
huskat • *n* cat
huske • *v* remember
husleje • *n* rent
husmand • *n* smallholder
husmandsbrug • *n* smallholding
husmandssted • *n* smallholding
husskade • *n* magpie
hustru • *n* wife
hustrubidrag • *n* alimony
hvad • *pron* what
hvæs • *n* wheeze
hvæse • *v* hiss, wheeze • *n* hiss
hval • *n* whale
hvalp • *n* puppy, whelp
hvalros • *n* walrus
hvas • *adj* waspish
hvede • *n* wheat
hvedebrødsdage • *n* honeymoon
hveden • *adv* whence
hvem • *pron* who, whom
hveps • *n* hornet, wasp
hvepsetalje • *n* waist
hver • *adv* all
hverken • *conj* neither
hvid • *adj* blank, white • *n* white
hvidblomme • *n* snowflake
hvide • *n* albumen
hvidhval • *n* beluga
hvidlig • *adj* whitish
hvidløg • *n* garlic
hvile • *n* rest • *v* rest
hvilken • *pron* whom
hvin • *n* whine
hvinand • *n* goldeneye
hvine • *v* whine
hvirveldyr • *n* vertebrate
hvis • *conj* if • *pron* whose
hviske • *v* whisper
hvisken • *n* whisper
hvisle • *v* whistle

hvor • *adv* how, where, wherever • *conj* where, wherever • *pron* where
hvoraf • *adv* whence
hvordan • *adv* how • *conj* how
hvorefter • *conj* whereupon
hvorfor • *conj* wherefore • *adv* why
hvorfra • *adv* whence
hvorhen • *adv* whither
hvorimod • *conj* whereas
hvorledes • *adv* how • *conj* how
hvornår • *n* when • *adv* when • *conj* when • *pron* when
hvorpå • *conj* whereupon
hvorvidt • *conj* if
hyacint • *n* hyacinth
hyæne • *n* hyena
hybel • *n* den
hyben • *n* hip
hybris • *n* hubris
hydrat • *n* hydrate
hydraulik • *n* hydraulics
hydrere • *v* hydrate
hydrofil • *adj* hydrophilic
hydrofobi • *n* hydrophobia
hydrogen • *n* hydrogen
hyggelig • *adj* cosy, cozy
hygiejne • *n* hygiene
hygiejnisk • *adj* hygienic
hygrometer • *n* hygrometer
hykler • *n* hypocrite
hyl • *n* howl, wail
hyld • *n* elder
hylde • *n* shelf
hyldebær • *n* elderberry
hyldest • *n* homage
hyldetræ • *n* elder
hymne • *n* hymn
hynde • *n* cushion
hyperbel • *n* hyperbola, hyperbole
hyperbolsk • *adj* hyperbolic
hypertekst • *n* hypertext
hypnose • *n* hypnosis
hypnotisere • *v* mesmerize
hypnotisør • *n* hypnotist
hypotenuse • *n* hypotenuse
hypotese • *n* hypothesis
hyppig • *adv* often
hyppighed • *n* frequency
hyrde • *n* herd, shepherd
hyrevogn • *n* taxi
hytte • *n* shack

I

i • *prep* during, for, of, up
I • *pron* you
iagttage • *v* observe, watch
ibenholt • *n* ebony
iboende • *adj* inherent
identisk • *adj* identical
identitet • *n* identity
ideogram • *n* ideogram
ideologi • *n* ideology
idet • *conj* as
idiom • *n* idiom
idiomatisk • *adj* idiomatic
idiosynkrasi • *n* idiosyncrasy
idiosynkratisk • *n* idiosyncrasy
idiot • *n* idiot, jackass, nincompoop
idioti • *n* idiocy
idiotsikker • *adj* foolproof
idol • *n* god
idolisere • *v* idolize
idyl • *n* idyll
idyllisk • *adj* idyllic
igen • *adv* again
igennem • *prep* through
igler • *n* leech
iglo • *n* igloo
ignorere • *v* ignore, neglect
ihærdig • *adj* diligent, industrious
ikke • *adv* not • *interj* not
ikkeeksisterende • *adj* nonexistent
ikon • *n* icon
ikosaeder • *n* icosahedron
ild • *n* fire, pyre
ildebefindende • *n* turn
ilder • *n* polecat
ildevarslende • *adj* dire, ominous
ildflue • *n* firefly
ildkugle • *n* bolide, fireball
ildprøve • *n* crucible
ildsted • *n* fire
ildsten • *n* flint
ildvåben • *n* firearm
illegitim • *adj* illegitimate
illusion • *n* illusion
ilt • *n* oxygen
imaginær • *adj* imaginary
imam • *n* imam
imellem • *prep* between, betwixt
imens • *conj* as
imitation • *n* imitation
imod • *prep* against
imødekommenhed • *n* kindness
impala • *n* impala
imperium • *n* empire
implantat • *n* implant
implicit • *adj* implicit
imponerende • *adj* imposing
imposant • *adj* imposing

imprægnere • *v* waterproof
imprægneret • *adj* waterproof
impulsiv • *adj* impetuous, impulsive
incest • *n* incest
ind • *adv* in
indbegrebet • *n* epitome
indbildning • *n* delusion
indbrud • *n* burglary
indbyde • *v* invite
indbygget • *adj* built-in
inddampning • *n* evaporation
inde • *adv* in
indeks • *n* index
indeksere • *v* index
inden • *conj* before • *prep* before
indespære • *v* incarcerate
indfatning • *n* rim
indfatte • *v* set
indflydelse • *n* influence
indflydelsesrig • *adj* influential
indflyvning • *n* approach
indføre • *v* feed
indgang • *n* entrance
indgifte • *n* endogamy
indhold • *n* content, tenor
indholdsfortegnelse • *n* index
indhøste • *v* garner
indium • *n* indium
indkast • *n* insertion, throw-in
indkøb • *n* procurement
indkøbsafdeling • *n* procurement
indkøbskurv • *n* basket
indkomst • *n* income
indlands- • *adj* landlocked
indlevere • *v* deliver
indlysende • *adv* clearly • *adj* evident, obvious
indprente • *v* brand
indre • *adj* intrinsic
indrømme • *v* confess
indsamle • *v* accrue, garner
indsamling • *n* collection
indse • *v* understand
indstille • *v* set
indstilling • *n* attitude, mind
indsukre • *v* sugar
indtægt • *n* income, revenue
indtaste • *v* enter
indtil • *prep* till, until
indtræffe • *v* happen
industri • *n* industry
indvandrer • *n* immigrant
indvandring • *n* immigration
indvende • *v* object
indviklethed • *n* complexity
indvillige • *v* acquiesce
infamøs • *adj* infamous

infanteri • *n* infantry
infantil • *adj* immature
infektion • *n* infection
inferno • *n* inferno
infinitiv • *n* infinitive
inflation • *n* inflation
influenza • *n* flu
informant • *n* informant
information • *n* information
informationer • *n* information
infrarød • *adj* infrared
ingefær • *n* ginger
ingen • *pron* none • *adj* zero
ingeniør • *n* engineer
ingensteds • *adv* nowhere
ingenting • *pron* nothing • *n* zero
initiativ • *n* enterprise
initiativløs • *adj* feckless
inkontinens • *n* incontinence
insekt • *n* bug, insect
insektæder • *n* insectivore
insektlære • *n* entomology
insinuation • *n* innuendo, insinuation
inspiration • *n* inspiration
institut • *n* institute
instrument • *n* tool
insulin • *n* insulin
intelligens • *n* intelligence
intelligent • *adj* sapient
intelligentsia • *n* intelligentsia
intens • *adj* rigorous
intensivere • *v* intensify
intention • *n* purpose
interessant • *n* interest • *adj* interesting
interesse • *n* interest
interessent • *n* stake
interessere • *v* interest, warm
interesseret • *adj* interested
interpersonelle • *adj* interpersonal
interpreter • *n* translator
interval • *n* window
intervention • *n* intervention
interview • *n* interview

intet • *pron* nothing
intetkøn • *n* neuter • *adj* neuter
intetkønsord • *n* neuter
intetsigende • *adj* inane
intetsteds • *adv* nowhere
intonation • *n* intonation
intramuskulær • *adj* intramuscular
intransitiv • *adj* neuter
intravenøs • *adj* intravenous
intravenøst • *adv* intravenously
invadere • *v* invade
invasion • *n* invasion
inventar • *n* furniture
investere • *v* invest
invitere • *v* invite
ionosfære • *n* ionosphere
ir • *n* verdigris
iridium • *n* iridium
iris • *n* iris
ironi • *n* irony
ironisk • *adj* ironic
irrational • *adj* irrational
irrationel • *adj* irrational
irritabel • *adj* peckish
irritation • *n* irritation
irriterende • *v* annoying
is • *n* ice
isbjerg • *n* iceberg
isbryder • *n* icebreaker
isenkram • *n* hardware
iskias • *n* sciatica
isolere • *v* isolate
isomorfi • *n* isomorphism
isop • *n* hyssop
isotropisk • *adj* isotropic
isse • *n* crown
isstormfugl • *n* fulmar
istap • *n* icicle
itu • *adv* up
iver • *n* anxiety, ardor
ivrig • *adj* anxious

J

ja • *n* yes
jade • *n* jade
jadegrøn • *n* jade
jæger • *n* hunter
jærv • *n* wolverine
jætte • *n* jotun
jættegryde • *n* pothole
jævn • *adj* even, level
jævndøgn • *n* equinox

jævne • *v* flatten, level
jævnt • *adv* flat
jage • *v* buffalo, course, hunt
jagt • *n* chase, hunt
jagte • *v* chase
jagtfalk • *n* gyrfalcon
jagthytte • *n* box
jaguar • *n* jaguar
jakke • *n* jacket

jakkerevers • *n* lapel
jaloux • *adj* jealous
jammer • *n* wail
Japan-Ræddike • *n* daikon
jarl • *n* earl
jasket • *adv* slapdash
javert • *n* penis
jazz • *n* jazz
jeg • *pron* me
jer • *pron* you
jern • *n* iron
jern- • *adj* iron
jernbane • *n* railway
jernbanefløjl • *n* corduroy
jeton • *n* chip, counter
jihad • *n* jihad
jod • *n* iodine
jodle • *v* yodel
jogurt • *n* yogurt
jøkel • *n* glacier
jolle • *n* dinghy
jomfru • *n* virgin
jomfruhinde • *n* hymen
jonglere • *v* juggle
jonglering • *n* juggling
jonglør • *n* juggler
jord • *n* earth, soil
jordart • *n* earth
jordbær • *n* strawberry • *adj* strawberry
jordbærfarvet • *adj* strawberry
jordbærplante • *n* strawberry
jorde • *v* earth

jordegern • *n* chipmunk
jordemoder • *n* midwife
jordemor • *n* midwife
jordforbinde • *v* earth
jordforbindelse • *n* earth
jordhule • *n* burrow
jordklode • *n* globe
jordnær • *adj* humble
jordnød • *n* peanut
jordskælv • *n* earthquake
jordskred • *n* landslide
jordstykke • *n* patch
jordsvin • *n* aardvark
joule • *n* joule
journalist • *n* journalist
journalistik • *n* journalism
journalistisk • *adj* journalistic
jubilæum • *n* jubilee
juble • *v* rejoice
judo • *n* judo
juice • *n* juice
jukeboks • *n* jukebox
julestjerne • *n* poinsettia
jungle • *n* jungle
junke • *n* junk
jura • *n* jurisprudence, law
jurte • *n* yurt
justering • *n* adjustment
jute • *n* jute
juveler • *n* jeweler

K

kabaret • *n* cabaret
kabinet • *n* ministry
kabys • *n* galley
kåd • *adj* frisk
kadaver • *n* cadaver, carcass, corpse
kadmium • *n* cadmium
kæbe • *n* jaw
kæberasler • *n* belt
kæde • *n* chain, nexus, train • *v* link
kæderyger • *n* chain-smoker
kæft • *n* face, mouth
kælder • *n* basement, cellar
kæle • *v* cuddle, pet
kæledyr • *n* pet
kælenavn • *n* nickname
kælk • *n* sledge
kælling • *n* bitch
kæmpe • *v* fight, struggle
kæmpestor • *adj* huge
kænguru • *n* kangaroo

kæp • *n* stick
kære • *adj* dear
kæreste • *n* boyfriend, girlfriend, love
kærlig • *adj* fond
kærlighed • *n* love
kærnemælk • *n* buttermilk
kærte • *n* taper
kærtegne • *v* caress
kærv • *n* slot
kætter • *n* heretic
kætteri • *n* heresy
kættersk • *adj* heretic, heretical
kaffe • *n* coffee
kaffebønne • *n* coffee
kaffebusk • *n* coffee
kaffetræ • *n* coffee
kage • *n* cake
kahyt • *n* cabin
kaj • *n* quay, wharf
kajak • *n* kayak

kakao • *n* cacao, cocoa
kakaopulver • *n* cocoa
kakerlak • *n* cockroach
kaki • *n* persimmon
kakofoni • *n* cacophony
kaktus • *n* cactus
kål • *n* cabbage
kalcium • *n* calcium
kalde • *v* call
kaleidoskop • *n* kaleidoscope
kalfatring • *v* caulk
kalium • *n* potassium
kaliumpermanganat • *n* permanganate
kalk • *n* chalice
kalke • *v* plaster
kalkerpapir • *n* carbon
kalksten • *n* limestone
kalkun • *n* turkey
kalmebælte • *n* doldrums
kalorie • *n* calorie
kalorielet • *adj* light
kålorm • *n* caterpillar
kålrabi • *n* kohlrabi
kålroe • *n* rutabaga, swede
kalv • *n* calf, fawn
kamæleon • *n* chameleon
kamel • *n* camel
kamera • *n* camera
kammerat • *n* comrade, friend
kammeratinde • *n* friend
kamp • *n* battle, combat, fight, match, struggle
kampagne • *n* campaign
kampesten • *n* boulder
kampfly • *n* fighter
kamplysten • *adj* combative
kampvogn • *n* tank
kanal • *n* canal, channel, duct
kanalisere • *v* channel
kanariefugl • *n* canary
kanariegul • *n* canary • *adj* canary
kancellistil • *n* rhetoric
kande • *n* can
kandidat • *n* candidate
kandisere • *v* crystallize
kanel • *n* cinnamon
kanin • *n* rabbit
kano • *n* canoe
kanon • *n* cannon, canon
kanonbåd • *n* gunboat
kanonisere • *v* saint
kanonkugle • *n* cannonball
kansler • *n* chancellor
kant • *n* brink, edge
kantalup • *n* cantaloupe
kantarel • *n* chanterelle
kanton • *n* canton

kantor • *n* cantor
kaos • *n* chaos
kaotisk • *adj* chaotic
kap • *n* cape
kapacitet • *n* capacity
kapel • *n* chapel
kapers • *n* caper
kapivar • *n* capybara
kappe • *n* cape
kapring • *n* piracy
kapsel • *n* pod
kapun • *n* capon
kaput • *adj* kaput
kår • *n* circumstance
kar • *n* trough
karaffel • *n* carafe
karakal • *n* caracal
karakter • *n* character, grade
karakteristik • *n* characteristic
karakteristikon • *adj* characteristic
karakteristikum • *adj* characteristic
karamel • *n* caramel
karantæne • *n* quarantine
karavane • *n* caravan
karavel • *n* caravel
karbon • *n* carbon
karbonhydrid • *n* hydrocarbon
karbonpapir • *n* carbon
kardon • *n* cardoon
kåre • *v* choose
karikaturtegner • *n* caricaturist
karikaturtegning • *n* cartoon
karisma • *n* personality
karneval • *n* carnival
karpe • *n* carp
karré • *n* block
karre • *n* block
karrusel • *n* roundabout
karse • *n* bittercress
kartoffel • *n* potato
karton • *n* cardboard
kartouche • *n* cartouche
kasino • *n* casino
kaskade • *n* cascade
kasket • *n* hat
kasse • *v* box • *n* box, case
kassen • *n* box
kassere • *v* junk
kasserolle • *n* saucepan
kassette • *n* cassette
kassevogn • *n* van
kast • *n* shy
kastanje • *n* chestnut
kastanjebrun • *adj* auburn, chestnut • *n* chestnut
kastanjerød • *adj* auburn
kaste • *v* cast, chuck, shy, throw • *n* caste

kastrere • *v* neuter
kat • *n* cat
katakombe • *n* catacomb
katalog • *n* catalogue
katalysator • *n* catalyst
katamaran • *n* catamaran
katarsis • *n* catharsis
katastrofe • *n* catastrophe, disaster
kategori • *n* category
katte • *v* cat
kattekilling • *n* kitty
katteurt • *n* catnip
kaudervælsk • *n* gibberish
kaution • *n* caution
kautionere • *v* guarantee
kautionist • *n* guarantor
kavaler • *n* partner
kavalergang • *n* cleavage
kavaleri • *n* horse
kavalkade • *n* cavalcade
kaviar • *n* caviar
kede • *v* bore
kedel • *n* kettle
kedelig • *adj* boring, dull, tedious
kedsomhed • *n* boredom
Keiseren • *n* emperor
kejser • *n* emperor
kejserdømme • *n* empire
kejserinde • *n* empress
kejserrige • *n* empire
kejthåndet • *n* left-handed
kelp • *n* kelp
kemi • *n* chemistry
kemikalie • *n* chemical
kemiker • *n* chemist
kemisk • *adj* chemical
kemiske • *n* chemistry
kende • *v* know
kendemærke • *adj* characteristic
kendeord • *n* article
kendsgerning • *n* fact
kendskab • *n* knowledge
kendt • *adj* known
kentaur • *n* centaur
keratin • *n* keratin
kermesbær • *n* pokeweed
kerne • *n* kernel
kernetårn • *n* keep
kerub • *n* cherub
ketsjer • *n* racket
kid • *n* kid
kidnappe • *v* abduct
kikært • *n* chickpea
kikærter • *n* chickpea
kikke • *v* look
kikkert • *n* binoculars
kilde • *n* source, spring • *v* tickle

kile • *n* wedge
killing • *n* kitten, kitty, leveret
kilogram • *n* kilogram
kimære • *n* chimera
Kinaradisen • *n* daikon
kind • *n* cheek
kinin • *n* quinine
kiosk • *n* kiosk
kirke • *n* church
kirkegænger • *n* churchgoer
kirkestol • *n* pew
kiromanti • *n* chiromancy
kirsebær • *n* cherry
kirsebærfarvet • *n* cherry
kirsebærtræ • *n* cherry
kiste • *n* chest, coffin
kiwi • *n* kiwi
kjerne • *n* churn
kjole • *n* dress
kjove • *n* jaeger, skua
kladde • *n* draft
klæde • *n* cloth • *v* dress
klædebørste • *n* clothesbrush
klædeskab • *n* wardrobe
klæg • *n* horsefly
klage • *n* cry
klageråb • *n* wail
klagesang • *n* elegy
klang • *n* tone
klapperslange • *n* rattlesnake
klapre • *n* chatter
klaptræet • *n* clapperboard
klar • *adj* bright, clear, set, transparent
klare • *v* stand
klargøre • *v* prime
klarinet • *n* clarinet
klarsyn • *n* clairvoyance
klarsynet • *adj* perspicacious
klart • *adv* clearly
klase • *n* cluster
klatmaler • *n* dauber
klaustrofobi • *n* claustrophobia
klaver • *n* piano
klemme • *v* pinch, squeeze • *n* squeeze
kleptomani • *n* kleptomania
klientel • *n* clientele
klik • *n* click
klima • *n* climate
klimatologi • *n* climatology
klinik • *n* clinic
klint • *n* cliff
klippe • *v* mow
klippegrævling • *n* hyrax
klipse • *v* clip
klistre • *v* plaster
klit • *n* dune
klitoris • *n* clitoris

klo • *n* claw • *v* claw
klode • *n* globe
kløft • *n* canyon, cleavage
klog • *adj* clever, shrewd, smart
klokke • *n* bell
klokken • *n* time
klor • *n* chlorine
klorid • *n* chloride
klorofyl • *n* chlorophyll
klosaks • *n* claw
kloster • *n* cloister, monastery
kløve • *v* cleave
kløver • *n* clover, club
klovn • *n* clown
klub • *n* club
klump • *n* nugget
klynge • *n* cluster, scrum
knæ • *n* knee
knægt • *n* boy, jack
knag • *n* brick
knage • *n* hook
knagen • *n* creak
knald • *n* bang, detonation, fuck
knalde • *v* bang, fuck
knallert • *n* moped, nincompoop
knap • *n* button • *adv* hardly
knaphul • *n* buttonhole
knaphulsblomst • *n* buttonhole
knappe • *v* button
knappenål • *n* pin
knast • *n* knot
kneppe • *v* fuck, sex
knib • *n* pinch
knibe • *n* jam • *v* pinch
knippe • *n* sheaf
knirken • *n* creak
kniv • *v* knife • *n* knife, razor
kno • *n* ankle, knuckle
knob • *n* knot
knogle • *n* bone
knold • *n* tuber
knop • *n* stud
knude • *n* knot
knuge • *v* squeeze
knuget • *adj* despondent
knurhår • *n* whisker
knus • *n* hug, squeeze
knuse • *v* cuddle, hug
knytnæve • *n* fist
ko • *n* cow
kø • *n* file, queue • *v* queue
koagulere • *v* congeal
koala • *n* koala
kobber • *n* copper
købe • *v* buy
koben • *n* crowbar
koble • *v* hook

kobling • *n* clutch
koblingspedal • *n* clutch
købmand • *n* merchant
kobolt • *n* cobalt
købslå • *v* haggle
kød • *n* flesh, meat
kødæder • *n* carnivore
kodeks • *n* code
kodeord • *n* password
kodex • *n* code
kødfarve • *n* flesh
kødfløjte • *n* dick
koefficient • *n* coefficient
koffein • *n* caffeine
kogebog • *n* cookbook
kogger • *n* quiver
kogle • *n* cone
kognition • *n* cognition
kognitiv • *adj* cognitive
kohæsion • *n* cohesion
kohæsionskraft • *n* cohesion
kok • *n* cock, cook
kokain • *n* cocaine, snow
kokettere • *v* coquet
køkken • *n* cuisine, galley, kitchen
køkkenbord • *n* counter
køkkenvask • *n* sink
kokon • *n* cocoon
kokos • *n* coconut
kokosnød • *n* coconut
koks • *n* carbon, coke
kola • *n* cola
kold • *adj* cold, cool
koldblodig • *adj* cold-blooded, cool
koldbrand • *n* gangrene
kolera • *n* cholera
køleskab • *n* refrigerator
kølhale • *v* keelhaul
kølig • *adj* cool
Kølig • *adj* cool
kolkhoz • *n* kolkhoz
kollega • *n* colleague
kollokvium • *n* colloquy
kølnervand • *n* cologne
kolon • *n* colon
koloni • *n* colony
kolonial • *adj* colonial
kolonialisme • *n* colonialism
kolonist • *n* colonist
kølsvin • *n* keelson
koma • *n* coma
kombinere • *v* combine
komedie • *n* comedy
komet • *n* comet
komfort • *n* comfort
komisk • *adj* laughable
komité • *n* committee

komite • *n* committee
komma • *n* comma, point
komme • *n* advent • *v* come, sail
kommen • *n* caraway
kommentar • *n* comment
kommentere • *v* comment
kommissær • *n* commissioner
kommune • *n* commune, municipality
kommunikation • *n* communication
kommunisme • *n* communism
kommunist • *n* communist
kommutere • *v* commute
kompagnon • *n* partner
kompakt • *adj* dense, solid
kompas • *n* compass
kompetence • *n* competency
kompetens • *n* competency
kompetent • *adj* able
kompleksitet • *n* complexity
komplet • *adj* full, utter
kompliment • *n* compliment
komplimentere • *v* compliment
komponent • *n* component
komponist • *n* composer
komposition • *n* composition
kompost • *n* compost
kompostere • *v* compost
kompot • *n* compote
køn • *n* gender, sex
koncentrat • *n* essence
koncentrere • *v* focus
koncept • *n* concept
koncert • *n* concert
koncertina • *n* concertina
koncis • *adj* concise
kondom • *n* condom
kondor • *n* condor
kone • *n* wife
konfekt • *n* sweet
konference • *n* conference
konfetti • *n* confetti
konfiskere • *v* confiscate
konflikt • *n* conflict
konformitet • *n* conformity
konfrontere • *v* face
kong • *n* king
konge • *n* king
kongedømme • *n* kingdom
kongelig • *adj* royal
kongerige • *n* kingdom
konisk • *adj* conical
konk • *n* whelk
konkret • *adj* concrete
konkretisere • *v* concrete
konkubine • *n* concubine
konkurrence • *n* competition, contest
konkurrent • *n* contestant

konkurrere • *v* compete
konkurs • *adj* bankrupt • *n* bankruptcy
konkylie • *n* seashell
konnotation • *n* connotation
konsangvinitet • *n* consanguinity
kønsben • *n* pubis
kønsbestemme • *v* sex
kønscelle • *n* gamete
konsekvens • *n* consequence
konsensus • *n* consensus
konservativ • *n* conservative • *adj* conservative, right
konservator • *n* conservator
konservatorium • *n* conservatory
konservere • *v* can
konserveringsmiddel • *n* preservative
konsistens • *n* consistency
kønsliv • *n* sex
kønsløs • *adj* neuter
konsonant • *n* consonant
konstruere • *v* construct, set
konstrukere • *v* craft
konsulat • *n* consulate
konsument • *n* user
kontakt • *n* contact
kontakte • *v* contact
kontaminere • *v* contaminate
kontanter • *n* cash
kontinent • *n* continent
kontinuitet • *n* continuity
konto • *n* account
kontor • *n* office
kontorassistent • *n* clerk
kontorfunktionær • *n* clerk
kontrafej • *n* portrait
kontrollere • *v* control
kontroversiel • *adj* controversial
konveks • *adj* convex
konversation • *n* conversation, dialogue
konvolut • *n* envelope
koordinat • *n* coordinate
koordination • *n* coordination
koordinere • *v* coordinate
kop • *n* cup
kopi • *n* copy
kopiere • *v* copy
kopper • *n* smallpox
kopula • *n* copula
kor • *n* choir
koral • *n* coral
korbær • *n* dewberry
køre • *v* drive, ride, truck
kørelejlighed • *n* lift
kørestol • *n* wheelchair
køretøj • *n* vehicle
koriander • *n* coriander
korn • *n* cereal

kornblomst • *n* cornflower
kornel • *n* dogwood
kornkammer • *n* garner
kornsort • *n* cereal
korollar • *n* corollary
korporal • *n* corporal
korrekt • *adj* correct, right
korrekturlæser • *n* proofreader
korrigere • *v* right
korrunding • *n* apse
korruption • *n* corruption
kørsel • *n* driving
korset • *n* corset
korsnæb • *n* crossbill
kort • *adj* brief, short • *n* card, map
kortfattet • *adj* brief, laconic
kortslutning • *n* short
kortslutte • *v* short
kørvel • *n* chervil
korvet • *n* corvette
kosmetiker • *n* cosmetologist
kosmologi • *n* cosmology
kosmos • *n* cosmos
kost • *n* broom
kosteskaft • *n* broomstick
køter • *n* cur
kovs • *n* thimble
krabbe • *n* crab
kradse • *v* claw
kræft • *n* cancer
krænke • *v* abuse, encroach, invade
kræve • *v* demand, want
kraft • *n* force, spirit
kraftig • *adj* brawny, violent
krage • *n* crow
kram • *n* hug
kramme • *v* hug
krampe • *n* spasm
kran • *n* crane
kranie • *n* skull
kranium • *n* skull
krans • *n* wreath
kråse • *n* gizzard
krash • *n* crash
krat • *n* thicket
krav • *n* demand
krave • *n* collar
kraveben • *n* clavicle
kravle • *v* crawl
krebs • *n* crayfish
kreds • *n* circle
kredsløb • *n* circle, cycle
kreere • *v* create
krematorie • *n* crematorium
krematorium • *n* crematorium
kridt • *n* chalk
krig • *n* war

kriger • *n* fighter, warrior
krigerisk • *adj* combative
krigsskib • *n* warship
krigstid • *n* wartime
krikke • *n* nag
kriminalitet • *n* crime
kriminel • *n* criminal
kriminologi • *n* criminology
krise • *n* crisis
krisetilstand • *n* crisis
kristtorn • *n* holly
kriterium • *n* criterion
kritik • *n* criticism
kritiker • *n* critic
kro • *n* inn, pub
krog • *n* hook, nook
krokodille • *n* crocodile
krølle • *v* wrinkle
krom • *n* chromium
kromatografi • *n* chromatography
kromatografisk • *adj* chromatographic
kromosom • *n* chromosome
kromosomal • *adj* chromosomal
krone • *n* crown • *v* queen
kroning • *n* coronation
krop • *n* body, flesh
kropsvisitere • *v* frisk
krucifiks • *n* crucifix
krudt • *n* gunpowder
krukke • *n* pot
krumme • *n* crumb
krumsabel • *n* scimitar
krumtaphus • *n* crankcase
krus • *n* mug
kruset • *adj* ruffled
kryb • *n* bug
krybdyr • *n* reptile
krybe • *v* crawl, creep
krybskytte • *n* poacher
krydder • *n* rusk
krydderi • *n* spice
kryddernellike • *n* clove
krydre • *v* salt • *n* seasoning
kryds • *n* cross, intersection
krydse • *v* cut
kryptografi • *n* cryptography
krypton • *n* krypton
krystallisere • *v* crystallize
kryster • *n* poltroon
kubismen • *n* cubism
kubus • *n* cube
kugle • *n* ball, bullet, shot, sphere
kuglefisk • *n* blowfish
kugleformet • *adj* global
kuglelyn • *n* fireball
kugleramme • *n* abacus
kuglerund • *adj* global

kujon • *n* poltroon
kul • *n* carbon, coal
kulbrinte • *n* hydrocarbon
kuld • *n* brood, litter
kulde • *n* cold
kuldsejle • *v* capsize
kulhydrat • *n* carbohydrate
kulinarisk • *adj* culinary
kuling • *n* gale
kuller • *n* haddock
kulør • *n* color, suit
kulørt • *adj* colored
kulso • *n* lumpsucker
kulstof • *n* carbon
kult • *n* cult
kultur • *n* civilization, culture
kulturel • *adj* cultural
kunde • *n* customer, fare
kundskab • *n* knowledge
kunne • *v* can, dig
kunst • *n* art
kunstgødning • *n* fertilizer
kunstig • *adj* false
kunstmaler • *n* painter
kunstner • *n* artist
kunstnerisk • *adj* artistic
kuppel • *n* dome
kurer • *n* courier
kuriøs • *adj* curious
kurs • *n* course
kursus • *n* course
kurtisere • *v* woo
kurv • *n* basket
kurve • *n* curve
kurver • *n* curve
kusine • *n* cousin
kusk • *n* coachman
kuskesæde • *n* box
kusse • *n* cunt, pussy
kutter • *n* sailboat
kuvert • *n* envelope
kvabso • *n* lumpsucker
kvadrat • *n* square
kvadratisk • *adj* square
kvæde • *n* quince
kvæg • *n* cattle

kvæk • *n* croak
kvækerfinke • *n* brambling
kvæle • *v* murder, strangle, suffocate
kvælertag • *n* choke
kvæles • *v* suffocate
kvælning • *n* choking
kvælstof • *n* nitrogen
kvaj • *n* nit
kvaksalver • *n* quack, quacksalver
kvalifikation • *n* qualification
kvalitet • *n* brand, quality
kvalm • *adj* ill
kvalme • *n* nausea
kvan • *n* angelica
kvaner • *n* angelica
kvantificere • *v* quantify
kvark • *n* quark
kvart • *n* quart, quarter
kvartal • *n* quarter
kvarter • *n* neighborhood, quarter
kvartermester • *n* quartermaster
kvartfinale • *n* quarterfinal
kvartil • *n* quartile
kvasar • *n* quasar
kvast • *n* tassel
kvidder • *n* tweet
kvik • *adj* astute, bright, clever, quick
kviksand • *n* quicksand
kviksølv • *n* mercury, quicksilver
kvinde • *n* female, woman • *adj* feminine
kvindelig • *adj* female, feminine
kvist • *n* stick
kvittering • *n* receipt
kvote • *n* quota
kvotient • *n* quotient
kykkeliky • *interj* cock-a-doodle-doo
kylling • *n* chick, chicken
kyniker • *n* cynic
kynisk • *adj* cynical
kynisme • *n* cynicism
kys • *n* kiss
kysse • *v* kiss
kyssesyge • *n* mononucleosis
kyst • *n* coast
kystlinje • *n* coastline

L

labskovs • *n* lobscouse
lacrosse • *n* lacrosse
lade • *n* barn • *v* let, load, sound
ladestok • *n* ramrod
ladning • *n* charge
læbe • *n* lip

læbestift • *n* lipstick
læder • *n* leather
læder- • *adj* leather
læg • *n* calf • *adj* lay
læg- • *adj* lay
læge • *n* doctor

lægge • *v* box, couch, lay
lægmuskel • *n* calf
lækat • *n* ermine
lække • *v* leak
lækker • *adj* delicious, hot
lækkerbisken • *n* plum
lænestol • *n* armchair
længde • *n* length
længdegrad • *n* longitude
længe • *adv* long
længes • *v* long
længselsfuld • *adj* wistful
lænseport • *n* scupper
lære • *v* learn, study, teach
lærebog • *n* textbook
lærer • *n* teacher
lærerinde • *n* teacher
lærk • *n* larch
lærke • *n* lark
lærkefalk • *n* hobby
lærketræ • *n* larch
læs • *n* burden, charge
læse • *v* read
læselig • *adj* legible
læser • *n* reader
låg • *n* lid
lag • *n* coat, tier
låge • *n* door
lager • *n* storage, warehouse
lagkage • *n* cake
lagre • *v* store
lagune • *n* lagoon
lahar • *n* lahar
lak • *n* lacquer, varnish
lakaj • *n* lackey
lakere • *v* lacquer
lakonisk • *adj* laconic
lakrids • *n* licorice
laks • *n* salmon
laktose • *n* lactose
lam • *n* fawn, lamb • *adj* lame
lamel • *n* slot
lampe • *n* lamp
lampeskærm • *n* lampshade
lamt • *adj* lame
land • *n* country, land
landarbejder • *n* laborer
landbrug • *n* agriculture
lande • *v* land
landevejsridder • *n* vagabond
landevejsrøver • *n* highwayman
landkrabbe • *n* landlubber
landmand • *n* farmer
landsby • *n* hamlet, village
landskab • *n* landscape
landstryger • *n* vagabond
landsvale • *n* swallow

landtange • *n* isthmus
låne • *v* borrow, lend
låneord • *n* loanword
lang • *adj* long
langbue • *n* longbow
langskibs • *adv* alongside
langsom • *adj* deliberate, slow
langsomt • *adv* deliberately, slowly
lanse • *n* lance
lanthan • *n* lanthanum
lap • *n* lobe, patch
lappe • *v* mend
lår • *n* thigh
larm • *n* noise
larme • *v* bellow
larve • *n* caterpillar
lås • *n* lock
lasagne • *n* lasagna
laser • *n* laser
last • *n* burden, vice
lastbil • *v* truck • *n* truck
latent • *adj* latent
latex • *n* latex
latrin • *n* latrine
latter • *n* laugh, laughter
latterlig • *adj* laughable
laurbær • *n* laurel
laurbærkrans • *n* laurel
lav • *adj* down, low, shallow, short • *n* guild, lichen
lava • *n* lava
lave • *v* make
lavendel • *n* lavender
lavine • *n* avalanche
lavland • *n* lowland
lavtryksudløber • *n* trough
lavvandet • *adj* shallow
lawrencium • *n* lawrencium
le • *v* laugh • *n* scythe
lebbe • *n* dyke
led • *n* link
leddyr • *n* arthropod
lede • *v* direct, govern, hunt, search
leder • *n* manager
ledig • *adj* vacant
ledsage • *v* accompany
ledsager • *n* date, follower
leg • *n* play
legeme • *n* field, person
legemliggørelse • *n* embodiment
legemskrænkelse • *n* battery
legeplads • *n* playground
legering • *n* alloy
legetøj • *n* toy
leje • *n* bearing, couch, rent • *v* rent
lejesoldat • *n* mercenary
lejlighed • *n* apartment, occasion

leksikografi • *n* lexicography
leksikon • *n* encyclopedia
lektier • *n* homework
lem • *n* trapdoor
lemlæste • *v* maim, mutilate
lensed • *n* fealty
lensherre • *n* lord
lenshyldning • *n* homage
ler • *n* clay, loam
lesbianisme • *n* lesbianism
lesbisk • *n* lesbian • *adj* lesbian
let • *adj* easy, light • *adv* sweet
lethed • *n* easiness
lettelse • *n* relief
leucin • *n* leucine
leukæmi • *n* leukemia
leve • *v* dwell, live
levebrød • *n* livelihood
lever • *n* liver
leverance • *n* supply
leverandør • *n* vendor
leverbetændelse • *n* hepatitis
levere • *v* deliver, supply
levested • *n* habitat
levetid • *n* age, life
levitation • *n* levitation
levnedsmiddel • *n* foodstuff
lian • *n* liana
liberalisme • *n* liberalism
libertiner • *n* rake
lide • *v* dig, suffer
liden • *adj* small
lidenskabelig • *adj* passionate
liderlig • *adj* horny, libidinous
liderlighed • *n* lust
liflig • *adj* delicious
lift • *n* lift
lig • *n* body, corpse
ligatur • *n* ligature
lige • *adv* dead • *adj* right
ligegyldig • *adj* random
ligegyldigt • *pron* whatever
liger • *n* liger
ligeså • *adv* too
ligevægt • *n* equilibrium
ligge • *v* lie
lighed • *n* equality, resemblance, similarity
ligkiste • *n* coffin
ligne • *v* resemble
lignelse • *n* simile
lignende • *adj* similar
ligning • *n* equation
ligvogn • *n* hearse
likør • *n* liqueur, liquor, spirits
likviditet • *n* liquidity
lilje • *n* fleur-de-lis, lily

lilla • *adj* purple
lille • *adj* little, small
lillehjerne • *n* cerebellum
lim • *n* glue
lime • *n* lime
limousine • *n* limousine
lindorm • *n* dragon
lindrende • *adj* soothing
line • *n* line
lineær • *adj* linear
lineal • *n* ruler
lingvist • *n* linguist
lingvistik • *n* linguistics
link • *n* link
linse • *n* lens, lentil
liste • *v* creep, nose • *n* list, slot
listig • *adj* shrewd
lithium • *n* lithium
litterær • *adj* literary
litteratur • *n* literature
liturgi • *n* liturgy
liturgisk • *adj* liturgical
liv • *n* life, spirit
livegen • *n* serf
livegenskab • *n* serfdom
livlig • *adj* bright, frisk, gay
livmoder • *n* womb
livrem • *n* belt
livstid • *n* life
livvagt • *n* bodyguard, guard
løb • *n* course, race, run
lobby • *n* lobby
lobbye • *v* lobby
lobbyist • *n* lobbyist
løbe • *v* run
løbehjul • *n* scooter
løber • *n* bishop, runner, stretcher
løbetid • *n* heat
lockout • *n* lockout
lodde • *v* solder, sound
loddemetal • *n* solder
lodden • *adj* hairy
lodret • *adj* vertical
lodtrækning • *n* draw
loft • *n* ceiling, loft
løft • *n* lift
løfte • *v* lift • *n* oath, promise
loftsrum • *n* attic
løg • *n* onion
logaritme • *n* logarithm
loge • *n* box
logistik • *n* logistics
løgn • *n* lie
løgnagtighed • *n* mendacity
løgner • *n* liar
logre • *v* fawn
løjtnant • *n* lieutenant

lok • *n* lock
lokal • *adj* local
lokalbedøvelse • *n* analgesic
lokalisere • *v* localize
lokke • *v* lure
løkke • *n* noose
lokkemad • *n* lure
lokkemiddel • *n* lure
lokomotiv • *n* locomotive
lokum • *n* bog, toilet
lom • *n* diver, loon
lomme • *n* pocket
lommeregner • *n* calculator
lommetørklæde • *n* handkerchief, tissue
lommetyv • *n* pickpocket
løn • *n* maple, wage
lønningsdag • *n* payday
loppe • *n* flea
loppebid • *n* fleabite
lord • *n* lord
lort • *n* shit
los • *n* lynx
løse • *v* sort
løsen • *n* password
løsesum • *n* ransom
løslade • *v* free
løsøre • *n* chattel
løss • *n* loess
løssluppenhed • *n* abandon
lov • *n* law
løv • *n* leaf
lovændring • *n* amendment
løve • *n* lion
løve- • *adj* leonine
løvemund • *n* snapdragon
løvetand • *n* dandelion • *adj* dandelion
løvfældende • *adj* deciduous
lovgivende • *adj* legislative
løvinde • *n* lion, lioness
lovlig • *adj* legal
lovligt • *adv* legally
lovløs • *adj* lawless • *n* renegade
lovløshed • *n* lawlessness
lovmæssigt • *adv* legally
lovtale • *n* panegyric
loyal • *adj* loyal
loyalitet • *n* loyalty
lud • *n* lye
ludefisk • *n* lutefisk
luder • *n* hooker, whore
ludfisk • *n* lutefisk
lue • *n* flame
luffe • *n* mitten
luft • *n* air
luftballon • *n* balloon
luftfartøj • *n* aircraft
lufthavn • *n* airport

luftkonditioneret • *adj* air-conditioned
luftpost • *n* airmail
luftspejling • *n* mirage
luftstrøm • *n* wind
lufttæt • *adj* airtight
luge • *n* trapdoor
lugt • *n* smell
lugte • *v* smell
lugtesans • *n* smell
lukke • *v* close, shut
lummer • *adj* sultry
lun • *adj* warm
lund • *n* grove
lunde • *n* puffin
lunefuld • *adj* fickle
lunge • *n* lung
lunken • *adj* lukewarm, tepid
luns • *n* hunk
lus • *n* louse
luseæg • *n* nit
lusket • *adj* fishy
lut • *n* lute
lutetium • *n* lutetium
luv • *n* weather
lyd • *n* noise, sound, voice
lyddæmper • *n* silencer
lyde • *v* sound
lydighed • *n* obedience
lydord • *n* onomatopoeia
lydpotte • *n* silencer
lygtepæl • *n* lamppost
lykke • *n* happiness, joy, welfare
lykkelig • *adj* happy
lymfe • *n* lymph
lyn • *n* flash, lightning
lyn- • *adj* crash
lynglimt • *n* levin, lightning
lynnedslag • *n* lightning
lyre • *n* lyre
lyrik • *n* poetry
lys • *adj* bright, cheerful, fair, light • *n* candle, light
lyse • *v* flash, shine
lysebrun • *adj* fawn
lysekrone • *n* chandelier
lyserød • *n* pink • *adj* pink
lyshåret • *n* blond
lyskæde • *n* festoon
lyske • *n* groin
lyskilde • *n* light
lyssky • *adj* sleazy
lyst • *n* desire, lust
lystfiskeri • *n* fishing
lystig • *v* laugh
lytte • *v* listen
lyve • *v* lie

M

må • *v* can, may
måbe • *v* gawk
macademia • *n* macadamia
macademiatræ • *n* macadamia
mad • *n* food
maddike • *n* maggot
måde • *n* way
madkæreste • *n* follower
madras • *n* mattress
madvare • *n* foodstuff
mæ • *interj* baa
mæh • *interj* baa
mælk • *adj* light
mælkebøtte • *n* dandelion • *adj* dandelion
mælkesukker • *n* lactose
mængde • *n* amount, set
mær • *n* slut
mærke • *n* brand, make, token • *v* feel
mærkelig • *adj* weird
mærkværdig • *adj* curious
mæsk • *n* mash
mæslinger • *n* measles
mæt • *adj* full
magasin • *n* garner, magazine
måge • *n* gull
mageløs • *adj* peerless
mager • *n* mage • *adj* scrawny
magi • *n* magic
magiker • *n* mage, warlock
magma • *n* magma
magnat • *n* magnate
magnesium • *n* magnesium
magnet • *n* magnet
magnetisme • *n* magnetism
magt • *n* force, power
mahogni • *n* mahogany
majonæse • *n* mayonnaise
majroe • *n* turnip
majstang • *n* maypole
makeup • *n* makeup
makrel • *n* mackerel
makro • *n* macro
makron • *n* macaroon
maksime • *n* maxim
mål • *n* amount, goal, language, purpose, target
malaria • *n* malaria
male • *v* color, paint
maler • *n* painter
malerisk • *adj* picturesque
malerkunst • *n* painting
malle • *n* catfish
mallemuk • *n* fulmar

målløs • *adj* dumbfounded, speechless
malm • *n* ore
målmand • *n* goalkeeper
målstolpe • *n* post
malstrøm • *n* maelstrom
måltid • *n* meal
malurt • *n* wormwood
målvogter • *n* goalkeeper
mammut • *n* mammoth
man • *n* mane • *pron* one, you
manchet • *n* cuff
manchetknap • *n* cufflink
mand • *interj* boy, man • *n* husband, man
mandarin • *n* mandarin, tangerine
mandel • *n* almond, tonsil
mandelkerne • *n* amygdala
mandig • *adj* manly, masculine
mandlig • *adj* masculine
mandola • *n* mandola
måne • *n* moon
måned • *n* month, moon
månen • *n* moon
manér • *n* foible
måneskin • *n* moonlight
mangan • *n* manganese
mangel • *n* absence, deficiency
mangfoldighed • *n* manifold
mango • *n* mango
mani • *n* mania
maniodepressiv • *adj* manic-depressive
manke • *n* mane
manticore • *n* manticore
manual • *n* manual
manuskript • *n* manuscript, script
mår • *n* marten
maraton • *n* marathon
maratondeltager • *n* marathoner
maratonløb • *n* marathon
maratonløber • *n* marathoner
march • *n* march
marchere • *v* march
marchfløjte • *n* fife
marcipan • *n* marzipan
mareridt • *n* nightmare
marine • *n* navy
marineblå • *n* navy
marionet • *n* puppet
mark • *n* field
marked • *n* fair, market
markeds- • *n* market
markedsføre • *v* market
markedsplads • *n* market
markgreve • *n* margrave
marmelade • *n* jam

marmor • *n* marble
maron • *n* maroon
marshmallow • *n* marshmallow
marv • *n* marrow
mas • *n* hassle
mascara • *n* mascara
mase • *v* squeeze
måske • *v* may • *adv* maybe, perhaps
maske • *n* mask, mesh, stitch
maskine • *n* hardware, machine • *v* tool
maskinel • *n* hardware
maskineri • *n* apparatus
maskulin • *adj* masculine
massage • *n* massage
massakre • *n* massacre
massakrere • *v* massacre
masse • *v* concrete • *n* substance, weight
massiv • *adj* solid
massør • *n* masseur
mast • *n* mast
masturbation • *n* masturbation
mat • *adj* dull
matematik • *n* mathematics
matematisk • *adj* mathematical
materiale • *n* material
materie • *n* pus
materiel • *adj* material
matrix • *n* matrix
matros • *n* sailor
måtte • *n* mat, rug
mave • *n* belly
mavepine • *n* stomachache
mayonnaise • *n* mayonnaise
med • *prep* by, with • *n* snail • *adj* up
medalje • *n* medal
medbetydning • *n* connotation
medens • *conj* while
medfødt • *adj* congenital
medgive • *v* concede
medicin • *n* medicine
meditation • *n* meditation
medium • *n* medium
medlem • *n* member
medlemskab • *n* membership
medley • *n* medley
medlidenhed • *n* compassion
medløber • *n* follower
medmindre • *conj* unless
medspiller • *n* partner
medynkvækkende • *adj* pathetic
megalomani • *n* megalomania
megawatt • *n* megawatt
meget • *adv* very
meje • *v* mow
mejere • *n* harvestman
mejeri • *n* dairy
mejeriprodukt • *n* dairy

mejse • *n* chickadee
mekaniker • *n* mechanic
mekanisme • *n* mechanism
mel • *n* flour
melankoli • *n* melancholy
melankolsk • *adj* melancholy
melanom • *n* melanoma
melasse • *n* molasses
melbærris • *n* bearberry
meldug • *n* mildew
melk • *adj* light
mellem • *prep* among, between
mellemhjernen • *n* diencephalon
mellemkød • *n* perineum
mellemrum • *n* blank, space
melodiøs • *adj* melodious, tuneful
melodisk • *adj* sweet
melon • *n* melon
men • *conj* but
mendelevium • *n* mendelevium
mene • *v* believe, mean, think, understand
mened • *v* perjure
menig • *n* private
mening • *n* meaning, opinion, purpose, tenor
menneske • *n* human, man, wight
menneskefjendsk • *adj* misanthropic
menneskehed • *n* mankind, world
menneskelig • *adj* human
mens • *conj* as, while
menstruation • *n* menstruation
mentalitet • *n* mentality
mentol • *n* menthol
menu • *n* menu
mere • *adv* more
mergel • *n* marl
meridian • *n* longitude
mesanmast • *n* mizzenmast
mesencephalon • *n* midbrain
messe • *n* mess
messehagel • *n* chasuble
messianske • *adj* messianic
messias • *n* messiah
messing • *n* brass
mester • *n* champion
mesterlig • *adj* champion
mesterskab • *n* championship
mesterværk • *n* masterpiece
metafor • *n* metaphor
metal • *n* metal
metallurgi • *n* metallurgy
metamorfose • *n* metamorphosis
metastase • *n* metastasis
meteor • *n* fireball, meteor
metode • *n* method
metoik • *n* metic

metro • *n* metro
metrologi • *n* metrology
metropolit • *n* metropolitan
miav • *interj* meow
middag • *n* banquet, dinner, noon
middel • *n* mean
middelalderlig • *adj* medieval
middelmådig • *adj* mediocre
mide • *n* mite
midlertidig • *adj* temporary
midnat • *n* midnight
midsommerstang • *n* maypole
midtbane • *n* midfield
midte • *n* center, middle
midthjernen • *n* midbrain
mig • *pron* me
migræne • *n* migraine
mikrobe • *n* microbe
mikrobølge • *n* microwave
mikrofon • *n* microphone
mikroorganisme • *n* microorganism
mikrosekund • *n* microsecond
mikroskop • *n* microscope
mikroskopisk • *adj* microscopic
mikse • *v* mix
mikser • *n* mixer
mil • *n* mile
milepæl • *n* milestone
miljø • *n* environment, milieu
milkshake • *n* shake
milligram • *n* milligram
millionær • *n* millionaire
milliontedel • *n* millionth
millisekund • *n* millisecond
milt • *n* spleen
miltbrand • *n* anthrax
min • *pron* me, mine
minde • *n* keepsake, token
mindesmærke • *n* monument
mindreårig • *n* infant, minor • *adj* under-age
mindretal • *n* minority
mine • *n* countenance, mine
minearbejder • *n* miner
minedrift • *n* mining
mineralogi • *n* mineralogy
mineralsk • *adj* mineral
minister • *n* minister
ministerium • *n* ministry
minut • *n* minute
mirakel • *n* miracle, wonder
mis • *n* beaver, pussy
misantropisk • *adj* misanthropic
misbrug • *n* abuse, misuse
misbruge • *v* abuse
misbruger • *n* user
misfarvning • *n* discoloration

misforstå • *v* mistake, misunderstand
mishandle • *v* abuse
mishandling • *n* abuse
mislykkes • *v* fail, miscarry
missekat • *n* pussy
missil • *n* missile
missionær • *n* missionary
miste • *v* lose
mistelten • *n* mistletoe
misunde • *v* grudge
misundelig • *adj* envious, jealous
misundelse • *n* envy
mjav • *interj* meow
mjød • *n* mead
mø • *n* virgin
moa • *n* moa
mobbe • *v* bully
møbel • *n* furniture
mod • *prep* against, for, from • *n* bravery, courage, spirit • *v* face
møde • *v* meet • *n* meeting
mode • *n* cut
modeord • *n* buzzword
moder • *n* mother
moderat • *adv* moderately • *adj* modest
moderfår • *n* ewe
moderkage • *n* placenta
modermærke • *n* birthmark, mole
moderne • *adj* contemporary
moderskab • *n* motherhood
mødes • *v* meet
modgift • *n* antidote
modificere • *v* modify
modig • *adj* bold, brave, courageous
modløshed • *n* dejection, despondency
mødom • *n* hymen
mødomshinde • *n* hymen
modsat • *adj* opposite
modstandsdygtig • *adj* hardy
modstræbende • *adj* grudging
modtage • *v* get
modtagelig • *adj* receptive
modtager • *n* receiver, recipient
modulation • *n* inflection, modulation
modulere • *v* modulate
modvillig • *adj* grudging
møg • *n* dung, manure
møgunge • *n* brat
mokka • *n* mocha
møl • *n* moth
mol • *adj* minor
mole • *n* pier
molekyle • *n* molecule
mølle • *n* mill
møller • *n* miller
møllesten • *n* millstone
molybdæn • *n* molybdenum

monark • *n* monarch
monarki • *n* monarchy
mønje • *n* minium
mononukleose • *n* mononucleosis
monopol • *n* monopoly
monopolisere • *v* monopolize
monopolist • *n* monopoly
monoteisme • *n* monotheism
monoton • *adj* monotonous
monotoni • *n* monotony
mønster • *n* rhythm
mønt • *n* coin, mint
møntenhed • *n* money
møntvaskeri • *n* launderette
monument • *n* monument
monumental • *adj* imposing
mor • *v* mother • *n* mother
mør • *adj* tender
moræne • *n* moraine
moral • *n* morality
moratorium • *n* moratorium
morbær • *n* mulberry
morbror • *n* uncle
mord • *n* murder
morder • *n* assassin, killer, murderer
morfi • *n* morphism
morgen • *n* morning
morgendag • *n* tomorrow
morgenfrue • *n* marigold
morgenmad • *n* breakfast
morgue • *n* morgue
mørk • *adj* dark, deep, sullen
mørke • *n* dark, darkness, night
mørke- • *adj* dark
mørkeræd • *n* nyctophobia
mørkhåret • *adj* brunette, dark-haired
morsom • *adj* funny
mørtel • *n* mortar
mørtelbræt • *n* hawk
mos • *n* moss
mose • *n* bog, marsh, swamp
moske • *n* mosque
moské • *n* mosque
moster • *n* aunt
motbydelig • *adj* heinous
motiv • *n* motive
motor • *n* engine
motorbåd • *n* motorboat
motorcykel • *n* motorcycle
motorvej • *n* highway
motto • *n* motto
muaddhin • *n* muezzin
mudderstrøm • *n* mudslide
muffe • *n* sleeve
muffin • *n* muffin
muflon • *n* mouflon
mug • *n* mildew, mold

muh • *n* moo • *interj* moo
mulat • *n* mulatto
muldjord • *n* soil
muldvarp • *n* mole
muldyr • *n* hinny
mulig • *adj* feasible, possible
mulighed • *n* possibility
multe • *n* mullet
multebær • *n* cloudberry
mumie • *n* mummy
mumle • *v* mumble, murmur
mumlen • *n* mumble, murmur
mums • *adj* yum
mund • *n* mouth
mundharmonika • *n* harmonica
mundharpe • *n* harmonica
mundhugges • *v* bicker
mundlam • *adj* speechless
munk • *n* blackcap, monk
munkering • *n* doughnut
munter • *adj* bright, cheerful
mur • *n* wall
murer • *n* bricklayer
murmeldyr • *n* marmot
mursten • *n* brick • *adj* brick
mus • *n* mouse
muse • *n* muse
musefælde • *n* mousetrap
museum • *n* museum
musical • *n* musical
musik • *n* music
musikal • *n* musical
musiker • *n* musician, player
musikkonservatorium • *n* conservatory
muskat • *n* nutmeg
muskatnød • *n* nutmeg
muskel • *n* muscle
musket • *n* musket
musketer • *n* musketeer
muskulær • *adj* muscular
muskuløs • *adj* brawny, muscular
musvåge • *n* buzzard
mut • *adj* sullen
mutation • *n* mutation
my • *n* mu
myg • *n* gnat
myndig • *n* age
myndighed • *n* authority
mynte • *n* mint
myrde • *v* murder
myre • *n* ant
myrepindsvin • *n* echidna
myresluger • *n* anteater
myriade • *n* myriad
myrra • *n* myrrh
myrte • *n* myrtle
mysli • *n* muesli

mysterium • *n* mystery
myte • *n* myth
mytologi • *n* mythology

mytteri • *n* mutiny

N

nabolag • *n* neighborhood, vicinity
nåde • *n* mercy
næb • *n* beak, bill
næbdyr • *n* platypus
nælde • *n* nettle
nældetræ • *n* hackberry
nær • *adj* close, near
nærhed • *n* proximity, vicinity
nærig • *adj* miserly, stingy
nærkamp • *n* melee
nærmest • *conj* if
nærsynethed • *n* myopia
næs • *n* ness
næse • *n* nose
næseben • *n* bridge
næseblod • *n* nosebleed
næsebor • *n* nostril
næsehorn • *n* rhinoceros
næst- • *adj* second
næste • *adj* following, next
næsten • *adv* about, almost
næstsidst • *adj* penultimate
næsvis • *adj* impudent
næve • *n* fist
nævne • *v* name
nævner • *n* denominator
nag • *n* grudge
nagle • *n* nail, spike
naiv • *adj* naive
nakke • *n* nape
nål • *n* needle
nåleøje • *n* eye
nåleskov • *n* taiga
nap • *n* pinch
nappe • *v* pinch
nar • *n* fool
når • *conj* when
narhval • *n* narwhal
narkolepsi • *n* narcolepsy
narkoleptiker • *n* narcoleptic
narkoleptisk • *adj* narcoleptic
nasalitet • *n* nasalization
nasser • *n* nag
nat • *n* night
nation • *n* nation
national • *adj* national
natrium • *n* sodium
nattesøvn • *n* night
natur • *n* character, kind, nature, temper

naturalier • *n* kind
naturalisme • *n* naturalism
naturlig • *adj* inherent
naturligvis • *adv* obviously
naturreservat • *n* preserve
navle • *n* navel
navn • *n* name
navneord • *n* noun
navngive • *v* name
navnlig • *adv* namely
ned • *adv* down
nedad • *adv* down
nedadgående • *adj* down
nedbør • *n* precipitation
nedbrud • *n* crash, failure
nede • *adj* down, low • *adv* down
nederdel • *n* skirt
nedgøre • *v* humble
nedkomme • *v* deliver
nedladende • *adj* condescending
nedlægge • *v* disband, floor
nedsætte • *v* cut
nedsættelse • *n* cut
nedsættende • *adj* derogatory, disparaging
nedskrive • *v* book
nedslidt • *adj* bald
nedtælling • *n* count
nedtrykthed • *n* dejection
neemtræ • *n* neem
neger • *n* black, ghostwriter
negl • *n* fingernail, nail
negle • *v* pinch
negligere • *v* neglect
negligering • *n* neglect
nej • *n* no
nekrofili • *n* necrophilia
nekromanti • *n* necromancy
nektar • *n* nectar
nektarin • *n* nectarine
nellike • *n* carnation
nem • *adj* easy
neodym • *n* neodymium
neologisme • *n* neologism
neon • *n* neon
neptunium • *n* neptunium
nerve • *n* nerve
nerve- • *adj* nervous
nervesvag • *adj* nervous

nervøs • *adj* nervous
nervøsitet • *n* nervousness
nervøst • *adv* nervously
net • *n* mesh, net, network
netmave • *n* reticulum
netværk • *n* network
neurotiker • *n* neurotic
neurotisk • *adj* neurotic
neutrino • *n* neutrino
neutrum • *n* neuter
nevø • *n* nephew
nexus • *n* nexus
nice • *interj* great
niche • *n* alcove
niece • *n* niece
niende • *adj* ninth
nier • *n* nine
nigger • *n* nigger
nihilisme • *n* nihilism
nikkel • *n* nickel
nikotin • *n* nicotine
niks • *n* nix
nilpotent • *adj* nilpotent
niobium • *n* niobium
nip • *n* sip
nippe • *v* sip
nisse • *n* goblin
nital • *n* nine
nitrat • *n* nitrate
nitrogen • *n* nitrogen
nittende • *adj* nineteenth
nittendedel • *n* nineteenth
nittener • *n* nineteenth
niv • *n* pinch
nive • *v* pinch
niveau • *n* level
nivellere • *v* level
nivelleringsinstrument • *n* level
nobelium • *n* nobelium
nød • *n* nut
nøddeknækker • *n* nutcracker
nøddeskal • *n* nutshell
node • *n* music, note
nødsituation • *n* distress
nødvendig • *adj* necessary
nøgen • *adj* naked, nude
nogen • *pron* somebody
nøgenhed • *n* nakedness, nudity
nogensteds • *adv* somewhere
noget • *pron* something
nogetsteds • *adv* somewhere
nøgle • *n* clef, clue, key
nøgleben • *n* clavicle
nøgtern • *adj* level
nøjagtighed • *n* accuracy
nøjeregnende • *adj* fussy
nominere • *v* nominate

nonne • *n* nun, sister
nonsens • *n* gibberish, nonsense
nord • *n* north
nørd • *n* geek
nordlig • *adj* north
nordnordøst • *n* north-northeast
nordnordvest • *n* north-northwest
nordøst • *n* northeast
nordvest • *n* northwest
norm • *n* norm
normal • *adj* normal, regular
nosse • *n* bollock
notar • *n* notary
notere • *v* book
notits • *n* notice
nu • *n* now • *adv* now • *conj* now
nuance • *n* tone
nudel • *n* noodle
nul • *n* love, zero • *adj* zero
nulpunkt • *n* zero
nulstille • *v* zero
nulværdi • *n* zero
numismatiker • *n* numismatist
nummer • *n* digit
numse • *n* backside
nuppe • *v* pinch
nurse • *n* nurse
nutids- • *adj* contemporary
nuttet • *adj* cute
nuværende • *adj* current, new
ny • *adj* fresh, new • *n* nu
Nybegynder • *n* neophyte
nybegynder • *n* newcomer
nyde • *v* enjoy, relish
nydelig • *adv* prettily
nydelse • *n* relish
nyfødt • *adj* new, newborn
nyheder • *n* news
nyklassicisme • *n* neoclassicism
nyktofobi • *n* nyctophobia
nylig • *adj* recent
nymfe • *n* nymph
nymfoman • *n* nymphomaniac • *adj* nymphomaniac
nymfomani • *n* nymphomania
nymodens • *adj* newfangled
nyre • *n* kidney
nys • *n* sneeze
nyse • *v* sneeze
nysgerrig • *adj* curious
nysgerrighed • *n* curiosity
nyskabende • *adj* innovative
nyt • *n* news
nytte • *n* advantage
nytteløs • *adj* futile
nyttig • *adj* useful

O

ø • *n* island
oase • *n* oasis
obduktion • *n* autopsy, necropsy
oberst • *n* colonel
objekt • *n* object
obo • *n* oboe
øbo • *n* islander
øboer • *n* islander
observatør • *n* observer
observatorium • *n* observatory
observere • *v* observe
obskøn • *adj* vulgar
obstetrik • *n* obstetrics
ocean • *n* ocean
odder • *n* otter
ode • *n* ode
ødelæg • *v* ruin
ødelægge • *v* destroy
ødelæggelse • *n* destruction
offentlig • *adj* public
offer • *n* kill, sacrifice, victim
offside • *n* offside
ofre • *v* sacrifice
ofte • *adv* often
og • *conj* and, plus
øg • *n* nag
og-tegn • *n* ampersand
øgenavn • *n* nickname
øgle • *n* lizard
øgruppe • *n* archipelago
også • *adv* also
øje • *n* eye
øjeæble • *n* eyeball
øjeblik • *n* instant, moment, second
øjeblikkelig • *adj* immediate
øjeblikkeligt • *adv* immediately • *n* instant
øjelåg • *n* eyelid
øjenbryn • *n* eyebrow
øjenlæge • *n* ophthalmologist
øjenlåg • *n* eyelid
øjenvippe • *n* eyelash
ok • *adj* cool
okkult • *adj* occult
okkultisme • *n* occult
okkupation • *n* occupation
økologi • *n* ecology
økologisk • *adj* ecological, organic
økonometri • *n* econometrics
økonomi • *n* economics, economy
okse • *v* slog
oksehoved • *n* hogshead
oksekød • *n* beef
oktav • *n* octave

oktet • *n* octet
økumeni • *n* ecumenism
økumenisk • *adj* ecumenical
øl • *n* beer
oldenborre • *n* cockchafer
oldtidslevning • *n* fossil
olie • *n* oil
olielampe • *n* lamp
oligarki • *n* oligarchy
oliven • *n* olive
om • *prep* about, an • *conj* if, whether
øm • *adj* fond, sore, tender
ombære • *v* deliver
ombudsmand • *n* ombudsman
ombytning • *n* change
ombytte • *v* change
omdele • *v* deliver
omdrejning • *n* turn
omdrejningstæller • *n* tachometer
omegn • *n* vicinity
omend • *conj* albeit
omfang • *n* spread
omfartsvej • *n* bypass
omfattende • *adj* comprehensive
omfavne • *v* hug
omfavnelse • *n* hug
omgå • *v* circumvent
omgang • *n* turn
omgive • *v* belt
omgivelse • *n* surroundings
omgivelser • *n* environment
omhyggelig • *adj* scrupulous
omklædning • *n* change
omkørsel • *n* roundabout
omkreds • *adv* about • *n* circumference
omkredse • *v* circle
omkring • *adv* about • *prep* about, by
omlyd • *n* umlaut
omplante • *v* transplant
område • *n* field
omringe • *v* belt, circumvent, surround
omsætning • *n* turnover
omskære • *v* circumcise
omskærelse • *n* circumcision
omskæring • *n* circumcision
omskiftelig • *adj* fluid
omsorg • *n* care
omstændelighed • *n* circumstance
omstændighed • *n* circumstance
omstridt • *adj* controversial
omstyrte • *v* topple
omtrent • *adv* approximately
omvej • *n* detour
onani • *n* masturbation

ond • *adj* bad, evil • *n* evil
ondskab • *n* evil
ondskabsfuld • *adj* dire
onkel • *n* uncle
onkologi • *n* oncology
onomatopoietikon • *n* onomatopoeia
onomatopoietisk • *adj* onomatopoeic
ønske • *v* desire, wish • *n* desire, wish
onyks • *n* onyx
op • *adv* up • *prep* up
opad • *adv* up
opbrugt • *adj* exhausted
opdækning • *n* spread
opdage • *v* discover
opdagelse • *n* discovery
opdagelsesrejse • *v* explore
opdigtet • *adj* fictional
opdrift • *n* buoyancy
opera • *n* opera
operationskniv • *n* scalpel
operator • *n* operator
operatør • *n* operator
opfarende • *adj* impetuous, irascible
opfatte • *v* understand
opfede • *v* fat, flesh
opfinde • *v* devise
opfindelse • *n* invention
opfindsom • *adj* innovative
opfindsomt • *adj* ingenious
opføre • *v* act, stage
opførelse • *n* building
opførsel • *n* demeanor
opfostre • *v* foster
opfylde • *v* meet
opgave • *n* task
opgive • *v* abandon, die
ophæve • *v* abrogate, cancel, lift
ophævningstegn • *n* cancel
ophav • *n* parent
ophavsret • *n* copyright
ophidse • *v* kindle
ophidset • *adj* excited
ophold • *n* sojourn
opholdssted • *n* sojourn
ophøre • *v* die
opkald • *n* call
opkast • *n* vomit
opklare • *v* clear
oplagt • *adj* obvious, transparent
opleve • *v* experience
oplevelse • *n* experience
opløse • *v* disintegrate
opløsning • *n* definition
opløsningsevne • *n* definition
opløsningsmiddel • *n* solvent
oplyse • *v* light
oplyst • *adj* light

opmærksom • *adj* attentive
opmærksomhed • *n* attention
opmuntre • *v* encourage
oppasser • *n* orderly
oppe • *adj* up
opportun • *adj* opportune
oppvaskemaskine • *n* dishwasher
opredning • *n* spread
oprettelse • *n* establishment
oprindelig • *adj* original
oprør • *n* revolt, tumult
oprørende • *adj* atrocious
oprørt • *adj* upset
opsamle • *v* accrue
opsat • *adj* anxious, set
opsige • *v* denounce
opsigelse • *n* determination
opsigelsesfrist • *n* notice
opspare • *v* save
opspind • *n* fiction
opstå • *n* being • *v* derive
opstand • *n* revolt
opstille • *v* set
opstilling • *n* set
opstrenge • *v* string
opsynsmand • *n* overseer
optæller • *n* counter
optælling • *n* count
optaget • *adj* engaged
optegnelse • *n* record
optog • *n* parade, train
optøjer • *n* row
optræde • *v* act
optræden • *n* demeanor
optrin • *n* scene
opvakt • *adj* bright
opvarme • *v* fire, heat, warm
opvarmning • *n* heat
orange • *n* orange • *adj* orange
orchestra • *n* orchestra
ord • *n* word
ordblindhed • *n* dyslexia
ordbog • *n* dictionary
ordenstal • *n* ordinal
ordentlig • *adj* orderly
ordentlighed • *n* propriety
ordforråd • *n* vocabulary
ordgåde • *n* conundrum
ordinær • *adj* vulgar
ordinaltal • *n* ordinal
ordinere • *v* ordain
ordkløver • *n* pettifogger
ordliste • *n* glossary
ordne • *v* dress
ordonnans • *n* orderly
ordre • *n* order
ordret • *adv* verbatim

ordspil • *n* pun
ordsprog • *n* proverb
ordvalg • *n* language
øre • *n* ear
oregano • *n* oregano
ørentvist • *n* earwig
ørepine • *n* earache
ørering • *n* earring
ørestikke • *n* stud
organ • *n* organ
organisation • *n* organization
organisere • *v* organize
organisme • *n* organism
orgasme • *n* orgasm
orgel • *n* organ
orgie • *n* orgy
orientere • *v* orient
original • *adj* genuine
ork • *n* orc
orkan • *n* cyclone, hurricane
ørken • *n* desert
ørkenrotte • *n* gerbil
orkester • *n* orchestra
orkestergrav • *n* orchestra
orlov • *n* leave
orm • *n* worm
ørn • *n* eagle
orne • *n* boar
ornithosis • *n* psittacosis
ornitologi • *n* ornithology
ørred • *n* trout
ortodoks • *adj* orthodox
ortodoksi • *n* orthodoxy
ortogonal • *adj* orthogonal
øse • *n* ladle
osmium • *n* osmium
øst • *n* east
ost • *n* cheese
ostekage • *n* cheesecake
otologi • *n* otology
ottekant • *n* octagon
ottende • *adj* eighth
otter • *n* eight
ottetal • *n* eight
øve • *v* practice, train
øvelse • *n* experience
ovenover • *prep* above
ovenpå • *prep* above
over • *prep* above • *v* laugh
overalt • *adv* everywhere
overarm • *n* arm
overbefolkning • *n* overpopulation
overbelastning • *n* overload
overbevise • *v* persuade
overbevisende • *adj* cogent
overbringe • *v* deliver
overdrage • *v* transfer
overdrive • *v* exaggerate

overenskomst • *n* transaction
overensstemme • *v* agree
overensstemmelse • *n* agreement
overfalde • *v* attack
overflade • *n* surface
overfladisk • *adj* perfunctory, shallow
overflod • *n* deluge
overflødig • *adj* random, redundant, superfluous
overflytning • *n* transfer
overfølsomhed • *n* idiosyncrasy
overføre • *v* transfer
overgå • *v* exceed
overgangsalder • *n* menopause
overgive • *v* deliver
overhale • *v* overtake
overholde • *v* adhere, observe
overhøre • *v* overhear
overklistre • *v* plaster
overlagt • *adj* deliberate
overlappe • *v* conflict
overleve • *v* live, survive
overlevere • *v* deliver
overlevering • *n* tradition
overmande • *v* overwhelm
overmod • *n* hubris
overnatning • *n* night
overnatte • *v* crash
overpris • *n* surcharge
overraske • *v* surprise
overraskelse • *n* surprise
overrasket • *adj* surprised
overrisling • *n* irrigation
oversætte • *v* translate
oversættelse • *n* translation
oversættelseslån • *n* calque
oversætter • *n* translator
overskæg • *n* moustache
overskrævs • *adv* astride
overskride • *v* exceed
overskyet • *adj* cloudy
overskygge • *v* overshadow
oversvømme • *v* flood, invade
oversvømmelse • *n* flood
overtro • *n* superstition
overtryk • *n* surcharge
overvægt • *n* obesity
overvælde • *v* overwhelm
overvågning • *n* surveillance
overveje • *v* deliberate, reason
overvejelse • *n* deliberation
overvinde • *v* defeat
overvurdere • *v* overestimate
ovn • *n* fire, oven
oxygen • *n* oxygen
ozon • *n* ozone

P

på • *prep* about, at • *adj* on • *v* wear
påbegynde • *v* execute
påbyde • *v* enjoin
padde • *n* toad
paddel • *n* paddle
padderok • *n* horsetail
padderokke • *n* horsetail
padle • *n* paddle
padleåre • *n* paddle
pædagog • *n* pedagogue
pæderast • *n* pederast
pæderasti • *n* pederasty
pæl • *n* puddle
pæn • *adj* nice
pæon • *n* peony
pære • *n* pear
påfugl • *n* peacock
pagaj • *n* paddle
pagode • *n* pagoda
pågribe • *v* arrest
pagt • *n* covenant, pact
pakke • *v* box, package • *n* package
påklædning • *n* dress
påklædningsrum • *n* toilet
pakning • *n* package
palads • *n* palace
pålægge • *v* enjoin
palæontologi • *n* paleontology
palaver • *n* palaver
palet • *n* spatula
paletkniv • *n* spatula
pålidelig • *adj* reliable, responsible, sound
palindrom • *n* palindrome
palladium • *n* palladium
palle • *n* pallet
påløbe • *v* accrue
påmindelse • *n* reminder
pande • *n* forehead
pandehår • *n* bang
pandekage • *n* pancake
pandemi • *n* pandemic
panegyrisk • *adj* panegyrical
panere • *v* bread
panik • *n* panic
pant • *n* mortgage
panter • *n* panther
pap • *n* cardboard
papegøje • *n* parrot
papegøjesyge • *n* psittacosis
papir • *n* paper
paprika • *n* pepper
par • *n* couple
parade • *n* parade

paradis • *n* paradise
paragraf • *n* article, paragraph
parallakse • *n* parallax
parallelepipedum • *n* parallelepiped
paramediciner • *n* paramedic
paranoia • *n* paranoia
paraply • *n* umbrella
parasit • *n* parasite
parentes • *n* bracket
park • *n* garden, park
parlament • *n* parliament
parodi • *n* parody
parodiere • *v* parody
pårørende • *n* relative
parti • *n* party
participere • *v* participate
partiel • *adj* partial
partikel • *n* particle
partisk • *adj* partial
partisoldat • *n* partisan
partitur • *n* score
partner • *n* partner
partnerskab • *n* partnership
paryk • *n* wig
pas • *n* passport
pasform • *n* fit
påskelilje • *n* daffodil, narcissus
påskud • *n* pretext
passage • *n* path, transit
passager • *n* passenger
passe • *v* become, belong, go
passende • *adv* adequately • *adj* fit, opportune
password • *n* password
påstået • *adj* alleged
påstand • *n* allegation
pastiche • *n* pastiche
pastinak • *n* parsnip
pat • *n* tit
patetisk • *adj* pathetic
patient • *n* patient
patologisk • *adj* pathological
patriakalsk • *adj* patriarchal
patriot • *n* patriot
patronym • *n* patronymic
patrulje • *n* patrol
pattebarn • *n* baby
pattedyr • *n* mammal
pattegris • *n* piglet
pave • *n* pope
peanut • *n* peanut
peber • *n* pepper
pebermynte • *n* peppermint
peberrod • *n* horseradish

pedal • *n* pedal
pedant • *n* pedant
pege • *v* finger, point
pegefinger • *n* forefinger
pejle • *v* sound
pejling • *n* bearing
pektin • *n* pectin
pelargonie • *n* geranium
pelikan • *n* pelican
pels • *n* coat, fur
pen • *n* pen
pendle • *v* commute
penge • *n* money
pengeafpresning • *n* blackmail
pengemand • *n* money
pengesum • *n* money
penicillin • *n* penicillin
penis • *n* penis
pentagon • *n* pentagon
perfektionist • *n* perfectionist
perforere • *v* perforate
perfume • *n* perfume
periferi • *n* periphery
periodisk • *adj* periodic • *adv* periodically
periskop • *n* periscope
peristaltik • *n* peristalsis
perle • *n* gem, pearl
perlemor • *n* mother-of-pearl
permanent • *n* permanent
permanganat • *n* permanganate
permission • *n* leave
persille • *n* parsley
person • *n* character, person
personale • *n* staff
personlig • *adj* personal
personlighed • *n* character, personality
pertentlig • *adj* fussy
pest • *n* plague
pestilens • *n* abomination, pest, plague
pianist • *n* pianist
piccolo • *n* bellboy
piccolofløjte • *n* piccolo
pig • *n* spike
pige • *n* girl
pigebarn • *n* chick
pigsko • *n* spike
pik • *n* dick, penis, tool
pike • *n* pike
pil • *n* arrow, willow
pilekogger • *n* quiver
piletræ • *n* willow
pilgrim • *n* pilgrim
pille • *n* pill
pilot • *n* pilot
pilrokke • *n* stingray
pilsner • *n* pilsner
pimpsten • *n* pumice

pind • *n* stick
pindsvin • *n* hedgehog
pingvin • *n* penguin
pip • *n* tweet
pirat • *n* pirate
pirateri • *n* piracy
piratfisk • *n* piranha
piratkopiering • *n* piracy
piruet • *n* pirouette
pis • *n* piss
pisk • *n* whip
piske • *v* whip, whisk
piskeris • *n* whisk
piskeslag • *n* lash
piskesnert • *n* lash
pisse • *v* pee
pistacie • *n* pistachio
pittoresk • *adj* picturesque
pixel • *n* pixel
pizza • *n* pizza
pizzeria • *n* pizzeria
pjække • *v* cut
placere • *v* plant, set
pladder • *n* babble
plade • *n* record
pladning • *n* plating
plads • *v* belong • *n* space
plæne • *n* grass, lawn
plage • *v* eat, hassle, scourge • *n* pest, plague
plageånd • *n* pest
plan • *n* level, plane • *adj* level, plane
planere • *v* level
planet • *n* planet
planetoide • *n* asteroid
plante • *v* plant • *n* plant
planteæder • *n* herbivore, vegetarian
plapre • *v* babble, prattle • *n* chatter
platan • *n* plane
platin • *n* platinum
pleje • *v* cultivate
pleonasme • *n* pleonasm
plet • *n* stain
pletfri • *adj* immaculate
pligt • *n* duty, obligation
pligtopfyldende • *adj* conscientious
pligtopfyldendehed • *n* conscientiousness
pløje • *v* plough
plov • *n* plough
pludre • *v* babble, prattle
pludren • *n* babble
pludselig • *adj* abrupt, sudden • *adv* overnight
pludseligt • *adv* suddenly
plukke • *v* pick, pluck
plumpe • *v* plop

plus • *conj* plus
plutonium • *n* plutonium
poesi • *n* poetry
point • *n* point
pointe • *n* point
pokal • *n* cup
pokkers • *adv* damn • *interj* damn
pol • *n* pole
polarlys • *n* aurora
polemik • *n* polemic
polere • *v* polish, shine
polet • *n* token
politi • *n* police
politik • *n* policy, politics
politiker • *n* politician
politimand • *n* policeman
politisk • *adj* political
politur • *n* polish
polonium • *n* polonium
pølse • *n* sausage
pølseforgiftning • *n* botulism
polstre • *v* cushion
polyætylen • *n* polyethylene
polygon • *n* polygon
polyteisme • *n* polytheism
polyteistisk • *adj* polytheistic
pomelo • *n* pomelo
pomfrit • *n* chip
pompelmus • *n* pomelo
pony • *n* nag, pony
poppel • *n* poplar
poppeltræ • *n* poplar
populisme • *n* populism
porcelæn • *n* china, porcelain
pornograf • *n* pornographer
pornografi • *n* pornography
pornografisk • *adj* pornographic
porøs • *adj* porous
porre • *n* leek
pors • *n* gale
port • *n* gate, port
portefølje • *n* briefcase
porto • *n* postage
portør • *n* orderly
portræt • *n* portrait
pose • *n* bag
positiv • *adj* positive
positur • *n* attitude
post • *n* post, record
postbud • *n* mailman
postfrisk • *adj* mint
postkasse • *n* mailbox
postkort • *n* postcard
postmodernisme • *n* postmodernism
poststempel • *n* postmark
pot • *n* cannabis, pot
pote • *n* paw

potenseksponent • *n* exponent
potentat • *n* potentate
potpourri • *n* pastiche, potpourri
potte • *n* pot
pr. • *prep* an
præcis • *adv* exactly • *adj* precise
præcision • *n* accuracy
prædikant • *n* preacher
prædikestol • *n* pulpit
præfiks • *n* prefix
præg • *n* stamp
præge • *v* stamp
prægtig • *adj* stately
Prælat • *n* prelate
præmie • *n* prize
præparat • *n* preparation
præparation • *n* preparation
præposition • *n* preposition
prærie • *n* prairie
prærieulv • *n* coyote
præsentere • *v* set
præservativ • *n* condom
præsident • *n* president
præst • *n* priest
præstation • *n* achievement, feat
præsteembede • *n* ministry
præstinde • *n* priestess
prævention • *n* contraception
pragmatisk • *adj* pragmatic
pragt • *n* glory
praksis • *n* practice, praxis
pral • *n* boast
prale • *v* boast, brag
pram • *n* barge
praseodymium • *n* praseodymium
presse • *v* squeeze
prik • *n* prick
primær • *adj* primary, prime
primtal- • *adj* prime
prins • *n* prince
prinselig • *adj* princely
prinsesse • *n* princess
printer • *n* printer
prioritet • *n* priority
pris • *n* price
prise • *v* celebrate
prisme • *n* prism
prissætte • *v* price
privat • *adj* private
problem • *n* problem
produktion • *n* production
produktiv • *adj* prolific
profet • *n* prophet
profeti • *n* prophecy
program • *n* program
programmel • *n* software
programmør • *n* developer

projekt • *n* project
projektil • *n* bullet
promethium • *n* promethium
prominent • *adj* salient
promiskuøs • *adj* promiscuous
promotor • *n* manager
pronomen • *n* pronoun
propel • *n* propeller
propfuld • *adj* jammed
proptrækker • *n* corkscrew
prosa • *n* prose
prosaisk • *adj* prosaic
proscenium • *n* proscenium
prosodi • *n* prosody
prostitueret • *n* hooker, whore
prostitution • *n* prostitution
protactinium • *n* protactinium
protein • *n* protein
protektorat • *n* protectorate
protist • *n* protist
proton • *n* proton
prøve • *v* attempt, essay, sound, try
prøveballon • *n* feeler
provins • *n* province
provisorie • *n* provisional
provisorisk • *adj* provisional
provokatør • *n* gadfly
provst • *n* provost
prut • *n* fart, wind
prutte • *v* fart, haggle
psittacosis • *n* psittacosis
psykologi • *n* psychology
psykometri • *n* psychometry
psykosomatisk • *adj* psychosomatic

psykoterapeut • *n* psychotherapist
pubertet • *n* puberty
puddel • *n* poodle
puddelhund • *n* poodle
pude • *n* cushion, pillow
puds • *n* plaster
pudse • *v* dress, plaster, polish, shine
pudsecreme • *n* polish
puge • *v* hoard
pule • *v* fuck
pullert • *n* bollard
pulsar • *n* pulsar
pulver • *n* powder
puma • *n* cougar, puma
pumpe • *n* pump
pund • *n* pound
pungdyr • *n* marsupial
punkt • *n* article, item, point
punktskrift • *n* braille
punkttegn • *n* bullet
punktum • *n* point
pupil • *n* pupil
purere • *v* cream
pus • *n* pus
pusher • *n* pusher
puste • *v* blow
putte • *v* cuddle, putt
pygmæ • *n* pygmy
pyjamas • *n* pajamas
pyramide • *n* pyramid
pyt • *n* puddle
pyton • *n* python

Q

qua • *adv* qua
quiz • *n* quiz

R

rå • *n* doe • *adj* raw
råb • *n* cry, shout
rabarber • *n* rhubarb
rabat • *n* discount, shoulder
rabbiner • *n* rabbi
råbe • *v* bark, cry, shout
rabies • *n* hydrophobia
racisme • *n* racism
rad • *n* row
råd • *n* advice, council
rådden • *adj* rotten

råde • *v* advise
radio • *n* radio
radioaktiv • *adj* radioactive
radioaktivitet • *n* radioactivity
radiofoni • *n* radio
radise • *n* radish
radius • *n* radius
rådne • *v* rot
radon • *n* radon
rådslagning • *n* deliberation
rædselsfuld • *adj* atrocious

række • *n* bank, nexus, phylum, row, series, train
rækkefølge • *n* sequence
råemne • *n* blank
ræsonnere • *v* reason
ræv • *n* fox
rævegrav • *n* earth
raffinement • *n* refinement
raffinere • *v* refine
råge • *n* rook
ragelse • *n* junk
ragout • *n* ragout
rakitis • *n* rickets
ral • *n* gravel, pebble
råmælk • *n* colostrum
rand • *n* boundary, brink, edge, rand, rim
rangle • *n* rattle
rangorden • *n* hierarchy
råolie • *n* oil
rap • *n* quack
rappe • *v* quack
rappenskralde • *n* shrew
rar • *adj* kind, pleasant
rase • *v* rage
rasende • *adj* livid
raseri • *n* frenzy, fury, rage
rask • *adj* clever, normal, sound
rasle • *n* rattle
rastløshed • *n* restlessness
ratificere • *v* ratify
rationalitet • *n* rationality
rationel • *adj* rational
rav • *n* amber
rave • *v* reel
ravine • *n* ravine
ravn • *n* raven
razzia • *n* raid
reaktion • *n* reaction
realismen • *n* realism
realist • *n* realist
realistisk • *adj* realistic
realitet • *n* reality
rebel • *v* rebel
rebus • *n* rebus
recensent • *n* reviewer
recessiv • *adj* recessive
reciprok • *adj* reciprocal
recitation • *n* recitation
recitere • *v* recite
redde • *v* save
rede • *v* comb • *n* nest
redigere • *v* edit
redning • *n* save
redskab • *n* tool
reducere • *adj* depleted
reduceret • *n* choke
reel • *n* reel

referere • *v* refer
reflektere • *v* think
refræn • *n* refrain
refugium • *n* haven
regel • *n* rule
regelmæssig • *adj* regular
regent • *n* regent
regere • *v* govern
regering • *n* government, ministry
regeringstid • *n* reign
region • *n* belt, region
registrering • *n* registration
regn • *n* rain
regnbue • *n* rainbow
regnbuehinde • *n* iris
regndråbe • *n* raindrop
regne • *v* rain
regnemaskine • *n* computer
regnorm • *n* earthworm
regnskab • *n* accounting
regulere • *v* modulate
reje • *n* prawn, shrimp
rejse • *n* journey, trip • *v* stand
rejsning • *n* erection
reklame • *n* advertisement, commercial, promotion
reklamere • *v* advertise
rekord • *n* record
rektangel • *n* rectangle
rektor • *n* headmistress
rekviem • *n* requiem
rekvirere • *v* requisition
rekyl • *n* recoil
relaterede • *adj* related
relativ • *adj* relative
relativt • *adv* relatively
relevant • *adj* germane
relevante • *adj* germane
relief • *n* relief
Religionsvidenskab • *n* theology
religiøs • *adj* religious
remis • *n* draw
ren • *adj* clean, sweet • *n* reindeer
rende • *n* drain, trough
rendezvous • *n* date, rendezvous
renlighed • *n* cleanliness
rensdyr • *n* reindeer
rense • *v* clean, clear, refine
reparere • *v* mend
repetere • *v* repeat, revise
replik • *n* retort
reproduktion • *n* reproduction
republik • *n* republic
reservere • *v* book
reserveret • *adj* reserved
ressource • *n* resource
rest • *n* remainder, remnant

restaurant • *n* restaurant
resterende • *adj* remaining
restriktive • *adj* restrictive
resultat • *n* achievement, result
resume • *n* abstract, summary
resumé • *n* summary
resurse • *n* resource
ret • *n* course, justice, right • *adj* right
retarderet • *adj* retarded
retfærdig • *adj* fair
retfærdighed • *n* equity, justice
retning • *n* direction, path
retningslinje • *n* guideline
retorik • *n* rhetoric
retorisk • *adj* rhetorical
retort • *n* retort
retroaktiv • *adj* retroactive
retsbygning • *n* courthouse
retslærd • *n* jurist
retsvidenskab • *n* jurisprudence
rette • *v* aim, direct, right
rettighed • *n* right
rettroende • *adj* orthodox
retvinklet • *adj* right
reveille • *n* reveille
revers • *n* revers
revidere • *v* revise
revisor • *n* auditor
revling • *n* crowberry
revne • *n* cleft, fissure, slot • *v* tear
revolution • *n* revolution
revolutionær • *adj* revolutionary
revy • *n* revue
rhenium • *n* rhenium
rhodium • *n* rhodium
rhombe • *n* rhombus
ribben • *n* rib
ridder • *n* knight
ride • *n* kittiwake • *v* ride
ridse • *n* scratch
ridt • *n* ride
riffel • *n* rifle
rift • *n* tear
rig • *adj* rich
rigdom • *n* gold, wealth
rige • *n* kingdom, realm
rigelig • *adj* ample
rigtig • *adj* correct, right
rigtighed • *n* propriety
rikochettere • *v* skim
rille • *n* slot
rimelig • *adj* fair
rimelighed • *n* equity
ring • *n* basket, ring
ringagte • *v* humble
ringe • *v* phone, ring, telephone
ris • *n* rice, rod

risikere • *v* risk
risiko • *n* peril, risk
rislen • *n* murmur
rismark • *n* paddy
rite • *n* rite
ritual • *n* ritual
ritus • *n* rite
rive • *v* claw, tear • *n* rake
rivejern • *n* grater
ro • *n* calm, peace, quiet, rest, rowing, tranquillity • *v* row
røbende • *adj* telltale
rød • *adj* rare, red
rod • *n* mess, root
rødbede • *n* beetroot
rødhals • *n* robin
rødhåret • *adj* redheaded
rødme • *v* color
roe • *n* fawn
røg • *n* smoke
røge • *v* smoke
røgelse • *n* frankincense, incense
rogn • *n* roe
røgrør • *n* flue
rokade • *n* castling
rokere • *v* castle
rokke • *v* shake
rokoko • *n* rococo
rokoko- • *adj* rococo
rolig • *adj* calm, cool, deliberate, quiet, tranquil
roligt • *adv* deliberately
rolle • *n* character
røllike • *n* yarrow
rom • *n* rum
roman • *n* novel
romantik • *n* love
romantiker • *n* romantic, romanticist
rombe • *n* rhombus
røn • *n* rowan
roning • *n* rowing
rønnebær • *n* rowanberry
rønnebærtræ • *n* rowan
rør • *n* pipe
ror • *n* rudder
rørdrum • *n* bittern
røre • *v* cream, mix, touch
rose • *v* praise • *n* rose
rosin • *n* raisin
rosmarin • *n* rosemary
røst • *n* voice
rouge • *n* blush
røv • *n* ass, butt
rovdyr • *n* carnivore
røve • *v* rob
røver • *n* brigand, robber
røvhul • *n* asshole, bastard

royal • *adj* royal
ru • *adj* harsh
rubel • *n* ruble
rubidium • *n* rubidium
rubin • *n* ruby
rubrik • *n* blank
rucola • *n* rocket
rude • *n* rue, window, windowpane
ruder • *n* diamond
rudimentær • *adj* vestigial
rug • *n* rye
rugby • *n* football
ruin • *n* ruin
rulle • *v* course, reel, run • *n* reel
rullebord • *n* coaster
rullegardin • *n* blind
rullestol • *n* wheelchair
rum • *n* room, space
rummet • *n* space
rumpe • *n* behind
rumskib • *n* spaceship
rumtid • *n* spacetime
rumvæsen • *n* alien

rund • *adj* circular
runde • *n* heat, leg
rundkørsel • *n* roundabout
rune • *n* rune
rural • *adj* rural
rusk • *n* shake
rustvogn • *n* hearse
rute • *n* course, run
ruthenium • *n* ruthenium
rutherfordium • *n* rutherfordium
rutine • *n* experience
ryg • *n* back, spine
ryge • *v* fume, smoke
ryger • *n* smoker
rygning • *n* smoking
rygrad • *n* backbone, spine
rygsæk • *n* backpack
rygsøjle • *n* spine
ryste • *v* shake
rysten • *n* shake
rytme • *n* rhythm
rytterfane • *n* banner

S

så • *adv* as • *v* plant • *conj* so
saccharose • *n* sucrose
sådan • *adv* so
sadisme • *n* sadism
sadist • *n* sadist
sadistisk • *adj* sadistic
sæbe • *n* soap
sæbeurt • *n* soapwort
sæd • *n* semen, sperm
sædcelle • *n* spermatozoon
sædvane • *n* custom
sædvanlig • *adj* common, textbook
sædvanligvis • *adv* usually
sæk • *n* bag, sack
sækfuld • *n* sack
sækkepibe • *n* bagpipes
sæl • *n* seal
sælge • *v* sell
sælger • *n* vendor
særegenhed • *n* idiosyncrasy
særfrimærke • *n* commemorative
særhed • *n* idiosyncrasy
særlig • *adv* very
særpræg • *n* idiosyncrasy
sæson • *n* season
sæt • *n* set
sætning • *n* sentence, set
sætstykke • *n* set
sætte • *v* set, stand

safir • *n* sapphire
safran • *n* saffron
saft • *n* juice, latex
saftevand • *n* nectar
saftig • *adj* juicy
saga • *n* saga
sagfører • *n* lawyer
saggruppeordbog • *n* thesaurus
sakramente • *n* sacrament
sakristi • *n* sacristy
saks • *n* scissors
sal • *n* level
salami • *n* salami
salat • *n* lettuce, salad
således • *adv* thus
salig • *adj* late
salingshorn • *n* spreader
salme • *n* psalm
salt • *n* salt • *adj* salt
salte • *v* salt
saltholdig • *adj* salt
salve • *n* ointment, plaster
samarbejde • *v* cooperate, partner • *n* co-operation
samarium • *n* samarium
samfund • *n* society
samle • *v* collect, gather, hoard
samleje • *v* sex • *n* sex
samler • *n* collector, gatherer

samlesæt • *n* set
samling • *n* collection, set
samme • *adj* same • *pron* same
sammen • *adv* together
sammendrage • *v* abridge
sammenhæng • *n* cohesion, nexus
sammenhængende • *adj* connected
sammenhængsevne • *n* cohesion
sammenhold • *n* cohesion
sammenkæde • *v* link
sammenligne • *v* compare
sammenligning • *n* resemblance, simile
sammensætning • *n* composition, fabric
sammenslutning • *n* alliance
sammenstød • *n* crash, melee
samovar • *n* samovar
samtale • *n* conversation, dialogue, talk
samtidig • *adj* contemporary
samtidigt • *adv* simultaneously
samtykke • *n* agreement
samurai • *n* samurai
samvittighed • *n* conscience
samvittighedsfuld • *adj* conscientious, scrupulous
samvittighedsfuldhed • *n* conscientiousness
sand • *n* sand • *adj* true
sandal • *n* sandal
sandbanke • *n* sandbank
sandelig • *adv* indeed, verily
sandet • *adj* sandy
sandfarvet • *adj* sandy
sandhed • *adv* indeed • *n* truth
sandkasse • *n* playground, sandbox
sandsæk • *n* sandbag
sandsten • *n* sandstone
sandstrand • *n* sand
sandsynlig • *adj* likely
sandsynlighed • *n* resemblance
sandwich • *n* sandwich
sang • *n* song
sanger • *n* singer, warbler
sangerinde • *n* singer
sangfugl • *n* songbird
sanglærke • *n* skylark, songbird
sanitær • *adj* sanitary
sanktvejtsdans • *n* chorea
sanselig • *adj* sultry, voluptuous
sappør • *n* sapper
sår • *n* injury, wound
sårbar • *adj* vulnerable
såre • *v* wound
sarkasme • *n* sarcasm
sarkofag • *n* sarcophagus
satan • *n* devil
satellit • *n* satellite
satire • *n* satire

satiriker • *n* satirist
satirisk • *adj* satirical
satyr • *n* satyr
sauna • *n* sauna
sav • *n* saw
savanne • *n* savanna
savl • *n* drool
savle • *v* drool
savne • *v* miss
savsmuld • *n* sawdust
savværk • *n* sawmill
scenario • *n* set
scene • *n* scene, stage
schankel • *n* nexus
schistosomiasis • *n* schistosomiasis
sclerose • *n* sclerosis
scooter • *n* scooter
score • *v* score • *n* score
scoring • *n* basket
se • *v* look, see, watch
segl • *n* sickle
seismolog • *n* seismologist
sej • *adj* ductile
sejl • *n* sail
sejle • *v* sail
sejlgarn • *n* twine
sejltur • *n* sail
sejr • *n* victory
sejre • *v* conquer, triumph
sejrsceremoni • *n* triumph
sekretariat • *n* secretariat
sekstal • *n* six
sekstant • *n* sextant
sekstentalssystem • *n* hexadecimal
seksualliv • *n* sex
sekt • *n* cult, sect
sekund • *n* second
sekundær • *adj* ancillary, secondary
sekundant • *n* second
sekundavare • *n* second
sekundere • *v* second
sekvens • *n* sequence
sekventiel • *adj* consecutive
selen • *n* selenium
selleri • *n* celery
selvbestemmelse • *n* self-determination
selvbiografi • *n* autobiography
selvhjælp • *n* self-help
selvisk • *adj* selfish
selvlært • *adj* self-educated
selvmord • *n* suicide
selvmorder • *n* suicide
selvom • *conj* although
selvrisiko • *n* coinsurance
selvstændighed • *n* independence
selvstyre • *n* autonomy
selvværd • *n* self-esteem

semantik • *n* semantics
semester • *n* semester
semifinale • *n* semifinal
semikolon • *n* semicolon
semiotik • *n* semiotics
sen • *adv* late
senat • *n* senate
sende • *v* send
sendt • *v* sent
sendte • *v* sent
sene • *n* tendon
senere • *adv* after, afterwards, later
seneskedehindebetændelse • *n* tenosynovitis
senest • *adj* last
seng • *n* bed
sengetæppe • *n* bedspread
sennep • *n* mustard
sennepskål • *n* rocket
sensuel • *adj* sultry
seraf • *n* seraph
sergent • *n* sergeant
serie • *n* cluster, string
serotonin • *n* serotonin
serviet • *n* napkin, tissue
servil • *adj* obsequious
servitrice • *n* waitress
servitut • *n* easement
sesam • *n* sesame
seværdighed • *n* sight
sex • *n* sex
sexet • *adj* sexy
sfære • *n* realm, sphere
sfærisk • *adj* global, spherical
sfinks • *n* sphinx
shaman • *n* shaman
shamanisme • *n* shamanism
shampoo • *n* shampoo
shanghaje • *v* shanghai
shoppe • *v* shop
shorts • *n* shorts
si • *n* sieve
sibilant • *n* sibilant
sidde • *v* sit
side • *n* dimension, facet, page, right
siden • *conj* as, since • *prep* since
sideror • *n* rudder
sidst • *adj* last
sidste • *adj* last
sig • *v* laugh
sige • *v* say
signal • *n* signal
signalere • *v* flag
signaturforklaring • *n* key
signe • *v* bless
sigøjner • *n* gypsy
sigte • *n* sieve, sight

sikker • *adj* certain, sound
sikkerhed • *n* caution, safety, security
sikkerhedssele • *n* belt
sikkert • *adj* certain • *adv* confidently
sikre • *adj* certain • *v* guarantee, safeguard
sikring • *n* fuse, safety
sild • *n* chick, herring
sildehaj • *n* porbeagle
silicium • *n* silicon
silikone • *n* silicone
silke • *n* silk
silkehale • *n* waxwing
silkeorm • *n* silkworm
simoni • *n* simony
simpel • *adj* rudimentary, vulgar
simulere • *v* feign
sind • *n* mind, temper
sindig • *adj* deliberate, level
sindigt • *adv* deliberately
sindsligevægt • *n* equilibrium
sindsro • *n* peace
sindssyg • *adj* insane, mad
sindssyge • *n* insanity, madness
sinecure • *n* sinecure
sinus • *n* sine
sip • *n* sip
sippe • *n* prude • *v* sip
sippet • *adj* prudish
sippethed • *n* prudery
sirup • *n* syrup
sitre • *v* quiver
sjæl • *n* ghost, mind, soul, spirit
sjælden • *adv* infrequently, seldom • *adj* rare
sjælefred • *n* peace
sjagger • *n* fieldfare
sjakal • *n* jackal
sjal • *n* shawl
sjette • *adj* sixth
sjettedel • *n* sixth
sjofel • *adj* rude
sjov • *adj* fun, funny, gay
sjover • *n* cur
sjuske • *n* slob
sjuskedorte • *n* slob
skab • *n* closet, scab
skabe • *v* beget, create, make
skabelon • *n* template, trope
skade • *v* damage • *n* damage, harm, magpie, wound
skadedyr • *n* pest, vermin
skadelig • *adj* detrimental, evil, harmful
skæbne • *n* destiny, fate
skæg • *n* beard
skægget • *adj* bearded
skæl • *n* dandruff

skænderi • *n* hassle, quarrel, row
skændes • *v* bicker, quarrel, row
skær • *n* hue, island
skære • *v* cut, knife • *adj* cut
skærf • *n* sash
skæring • *n* intersection
skæringspunkt • *n* intersection
skærm • *n* guard, mudguard, screen
skærsild • *n* purgatory
skæv • *adj* high, skew
skaffe • *v* supply
skafot • *n* scaffold
skak • *n* check, chess
skakbræt • *n* chessboard
skakmat • *interj* checkmate
skål • *interj* cheers • *n* cup, toast
skal • *n* snail
skaldet • *adj* bald
skaldyr • *n* shellfish
skam • *n* shame
skamben • *n* pubis
skandale • *n* scandal
skandaløs • *adj* scandalous
skandium • *n* scandium
skånselløs • *adj* ruthless
skånselsløs • *adj* ruthless
skår • *n* shard
skarntyde • *n* hemlock
skarntydegran • *n* hemlock
skarp • *adj* sharp, waspish
skarpsindig • *adj* astute
skarpsindighed • *n* perspicacity
skarpskytte • *n* sharpshooter
skarv • *n* cormorant, shag
skat • *n* hoard, love, sugar, tax
skatte • *v* value
skatte- • *adj* fiscal
skatteindtægt • *n* revenue
skattemæssig • *adj* fiscal
ske • *v* be, happen • *n* spoon
skede • *n* scabbard, sheath, vagina
skefuld • *n* spoonful
skelet • *n* skeleton
skepticisme • *n* skepticism
skeptisk • *adj* skeptical
skestork • *n* spoonbill
ski • *n* ski
skib • *n* boat, nave, ship
skide • *v* shit
skift • *n* change
skifte • *v* change, transfer • *n* course
skifting • *n* changeling
skik • *n* custom
skikkelse • *n* figure, personality
skilderhus • *n* box
skildpadde • *n* tortoise, turtle
skillevej • *n* fork

skillingsvise • *n* broadside
skimme • *v* browse, skim
skin • *n* glare, shine
skind • *n* hide, skin
skinke • *n* ham
skinne • *v* flash, glare, shine • *n* rail
skinneben • *n* shin
skipperlabskovs • *n* lobscouse
skitse • *n* thumbnail
skive • *n* disk
skizofreni • *n* schizophrenia
skjald • *n* skald
skjold • *n* shield
skjorte • *n* shirt
skjule • *v* conceal, hide, veil
skjulested • *n* hideout
sklerose • *n* sclerosis
sko • *n* horseshoe, shoe • *v* shoe
skod • *n* butt
skød • *n* lap
skødesløs • *adj* perfunctory
skøge • *n* harlot, whore
skohorn • *n* shoehorn
skolastik • *n* scholasticism
skole • *n* school
skolopender • *n* centipede
skomager • *n* shoemaker
skønhed • *n* beauty
skønlitteratur • *n* fiction
skønmaler • *n* apologist
skonnert • *n* schooner
skønt • *conj* although
skør • *adj* crazy, mad
skørbug • *n* scurvy
skøre • *adj* brittle
skorpe • *n* rusk
skorpion • *n* scorpion
skorsten • *n* chimney
skorstenspibe • *n* chimney
skørt • *n* skirt
skotøj • *n* footwear
skov • *n* forest
skovl • *n* shovel
skovmærke • *n* woodruff
skovsanger • *n* warbler
skovskade • *n* jay
skrabe • *v* skin
skrædder • *n* tailor
skrædderske • *n* tailor
skrækkelig • *adj* dire • *adv* dreadfully
skræl • *n* peel, skin
skrælle • *v* peel
skræmme • *v* faze
skræppe • *n* chatter
skramme • *n* cut
skrammel • *n* trash
skranke • *n* counter

skråstreg • *n* slash
skridt • *n* crotch, groin, move, step
skridtbeskytter • *n* box
skriftestol • *n* confessional
skrifttype • *n* font
skrig • *n* cry, scream, shout
skrige • *v* cry, shout
skrin • *n* box
skrive • *v* write
skrivebord • *n* desk
skrivehæfte • *n* notebook
skrivemaskine • *n* typewriter
skrøbelig • *adj* breakable, fragile
skrotum • *n* scrotum
skrubbe • *v* bark • *n* flounder
skrud • *n* robe
skrue • *n* screw
skruebrækker • *n* blackleg
skruelinje • *n* helix
skruenøgle • *n* wrench
skruestik • *n* vise
skruetvinge • *n* vise
skrummel • *n* monstrosity
skrumpelever • *n* cirrhosis
skud • *n* shot
skuespiller • *n* actor, player
skuespillerinde • *n* actor, actress
skuffe • *n* drawer
skulder • *n* shoulder
skuldertræk • *n* shrug
skule • *v* frown
skulle • *v* have, must, should
skum • *n* foam
skumfidus • *n* marshmallow
skumgummi • *n* foam
skummel • *adj* dark, sleazy
skumring • *n* dark, dusk, night, nightfall, twilight
skur • *n* shack, shed
skurk • *n* villain
skurvefugl • *n* butterfly
skvadderhoved • *n* nincompoop
sky • *n* cloud
skybrud • *n* cloudburst
skyde • *v* shoot
skydelære • *n* calipers
skydeskive • *n* target
skydevåben • *n* firearm
skygge • *n* shade, shadow
skyld • *n* guilt
skylde • *v* blame
skyldfølelse • *n* remorse
skyldighed • *n* debt
skyskraber • *n* skyscraper
slå • *v* box, hit, mow
sladder • *n* gossip
sladderhank • *n* telltale

sladre • *v* snitch
sladrehank • *n* snitch, telltale
sladrende • *adj* catty
slæb • *n* train
slæbebåd • *n* tugboat
slæde • *n* carriage, sledge
slægt • *n* genus, people
slægtled • *n* generation
slægtning • *n* relation
slægtskab • *n* kinship
slægtsnavn • *n* surname
slåen • *n* sloe
slag • *n* battle, belt, box, combat, fight
slagkraftig • *adj* cogent
slags • *n* kind, sort
slagskib • *n* battleship
slagsmål • *n* combat, fight, hassle, row
slagte • *v* slaughter
slagteoffer • *n* victim
slagter • *n* butcher
slagtilfælde • *n* fit, stroke
slang • *n* slang
slange • *n* hose, serpent, snake • *v* snake
slangemenneske • *n* contortionist
slank • *adj* slim
slås • *v* fight
slave • *v* slave • *n* slave
slaveri • *n* slavery
slavinde • *n* slave
slebet • *adj* cut
slem • *adj* bad, evil, naughty
slentre • *v* shuffle
slesk • *adj* obsequious, sycophantic
sleske • *v* fawn
slet • *adj* bad, evil
slette • *v* erase, wipe • *n* plain
slibe • *v* cut
slik • *n* candy, song, sweet
slikke • *v* lick
slikkepind • *n* lollipop
slikpind • *n* lollipop
slim • *n* mucus
slingre • *v* reel
slips • *n* necktie
sløjfe • *n* bow
slør • *n* veil
sløre • *v* camouflage, veil
slot • *n* castle
sløv • *adj* blunt, dull
slubre • *v* slurp
slud • *n* sleet
sludre • *v* babble, chat • *n* chatter
sluge • *v* down
slukke • *v* extinguish
slum • *n* slum
slumkvarter • *n* slum
slup • *n* sloop

slurk • *n* sip
slutning • *n* finish
slutte • *v* figure, reason
slyngel • *n* villain
små • *adj* little
småbarn • *n* toddler
smadre • *v* murder
smækfuld • *adj* jammed
småfisk • *n* fishy
smagfuld • *adj* delicious
smal • *adj* narrow
smålig • *adj* stingy
småpenge • *n* change
småplanet • *n* asteroid
smaragd • *n* emerald
smart • *adj* clever, smart
smed • *n* blacksmith, smith
smede • *v* forge
smedeværksted • *n* forge
smedje • *n* forge
smeltedigel • *n* crucible
smerte • *n* dolor, pain, sorrow, torment
smertefuld • *adj* painful
smide • *v* shy
smidig • *adj* ductile, flexible
smigrer • *n* adulator
smil • *n* smile
smile • *v* laugh, smile
sminke • *n* makeup
smøg • *n* smoke
smoking • *n* tuxedo
smør • *n* butter
smøre • *v* butter, oil, spread
smørepålæg • *n* spread
smuds • *n* squalor
smuk • *adj* beautiful, fair
smuldre • *v* crumble
smyge • *v* duck
smykker • *n* jewellery
snabel • *n* trunk
snæver • *adj* narrow
snævres • *v* narrow
snak • *n* talk
snakke • *v* chat, speak, talk • *n* chatter
snakkesalig • *adj* voluble
snaksom • *adj* talkative
snaksomhed • *n* talkativeness
snaps • *n* aquavit, schnapps
snarere • *conj* if
snart • *adv* soon
sne • *v* snow • *n* snow
sneblind • *adj* snow-blind
snebold • *n* snowball
snedighed • *n* ingenuity
snedrive • *n* snowdrift
snefald • *n* snow
snefane • *n* snowdrift

snefnug • *n* snowflake
snegl • *n* snail
snemand • *n* snowman
snerpe • *n* prude
snerperi • *n* prudery
snerpet • *adj* prudish
snes • *n* score
snescooter • *n* snowmobile
sneskred • *n* avalanche
snigmorder • *n* assassin
snild • *adj* clever
snit • *n* cut
snitsår • *n* cut
snitte • *v* cut
sno • *v* snake, wind
snob • *n* snob
snoning • *n* turn
snor • *n* twine
snørebånd • *n* shoelace
snorke • *v* snore
snorkel • *n* snorkel
snorkle • *v* snorkel
snørliv • *n* corset
snot • *n* snot
snu • *adj* shrewd, wily
snuble • *v* stumble
snublen • *n* stumble
snude • *n* nose
snuppe • *v* pinch
snurretop • *n* top
snuse • *v* nose
snusk • *n* squalor
snyde • *v* cheat, cut, tamper
so • *n* sow
sø • *n* lake, sea
sober • *adj* sober
socialisme • *n* socialism
sød • *adj* bland, cute, sweet
søde • *n* love • *v* sugar, sweeten
sødet • *adj* sweet
sødlig • *adj* sweet
sødme • *n* sweetness
sødt • *adv* sweet
sofa • *n* couch, sofa
software • *n* software
søgående • *adj* seagoing
søge • *v* hunt, search, seek
sogn • *n* parish
søjle • *n* column
sok • *n* sock
søko • *n* manatee
sol • *n* sun
solbader • *n* sunbather
solbær • *n* currant
solbrændt • *n* tan
solbriller • *n* sunglasses
soldat • *n* soldier

soldug • *n* sundew
solhverv • *n* solstice
solid • *adj* solid, sound
solidaritet • *n* solidarity
sølle • *adj* puny
solnedgang • *n* sunset
solopgang • *n* dawn, sunrise
solsikke • *n* sunflower
solskin • *n* sunshine
solsort • *n* blackbird
solur • *n* sundial
sølv • *n* argent, silver
solvens • *n* solvency
sølvfarvet • *adj* silver
sølvfisk • *n* silverfish
sølvkræ • *n* silverfish
sølvmønt • *n* silver
sølvpapir • *n* tinfoil
sølvtøj • *n* silverware
som • *conj* as • *prep* as • *adj* like • *pron* that, who
søm • *n* nail, seam
sømand • *n* seaman
sømme • *v* nail
sømmelig • *adj* modest
sømmelighed • *n* propriety
sommer • *n* summer
sommerflue • *n* butterfly
sommerfugl • *n* butterfly
søn • *n* son
sonate • *n* sonata
sonde • *n* sound
sondere • *v* sound
sonet • *n* sonnet
sønnedatter • *n* granddaughter
sønnesøn • *n* grandson
søpapegøje • *n* puffin
sorbet • *n* sorbet
søreme • *adv* indeed
sørens • *interj* damn
sorg • *n* sadness, sorrow
sørge • *v* mourn
sørgedigt • *n* elegy
sørgelig • *adj* pathetic, sorry
sorgløs • *adj* carefree
sørøver • *n* pirate
sørøveri • *n* piracy
sort • *n* black, sort • *adj* black
sortere • *v* sort
sortering • *n* sort
sortskjorte • *n* blackshirt
søsætning • *n* launching
søsætte • *v* launch
søskende • *n* sibling
søster • *n* sibling, sister
søstjerne • *n* starfish
søsyge • *n* seasickness

søtunge • *n* sole
søulk • *n* salt
sove • *v* sleep
soveværelse • *n* bedroom, room
søvn • *n* sleep
søvngængeri • *n* somnambulism
søvnig • *adj* sleepy
søvnløshed • *n* insomnia
sovs • *n* gravy, sauce
spade • *n* spade
spådom • *n* prophecy
spædbarn • *n* baby, infant
spænde • *n* buckle
spændende • *adj* exciting
spændingstilstand • *n* tone
spændt • *adj* anxious, excited
spændvidde • *n* spread
spærre • *v* block
spærretid • *n* curfew
spætte • *n* woodpecker
spåkvinde • *n* prophet
spam • *n* spam
spåmand • *n* prophet
spand • *n* bucket
spankulere • *v* prance, strut
spanskrør • *n* rod
spar • *n* spade
spare • *v* husband, save
spark • *n* kick
sparke • *v* foot, kick
sparsomhed • *n* parsimony
spatel • *n* spatula
spedalsk • *n* leper • *adj* leprous
spedalskhed • *n* leprosy
speedbåd • *n* speedboat
spejl • *n* mirror
spektakel • *n* noise, row
spekulere • *v* speculate • *n* wonder
spelt • *n* spelt
spermatozo • *n* spermatozoon
spid • *n* spit
spidde • *v* impale
spids • *n* nose, prong, spike • *adj* sharp
spidskommen • *n* cumin
spidsmus • *n* shrew
spiger • *n* spike
spil • *n* game, play
spild • *n* drain
spilde • *v* spill
spille • *v* act, lord, trumpet
spillemand • *n* fiddler, player
spilleplads • *n* field
spiller • *n* player
spilopper • *n* prank
spinat • *n* spinach
spinde • *v* weave
spindler • *n* arachnid

spinkel • *adj* fragile
spionage • *n* espionage
spir • *n* spire
spiral • *n* spiral
spiritus • *n* drink, liquor, spirit, spirits
spise • *v* dine, eat, lunch
spisekort • *n* menu
spiselig • *adj* edible, palatable
spiselige • *adj* comestible
spisepind • *n* chopstick
spiseske • *n* tablespoon
spiseskefuld • *n* tablespoon
spjæt • *n* jump
spjætte • *v* jump
spøg • *n* joke
spøge • *v* joke
spøgelse • *n* ghost
spøgelsesabe • *n* tarsier
spoiler • *n* spoiler
spole • *v* reel
spor • *n* clue, slot, trail, vestige
sporadisk • *adj* sporadic
spore • *n* spur
spørge • *v* ask
spørgsmål • *n* query, question
sport • *n* sport
sportsudøver • *n* athlete
sporvogn • *n* tram
sprække • *n* crack, fissure, slot
sprælsk • *adj* frisk
sprænge • *v* explode
sprænghoved • *n* warhead
sprechstallmeister • *n* ringmaster
sprede • *v* spread
spredning • *n* spread
spring • *n* jump, leap
springe • *v* explode, jump, leap, spring
springer • *n* knight
springkniv • *n* switchblade
springvand • *n* fountain
sprit • *n* spirit
sprog • *n* language
sprogbeherskelse • *n* language
sprogforskning • *n* linguistics
spurv • *n* sparrow
sputnik • *n* sputnik
spyd • *n* spear
spygat • *n* scupper
spyt • *n* saliva, spit
spytslikker • *n* adulator, sycophant • *v* lickspittle
spytte • *v* spit
stå • *v* stand
stab • *n* staff
stabil • *adj* stable
stade • *n* stand
stadie • *n* stage

stadig • *adv* still
stadion • *n* stadium
stådreng • *n* boner
stædig • *adj* implacable, recalcitrant, stubborn
stædighed • *n* stubbornness
stækbar • *adj* ductile
stær • *n* starling
stærk • *adj* severe, stark, strong
stævn • *n* stem
stævnemøde • *n* date
stævning • *n* subpoena
stafet • *n* baton
staffeli • *n* easel
stak • *n* queue
stakkels • *adj* poor
stål • *n* steel
stald • *n* barn, byre, stable
stalde • *v* stable
stamme • *v* hesitate • *n* tribe
stampe • *v* full, stamp
stampen • *n* stamp
stand • *n* stand
standard • *n* default
standart • *n* banner
standpunkt • *n* stand
standse • *v* arrest, flag, stop
stang • *n* rod, staff, stick
stangsejl • *n* staysail
stanniol • *n* tinfoil
stanse • *v* stamp
star • *n* sedge
starte • *v* execute
starut • *n* dude
stat • *n* nation, state
statelig • *adj* imposing, stately
station • *n* station
statistik • *n* statistics
statsborgerskab • *n* citizenship
statue • *n* statue
stav • *n* rod, staff, stick
stavbakterie • *n* rod
stave • *v* spell
stavefejl • *n* misspelling
stavelse • *n* syllable
stavlygte • *n* flashlight
stearinlys • *n* candle
sted • *n* place
steddatter • *n* stepdaughter
stedfar • *n* stepfather
stedmor • *n* stepmother
stedord • *n* pronoun
stedsegrøn • *adj* evergreen
steg • *n* fox
stejle • *v* prance
stemme • *v* voice, vote • *n* voice
stemning • *n* voice

stempel • *n* ram, stamp
stemple • *v* brand, cancel, stamp
stemt • *v* voice • *adj* voiced
sten • *n* stone
stenbider • *n* lumpsucker
stenbrud • *n* quarry
stenbuk • *n* ibex
stenbukken • *n* ram
stenet • *adj* stony
stenkul • *n* carbon
steppe • *n* steppe
stereoanlæg • *n* stereo
steril • *adj* sterile
sti • *n* path, sty
stift • *n* diocese
stigbøjle • *n* stirrup
stige • *n* ladder
stigning • *n* increase
stik • *n* jack
stikke • *v* knife, snitch
stikkelsbær • *n* gooseberry
stikker • *n* grass, snitch
stikmyg • *n* mosquito
stilfærdig • *adj* unobtrusive
stilhed • *n* calm, hush, quiet, silence, tranquillity
stillads • *n* scaffold
stille • *adj* calm, quiet, tranquil • *v* queue, set, stand
stillids • *n* goldfinch
stillits • *n* goldfinch
stime • *n* school
stinke • *v* smell
stinksvamp • *n* stinkhorn
stipendium • *n* scholarship
stirre • *v* glare, stare
stivelse • *n* starch
stiver • *n* strut
stivert • *n* boner
stivne • *v* congeal
stjæle • *v* lift, rob, steal
stjålen • *adj* stolen
stjålet • *adj* stolen
stjerne • *n* asterisk, star
stjernekaster • *n* sparkler
stjernestatus • *n* stardom
stjernetåge • *n* nebula
stodder • *n* vagabond
stødslæde • *n* ram
stødtand • *n* tusk
stof • *n* cloth, drug, fabric, material, solid, tissue
stofskifte • *n* metabolism
støj • *n* noise
stok • *n* stick
stokastisk • *adj* stochastic
stol • *n* bridge, chair

stola • *n* stole
stolpe • *n* post
stolthed • *n* pride
stoltsere • *v* strut
stønne • *v* groan
stopmæt • *adj* stuffed
stoppe • *v* arrest, stop
stoppested • *n* stop
stør • *n* sturgeon
stor • *adj* ample
storhedstid • *n* heyday
storhedsvanvid • *n* megalomania
storhjerne • *n* cerebrum
stork • *n* stork
storkenæb • *n* geranium
størkne • *v* concrete, set
storm • *n* storm
stormast • *n* mainmast
stormfugl • *n* petrel
stormvejr • *n* storm
større • *adj* bigger
størrelse • *n* size
storsejl • *n* mainsail
storsindet • *adj* magnanimous
storskarv • *n* cormorant
storslået • *adj* epic
støtte • *v* countenance, second, support • *n* promotion, second
støv • *n* dust
støvle • *n* boot
støvsuge • *v* vacuum
strå • *n* straw
stræde • *n* strait
straf • *n* penalty, punishment
straffe • *v* punish
straks • *adv* overnight
stråle • *v* beam, shine
strålende • *adj* resplendent
strand • *n* beach, coast, sand, strand
strandskade • *n* oystercatcher
strandsø • *n* lagoon
stratosfære • *n* stratosphere
strege • *v* blank
strejke • *n* strike
streng • *adj* severe • *n* string
strenge • *v* string
stress • *n* stress
stresse • *v* stress
strid • *n* row
stridsplejl • *n* flail
strikke • *v* knit
strisser • *n* bull
strø • *v* spread
strofe • *n* verse
strofer • *n* stanza
strøm • *n* burn, flow
strømme • *v* flow

strømpeholder • n girdle
strømsild • n argentine
strontium • n strontium
strubehoved • n larynx
struds • n ostrich
struktur • n fabric
stryge • v bow, cancel, iron, strop
strygejern • n iron
strygerne • n string
stud • n steer
studere • v learn, study
studerende • n student
studsmus • n vole
stum • adj mute
stump • n morsel
stundom • adv sometimes
stykke • n cake, cut, hand-me-down, item, piece, play
styr • n handlebar
styrbord • n starboard
styre • v control, govern, steer
styrke • n force • v tone
styrte • v topple
subjekt • n subject
subkutan • adj subcutaneous
sublim • adj sublime
sublimere • v sublime
subsidiær • adj subsidiary
substans • n substance
substantiv • n noun
substituere • v substitute
substitut • n substitute, surrogate
subtroper • n subtropics
subtropisk • adj subtropical
succes • n success
succubus • n succubus
suder • n tench
suge • v suck
suk • n sigh
sukke • v sigh
sukker • n sugar
sukrose • n sucrose
sult • n hunger, starvation
sultan • n sultan
sulten • adj hungry, peckish
sum • n amount
summere • v add
sump • n bog, quagmire
sund • adj good, healthy, sound • n sound
sundhed • n health
super • interj great • adj super
superlativ • n superlative
supermarked • n supermarket
sur • adj acid, angry, sour • v turn
surdej • n sourdough
surdejs- • adj sourdough
surikat • n meerkat

surkål • n sauerkraut
surmule • v sulk
surrealismen • n surrealism
surrogat • n substitute, surrogate
susen • n murmur
sushi • n sushi
suspekt • v suspect
sutur • n seam
svaber • n squeegee
svækkes • v flag
svækling • n weakling
svælg • n throat
sværd • n sword
sværddrager • n swordtail
sværdfisk • n swordfish
sværdlilje • n flag
sværge • v swear
sværhed • n difficulty
sværm • n cluster, swarm
sværmer • n enthusiast
sværmeri • n pasha
svag • adj weak
svaghed • n foible, weakness
svale • n swallow
svamp • n fungus, mushroom, sponge
svampemiddel • n fungicide
svane • n swan
svangerskab • n pregnancy
svar • n answer, reply
svare • v answer, reply
svastika • n swastika
sved • n sweat
svede • v sweat
svejseapparat • n welder
svejsemaskine • n welder
svejser • n welder
svelle • n sleeper
svend • n journeyman
svenskerhår • n mullet
sveske • n brick, prune
svigerdatter • n daughter-in-law
svigerfar • n father-in-law
svigerinde • n sister-in-law
svigermor • n mother-in-law
svigersøn • n son-in-law
svigt • n failure
svigte • v fail
svin • n hog, pig
svindle • v cheat
svine • v soil
svinekød • n pork
svinesti • n pigsty
svøbe • n scourge
svoger • n brother-in-law
svømme • v swim
svømmetur • n swim
svovl • n sulfur

svovle • *v* sulfur
svulme • *v* swell
sweater • *n* sweater
syd • *n* south
sydøst • *n* southeast
sydsydøst • *n* south-southeast
sydsydvest • *n* south-southwest
sydvest • *n* southwest
syerske • *n* dressmaker
syfilis • *n* syphilis
syg • *adj* ill, sick • *n* illness, sick
sygdom • *n* disease
syge • *n* sick
sygehus • *n* hospital
sygeplejerske • *n* nurse
syllogisme • *n* syllogism
syltetøj • *n* jam, marmalade
symbiose • *n* symbiosis
symbol • *n* symbol
symbolisere • *v* symbolize
symbolsk • *adv* symbolically
symfoni • *n* symphony
symmetrisk • *adj* symmetrical
syn • *n* eyesight, view
synagoge • *n* synagogue
synd • *n* sin
syndebuk • *n* scapegoat

syndefri • *adj* sinless
syndeløs • *adj* sinless
synder • *n* sin, sinner
syndig • *adj* sinful
syndikat • *n* syndicate
syndrom • *n* syndrome
synes • *v* look, seem, think
synge • *v* sing
synkron • *adj* synchronous
synkronisere • *v* synchronize
synlig • *adj* visible
synonym • *n* synonym
synonymordbog • *n* thesaurus
synsk • *adj* clairvoyant
synskhed • *n* clairvoyance
synspunkt • *n* angle
synsvinkel • *n* angle
synthesizer • *n* synthesizer
syre • *n* acid
syre- • *adj* acid
syren • *n* lilac
system • *n* fabric, system
syvende • *adj* seventh
syver • *n* seven
syvsover • *n* dormouse
syvtal • *n* seven

T

T-bane • *n* metro
tå • *n* finger, toe
tab • *n* defeat
tabe • *v* down, lose
tabel • *n* table
tåbelig • *adj* foolish
tåbelighed • *n* foolishness
tablet • *n* pill
tackling • *n* tackle
tække • *v* bark
tælle • *v* count
tæller • *n* counter, numerator
tælling • *n* count
tæmme • *v* tame
tænde • *v* heat, kindle, light
tænder • *n* tooth
tændstik • *n* match
tænke • *v* think • *n* wonder
tæppe • *n* blanket, carpet, curtain, rug
tærskel • *n* threshold
tærskelværdi • *n* threshold
tærte • *n* pie
tæt • *adj* dense, immediate, narrow, solid
tæve • *n* bitch
taft • *n* taffeta

tag • *n* roof
tåge • *n* fog
tage • *v* pinch, take, vacation
tagetes • *n* marigold
tagrende • *n* trough
tagvindue • *n* skylight
tak • *n* thanks • *interj* thanks
takling • *n* tackle
taknemlig • *adj* grateful
taknemlighed • *n* thankfulness
taknemmelig • *adj* grateful
taknemmelighed • *n* thankfulness
taks • *n* yew
takstræ • *n* yew
tal • *n* figure, number
tale • *v* speak, talk
talent • *n* talent
talentfuld • *adj* talented
taler • *n* speaker
talg • *n* tallow
talje • *n* tackle, waist
talkum • *n* talcum
tallerken • *n* dish, plate, saucer
talløs • *adj* countless
tålmod • *n* patience

tålmodig • *adj* patient
tålmodighed • *n* patience
talskvinde • *n* spokeswoman
talsmand • *n* spokesman
talsperson • *n* spokesperson
tam • *adj* tame
tampon • *n* tampon
tand • *n* prong, tooth
tandbørste • *n* toothbrush
tandem • *n* tandem
tandemcykel • *n* tandem
tandkød • *n* gum
tandlæge • *n* dentist
tandpasta • *n* toothpaste
tang • *n* pliers, seaweed
tange • *n* spit
tangent • *n* key
tank • *n* tank
tankbil • *n* tanker
tanke • *n* thought
tankefuld • *adj* pensive
tanker • *n* tanker
tankevirksomhed • *n* thought
tankskib • *n* tanker
tankvogn • *n* tanker
tannin • *n* tannin
tantal • *n* tantalum
tante • *n* aunt
tapet • *n* wallpaper
tapir • *n* tapir
tappe • *v* drain
tapperhed • *n* bravery, courage
tår • *n* drink
tåre • *n* tear
tarm • *n* intestine
tårn • *n* rook, tower
tårnfalk • *n* kestrel
tartan • *n* tartan
taske • *n* bag
tast • *n* key
tastatur • *n* keyboard
tatovering • *n* tattoo
tavle • *n* blackboard
tavshed • *n* silence
taxa • *n* taxi
taxi • *n* taxi
taxie • *v* taxi
te • *n* tea
teaktræ • *n* teak
teater • *n* theater
technetium • *n* technetium
tegl • *n* tile
tegn • *n* character, sign, token
tegne • *v* draw
tegnebog • *n* wallet
tegnefilm • *n* cartoon
tegner • *n* drawer

tegneserie • *n* cartoon
tegning • *n* cartoon
tegnsætning • *n* punctuation
teisme • *n* theism
tekande • *n* teapot
teknik • *n* technique
tekniker • *n* technician
teknologi • *n* technology
tekst • *n* text
telefon • *n* phone, telephone
telefonere • *v* telephone
telefonist • *n* operator
telefonistinde • *n* operator
telefonopkald • *n* call
telegraf • *n* telegraph
telegram • *n* telegram
teleskop • *n* telescope
tellur • *n* tellurium
telt • *n* tent
tema • *n* subject
tempel • *n* temple
temperament • *n* temper
temperatur • *n* temperature
tendentiøs • *adj* tendentious
tender • *n* tender
tennis • *n* tennis
tenor • *n* tenor
teosofi • *n* theosophy
tepotte • *n* teapot
terapeut • *n* therapist
terapi • *n* therapy
terbium • *n* terbium
teresse • *n* patio
terminal • *n* terminal
terminologi • *n* language
termitter • *n* termite
termliste • *n* glossary
termosfære • *n* thermosphere
termostat • *n* thermostat
terne • *n* tern
terning • *n* die
terrasse • *n* terrace
territorium • *n* territory
terrorisme • *n* terrorism
terrorist • *n* terrorist
tertiær • *adj* tertiary
terts • *n* third
tesaurus • *n* thesaurus
tese • *n* thesis
tesis • *n* thesis
testamente • *n* testament, will
testamentere • *v* devise
teste • *v* try
testosteron • *n* testosterone
tetrameter • *n* tetrameter
thallium • *n* thallium
the • *n* tea

theta • *n* theta
thi • *conj* for
thorium • *n* thorium
thrips • *n* thrips
thulium • *n* thulium
tid • *n* time
tidevand • *n* tide
tidlig • *adj* early
tidligere • *adv* before • *adj* old
tidligste • *adj* prime
tidsalder • *n* age
tidsånd • *n* zeitgeist
tidsbestemme • *v* date
tidsel • *n* thistle
tidsfæste • *v* date
tidsindstille • *v* time
tidspunkt • *n* date, point
tidsrum • *n* window
tidsskrift • *n* journal, magazine, newspaper
tiende • *adj* tenth • *n* tithe
tiendedel • *n* tenth
tier • *n* ten, tenth
tiger • *n* tiger
tigger • *n* beggar
tikamp • *n* decathlon
til • *prep* about, at, for, to • *v* concrete
tilbage • *adv* back, behind
tilbageholdende • *adj* unobtrusive
tilbageværende • *adj* remaining
tilbagevendende • *adj* perennial
tilbagevirkende • *adj* retroactive
tilbede • *v* pray
tilberede • *v* prepare
tilberedning • *n* preparation
tilbøjelighed • *n* propensity, turn
tilbud • *n* offer
tilbyde • *v* offer
tilfælde • *n* accident
tilfældig • *adj* random
tilfældighed • *n* accident
tilfalde • *v* accrue
tilflugtssted • *n* haven, hideout
tilføje • *v* damage
tilføjelse • *n* accretion, amendment
tilfreds • *adj* content, satisfied
tilfredsstille • *v* content
tilfredsstillende • *adv* adequately
tilgængelig • *adj* available
tilgive • *v* forgive
tilhænger • *n* follower
tilhøre • *v* belong
tilhøvle • *v* dress
tilhugge • *v* cut, dress
tilintetgøre • *v* annihilate
tilintetgørelse • *n* extinction
tillade • *v* allow, let, permit

tilladelse • *n* leave, permission
tillægsord • *n* adjective
tillid • *n* trust
tillykke • *interj* congratulations
tilnærmelsesvis • *adv* approximately
tilnavn • *n* byname, nickname
tilpasning • *n* adjustment
tilpasse • *v* fit
tilpassede • *v* fitted
tilpasset • *v* fitted
tilskære • *v* cut
tilskynde • *v* move
tilsøle • *v* soil
tilstå • *v* confess
tilstand • *n* state
tilstrækkelig • *adj* adequate
tilstrækkeligt • *adv* adequately
tilsyneladende • *adv* apparently
tiltalende • *adj* attractive
tiltrækkende • *adj* attractive
tiltro • *n* trust
time • *n* hour • *v* time
timeglas • *n* hourglass
tin • *n* pewter, tin
tinding • *n* temple
ting • *n* object, parliament, thing
tinnitus • *n* tinnitus
tintøj • *n* pewter
tisse • *v* pee
tissekone • *n* pussy, vulva
tissemand • *n* penis
tital • *n* ten
titan • *n* titanium
tja • *interj* well
tjære • *n* tar
tjald • *n* oystercatcher, weed
tjene • *v* serve
tjener • *n* waiter
tjeneste • *n* duty, kindness
tjørn • *n* hawthorn
tjur • *n* capercaillie
tobak • *n* tobacco
todelt • *adj* bipartite
tøffelhelt • *adj* henpecked
tog • *n* train
togvogn • *n* carriage
toilet • *n* bathroom, can, toilet
toiletkumme • *n* toilet
toiletpapir • *n* tissue
toilette • *n* toilet
tøj • *n* cloth, clothes, clothing, hand-me-down
tøjte • *n* slut
toksikolog • *n* toxicologist
toksokologisk • *adj* toxicological
told • *n* customs, duty
tolerance • *n* tolerance

tolerere • *v* countenance
tolk • *n* interpreter, translator
tolvfingertarm • *n* duodenum
tolvte • *adj* twelfth
tom • *adj* blank, empty
tomat • *n* tomato
tomhed • *n* emptiness
tomler • *n* hitchhiker
tomme • *n* inch
tømme • *v* drain, empty
tommelfinger • *n* thumb
tommelfingernegl • *n* thumbnail
tommeltot • *n* thumb
tømmermænd • *n* hangover
tømmermand • *n* carpenter
tømrer • *n* carpenter
tomrum • *n* void
ton • *n* ton
tønde • *n* barrel, drum
tone • *n* tenor, tone • *v* tone
tonefald • *n* tone
tonerække • *n* sequence
tonus • *n* tone
top • *n* spike, summit
topmøde • *n* summit
topologi • *n* topology
topskarv • *n* shag
tør • *adj* dry
torden • *n* thunder
tordenvejr • *n* thunderstorm
toretnings- • *adj* bidirectional
tørfisk • *n* stockfish
tørke • *n* drought
tørklæde • *n* headscarf
torn • *n* thorn
tornado • *n* tornado
torp • *n* thorp
tørre • *v* bake, wipe
tørretumbler • *n* dryer
torsk • *n* cod
tørst • *n* thirst
tørste • *v* lust, thirst
tørstig • *adj* thirsty
tortere • *v* torture
tortur • *n* torture
torturere • *v* torture
tørv • *n* peat
torv • *n* market, plaza, square
tøsedreng • *n* pussy
tosproget • *adj* bilingual
tosse • *n* mug
total • *n* two
totem • *n* totem
tov • *n* rope
tråd • *n* thread, wire
tradition • *n* tradition
traditionel • *adj* traditional

traditionelt • *adv* traditionally
trådløs • *adj* wireless
træ • *n* tree
træblæser • *n* woodwind
træde • *v* tread
træffe • *v* find, meet
træfning • *n* combat
træk • *n* character, feature, move
trækharmonika • *n* accordion
trække • *v* draw, move, pull
trækul • *n* carbon, charcoal
træl • *n* slave
trælkone • *n* slave
træne • *v* practice, train
træner • *n* coach
træsko • *n* clog
træt • *adj* tired
trættende • *adj* tedious
trættes • *v* languish
trafik • *n* traffic
tragedie • *n* tragedy
tragt • *n* funnel
traktor • *n* tractor
trampe • *v* stamp
trampolin • *n* trampoline
trane • *n* crane
tranebær • *n* cranberry
transaktion • *n* transaction
translitteration • *n* transliteration
transparent • *adj* transparent
transplantat • *n* transplant
transplantation • *n* transplant
transplantere • *v* transplant
transport • *n* transfer, transport
transportere • *v* transport
transseksuel • *adj* transsexual
transvestit • *n* transvestite
trapez • *n* trapezoid
trappe • *n* bustard, stair, staircase, stairs
traske • *v* plod, slog, trudge
travl • *adj* busy
trawler • *n* trawler
tre • *n* three
tredimensional • *adj* three-dimensional
tredivte • *adj* thirtieth
tredje • *adj* third
tredjedel • *n* third
tredoble • *v* treble
trekant • *n* triangle
trekantet • *adj* triangular
trekløver • *n* trefoil
tresindstyvende • *adj* sixtieth
tressende • *adj* sixtieth
trettende • *adj* thirteenth
treven • *adj* sullen
triangel • *n* triangle
tribune • *n* stand

tribut • *n* homage
trikotillomani • *n* trichotillomania
trille • *v* run
trillebør • *n* wheelbarrow
trimaran • *n* trimaran
trin • *n* step
trinbræt • *n* step
trisse • *n* reel
trist • *adj* sad
trit • *n* step
triumf • *n* triumph
triumfere • *v* triumph
triumftog • *n* triumph
trives • *v* thrive
triviel • *adj* light, tedious
tro • *n* belief, faith • *v* believe, think
trodse • *v* face
trodsig • *adj* defiant
trøje • *n* shirt
trold • *n* goblin, troll
trolddom • *n* witchcraft
troldkarl • *n* warlock
troldmand • *n* mage, warlock, wizard
troll • *n* troll
tromle • *n* drum, reel
tromme • *v* drum • *n* drum
trompet • *v* trumpet • *n* trumpet
trompeter • *n* trumpeter
trompetere • *v* trumpet
trompetist • *n* trumpet, trumpeter
trompetstød • *n* trumpet
trone • *n* throne
tropopause • *n* tropopause
troposfære • *n* troposphere
troskab • *n* fealty
trøske • *n* candidiasis
trosse • *n* hawser
trøst • *n* comfort, solace
truck • *n* truck
truende • *adj* fierce
truet • *adj* threatened
trug • *n* trough
trumf • *n* trump
trummerum • *n* rut
trygle • *v* implore
tryk • *n* accent
trykke • *v* squeeze
trykkende • *adj* sultry
tryllekunstner • *n* conjurer, magician
tryne • *n* snout
tuberkulose • *n* tuberculosis
tud • *n* nose
tudse • *n* toad
tulipan • *n* tulip
tumleplads • *n* playground
tummel • *n* tumult
tumpe • *n* goof

tumult • *n* row, tumult
tun • *n* tuna
tundra • *n* tundra
tung • *adj* heavy
tunge • *n* language, tongue
tungsindig • *adj* pensive
tunnel • *n* tunnel
tunnelbane • *n* metro
tur • *n* turn
turban • *n* turban
turbulens • *n* turbulence
turisme • *n* tourism
turist • *n* tourist
turkis • *n* turquoise • *adj* turquoise
tusindben • *n* millipede
tusinde • *adj* thousandth
tusindfryd • *n* daisy
tusmørke • *n* twilight
tv • *n* television
tv-program • *n* series
tv-serie • *n* series
tv-station • *n* station
tvang • *n* coercion
tvangsauktionere • *v* foreclose
tvangstanke • *n* obsession
tveægget • *adj* double-edged
tvebak • *n* rusk
tvekamp • *n* duel
tvekønnet • *adj* hermaphrodite
tvelyd • *n* diphthong
tvetydig • *adj* ambiguous
tvetydighed • *n* ambiguity
tvilling • *n* twin
tvinge • *v* force
tvivl • *n* doubt
tvivle • *v* doubt
tvivlende • *adj* doubtful, dubious
tvivlrådig • *adj* dubious, irresolute
tvivlsom • *adj* doubtful, dubious, questionable
tydelig • *adj* clear, explicit, obvious • *adv* clearly
tyfon • *n* typhoon
tyfus • *n* typhus
tygge • *v* chew
tyk • *adj* thick
tykt • *adv* thick
tynd • *adj* slim
tyndtbefolket • *adj* rural
type • *n* type
typisk • *adj* typical
tyr • *n* bull, hunk, stud
tyran • *n* bully, tyrant
tyrannisere • *v* bully
tyst • *adj* quiet
tyttebær • *n* lingonberry
tyv • *n* snitch, thief

tyveknægt • *n* snitch, thief
tyvende • *adj* twentieth
tyveri • *n* theft

tyvstjæle • *v* rob

U

U-bane • *n* metro
uafhængighed • *n* independence
uafskærmet • *adj* naked
ualmindelig • *adv* abnormally, infrequently
uanstændig • *adj* vulgar
uartig • *adj* naughty
uautoriseret • *adj* unauthorized
ubåd • *n* submarine
ubehag • *n* distress
ubehagelig • *adj* bad
ubekendt • *adj* unknown
ubekymret • *adj* carefree
uberegnelig • *adj* capricious
uberettiget • *adj* illegitimate
ubeskrevet • *adj* blank
ubeslutsom • *adj* indecisive, irresolute
ubetydelig • *adj* minor, negligible, petty
ubøjelig • *adj* indeclinable
ubønhørlig • *adj* inexorable
ubrugelig • *adj* useless
ubrydelig • *adj* unbreakable
udånde • *v* die
udarbejde • *v* devise
udbasunere • *v* trumpet
udbener • *n* boner
udbrede • *v* spread
udbredelse • *n* spread
udbredelsesområde • *n* habitat
udbringe • *v* deliver
udbrud • *n* cry, outbreak
udbryde • *v* cry
udbud • *n* offer, supply
udbudsforretning • *n* offer
udbygning • *n* development
udbytte • *n* dividend
udbytter • *n* user
uddannelse • *n* education
uddele • *v* share
uddød • *adj* extinct
uddøen • *n* extinction
uddybe • *v* elucidate
udelade • *v* omit
udelukke • *v* cut
uden • *conj* but • *prep* within, without
udenlandsk • *adj* foreign
udfladning • *n* flare
udfordre • *v* challenge
udfordrende • *adj* challenging

udføre • *v* do, execute, make
udførelse • *n* achievement
udforske • *v* explore
udfri • *v* deliver
udgået • *adj* dated
udgang • *n* exit
udgangsforbud • *n* curfew
udgave • *n* release
udglatte • *v* smooth
udgravning • *n* dig
udholde • *v* stand
udholdenhed • *n* endurance
udhungret • *adj* famished
udkæmpe • *v* fight
udkant • *n* outskirt, periphery
udkig • *n* lookout
udkigsmand • *n* lookout
udkigspost • *n* lookout
udkigspunkt • *n* lookout
udkørt • *adj* exhausted
udlænding • *adj* foreign
udlede • *v* derive
udlevere • *v* deliver
udløbe • *v* expire
udløser • *n* trigger
udløsning • *n* ejaculation
udlove • *v* offer
udmærket • *adj* bully • *interj* bully
udmatning • *n* fatigue
udmattet • *adj* exhausted
udmunding • *n* mouth
udnævne • *v* appoint, queen
udnytte • *v* exploit, work
udødelig • *adj* immortal
udøve • *v* practice
udpege • *v* find, finger
udplante • *v* transplant
udråb • *n* cry
udråbsord • *n* interjection
udrydde • *v* exterminate, extinguish
udsætte • *v* offer, postpone, procrastinate
udsagnsord • *n* verb
udsigt • *n* view, vista
udskære • *v* cut
udskæring • *n* cut
udskifte • *v* change, substitute
udskifter • *n* substitute
udskiftning • *n* change
udskyde • *v* procrastinate

udskyldning • *n* irrigation
udslettelse • *n* extinction
udslukke • *v* extinguish
udsøgt • *adj* choice
udspring • *n* source
udstå • *v* stand
udstanse • *v* stamp
udstøde • *v* abandon, utter
udstoppet • *adj* stuffed
udstrykkelig • *adj* explicit
udstyr • *n* equipment, gear, hardware
udstyre • *v* tool
udtænke • *v* devise
udtale • *v* pronounce, voice • *n* pronunciation
udtømme • *adj* depleted
udtømt • *adj* exhausted
udtørre • *v* drain
udtryk • *n* expression • *v* voice
udtrykke • *v* couch, express, utter, voice
uduelig • *adj* feckless
udvælge • *v* choose
udvandre • *v* emigrate, expatriate
udvandrer • *n* expatriate • *adj* expatriate
udvej • *n* exit
udvidelse • *n* development
udvikle • *v* develop, grow
udvikler • *n* developer
udvikling • *n* development, evolution, march
udviklingshæmmet • *adj* retarded
udvirke • *v* work
udvist • *n* expatriate
udyr • *n* brute
uegennyttig • *adj* altruistic
uendelighed • *n* infinity
uenighed • *n* quarrel
uerhørt • *adj* unheard-of
ufejlbarlig • *adj* infallible
ufødt • *adj* unborn
uformodet • *adj* abrupt
uforskammet • *adj* rude
uforskammethed • *n* cheek
uforstyrret • *adj* undisturbed, unperturbed
uforudsigbar • *adj* capricious
uforutsigbar • *adj* capricious
uge • *n* week
ugentlig • *adv* weekly
ugift • *adj* unmarried
ugle • *n* owl
ugyldig • *adj* dated
uhæderlighed • *n* mendacity
uheld • *n* accident
uheldig • *adj* infelicitous, unfortunate
uheldigvis • *adv* unfortunately
uheldsvanger • *adj* ominous

uhøflig • *adj* rude
uhøjtidelig • *adj* unpretentious
uhørt • *adj* unheard-of
uhyre • *n* monster
uidentificeret • *adj* unidentified
uigenkaldelig • *adj* irrevocable
uinteresseret • *adj* uninterested
ukendt • *adj* anonymous, unknown
ukomplet • *adj* incomplete
ukønnet • *adj* neuter
ukrudt • *n* weed
uld • *n* wool
ulig • *adj* different
ulighed • *n* inequality
ulk • *n* sculpin
ulogisk • *adj* illegitimate
ultimatum • *n* ultimatum
ultraviolet • *adj* ultraviolet
ulv • *n* wolf
ulykke • *n* accident
ulykkelig • *adj* hapless, unfortunate
ulykkestilfælde • *n* accident
umælende • *adj* mute
umættelig • *adj* insatiable
umoden • *adj* immature
umoderne • *adj* dated
umoralsk • *adj* evil
umulig • *adj* impossible
umulighed • *n* impossible
umuligt • *adj* impossible
unaturlig • *adj* unnatural
under • *prep* during • *n* miracle, wonder
underdanig • *adj* obsequious
underernæret • *adj* malnourished
underernæring • *n* malnutrition, undernourishment
underforstå • *v* understand
undergang • *n* perdition, undoing
undergrundsbane • *n* metro
underholdning • *n* amusement, entertainment
underkop • *n* saucer
underlig • *adj* funny, strange
underordnet • *adj* ancillary, subordinate
undersejl • *n* course
underskrift • *n* signature
undersøge • *v* explore
understøttelsespunkt • *n* fulcrum
undertekst • *n* subtitle
undertiden • *adv* sometimes
undertøj • *n* underwear
undertrykke • *v* oppress
undertrykkelse • *n* oppression
underudviklet • *adj* underdeveloped
underverden • *n* underworld
undervise • *v* teach
undgå • *v* cheat

undlade • *v* fail
undskyld • *interj* sorry
undskylder • *n* apologist
undskyldning • *n* apology
undtagelse • *n* exception
undtagelsesvis • *adv* exceptionally
undtagen • *conj* but, unless
undulat • *n* budgerigar
undvige • *v* duck
ung • *adj* young
unge • *n* brat, calf, kid
ungfugl • *n* chick
ungkarl • *n* bachelor
ungmo • *n* damsel
unheldig • *adj* unlucky
unicykel • *n* unicycle
union • *n* union
univers • *n* universe
universitet • *n* university
unødvendig • *adj* unnecessary
unormal • *adj* abnormal • *adv* abnormally
uofficiel • *adj* unofficial
uorden • *n* disorder
uortodoks • *adj* unorthodox
upålidelig • *adj* unreliable
upartisk • *adj* impartial
upasteuriseret • *adj* unpasteurized
upræcis • *adj* imprecise
uprofessionel • *adj* unprofessional
ur • *n* clock, talus
uræmi • *n* uremia
uran • *n* uranium
urapporteret • *adj* unreported
uregelmæssig • *adj* intermittent, strong
uren • *adj* dirty
uretmæssig • *adj* illegitimate
urin • *n* urine

urinal • *n* urinal
urinale • *n* urinal
urmager • *n* watchmaker
uro • *n* unrest
urolig • *adj* anxious
urostifter • *n* gadfly
urovækkende • *adj* anxious
urt • *n* herb, wort
urteagtig • *adj* herbaceous
usagt • *adj* unspoken
usaltet • *adj* sweet
usand • *adj* untrue
usandhed • *n* untruth
usejr • *n* defeat
usikker • *adj* doubtful, dubious, insecure
usikkerhed • *n* insecurity, uncertainty
ustemt • *adj* voiceless
usynlig • *adj* invisible
utaknemmelig • *adj* thankless
utallig • *adj* countless
utålmodig • *adj* impatient
utålmodighed • *n* impatience
utilgivelig • *adj* inexcusable, unpardonable
utilsigtet • *adj* inadvertent
utilsløret • *adj* naked
utilstrækkelighed • *n* deficiency
utopi • *n* utopia
utryg • *adj* insecure
utvivlsom • *adj* unequivocal
uundgåelig • *adj* unavoidable
uværdig • *adj* unworthy
uvidende • *adj* oblivious
uvidenhed • *n* dark, ignorance
uvilje • *n* grudge

V

våben • *n* arm, hardware, weapon
vable • *n* blister
våd • *adj* wet
vadested • *n* ford
vædde • *v* bet
væddemål • *n* bet
vædder • *n* ram
væg • *n* wall
væge • *n* wick
vægelsindet • *adj* fickle
væggelus • *n* bedbug
vægt • *n* weight
vække • *v* awake, evoke, kindle, wake
vækst • *n* growth, plant
vælge • *v* choose, elect, name

vælger • *n* voter
vælte • *v* topple
væmmelse • *v* disgust • *n* disgust
værd • *n* value
værdi • *n* value
værdifuld • *adj* valuable
værdig • *adj* dignified
værdigenstand • *n* money
værdighed • *n* dignity
værdiløs • *adj* worthless
værdsætte • *v* appreciate, value
være • *v* be, face
værelse • *n* den
værk • *n* oakum, work
værktøj • *n* tool

værn • *n* safeguard
værnepligt • *n* conscription
værre • *adj* worse
værst • *adj* worst
vært • *n* host
værtinde • *n* hostess
væsen • *n* being, creature, wight
væsener • *n* creature
væske • *n* fluid, liquid
vætte • *n* wight
væv • *n* loom, tissue
væve • *v* weave
vagabond • *n* vagabond
vagabund • *n* tramp
vågen • *adj* awake
vagina • *n* vagina
vågne • *v* awake, wake
vagt • *n* guard, watch
vagtel • *n* quail
vagtpost • *n* lookout
vajd • *n* woad
vaje • *v* wave
vakle • *v* reel
vakuum • *n* vacuum
valens • *n* degree
valg • *n* choice, election
valgfrit • *adj* optional
valgkreds • *n* constituency
valke • *v* full
valkyrie • *n* valkyrie
valle • *n* whey
valmue • *n* poppy
valnød • *n* walnut
valnøddetræ • *n* walnut
valør • *n* value
valuta • *n* currency, money
vampyr • *n* vampire
vams • *n* doublet
vanadium • *n* vanadium
vandalisme • *n* vandalism
vandfald • *n* cascade, waterfall
vandfast • *adj* waterproof
vandfly • *n* seaplane
vanding • *n* irrigation
vandkande • *n* can
vandkoger • *n* teakettle
vandmærke • *n* watermark
vandmand • *n* jellyfish
vandmelon • *n* watermelon
vandre • *v* walk
vandredrossel • *n* robin
vandregræshoppe • *n* locust
vandret • *adj* horizontal, level
vandretur • *n* walk
vandtæt • *adj* fail-safe, waterproof
vane • *n* habit, rut, wont
vanhellige • *v* desecrate

vanilje • *n* vanilla
vankelmodig • *adj* fickle, irresolute
vanlig • *adj* common
vanrøgt • *n* abuse
vanskelig • *adj* difficult, hard
vanskelighed • *n* difficulty
vant • *n* shroud
vante • *n* glove, mitten
vanvid • *n* frenzy, insanity, madness
vanvittig • *adj* mad
vår • *n* spring
varehus • *n* emporium
varemærke • *n* brand, trademark
varevogn • *n* van
varieté • *n* burlesque
varm • *adj* hot, warm • *v* warm
varme • *n* heat • *v* warm
varmebed • *n* hotbed
varmelære • *n* thermodynamics
varslende • *adj* ominous
varsom • *adj* cautious, circumspect, wary
varsomhed • *n* caution
varsomt • *adv* gingerly
varulv • *n* werewolf
vasal • *n* vassal
vase • *n* vase
vask • *n* sink
vaske • *v* wash
vaskebjørn • *n* raccoon
vaskeklud • *n* washcloth
vaskemiddel • *n* detergent
vasketøj • *n* laundry
vaterpas • *n* level
vattæppe • *n* quilt
ved • *prep* by
vederstyggelighed • *n* abomination
vedligeholde • *v* maintain
vedligeholdelse • *n* maintenance
vedrørende • *prep* about
vedvarende • *adj* perpetual
veganer • *n* vegan
vegetar • *n* vegetarian
vegetarisme • *n* vegetarianism
vej • *n* path, road, way
vejbelægning • *n* pavement
vejbred • *n* plantain
veje • *v* weigh
vejgaffel • *n* fork
vejkryds • *n* crossroads
vejlederen • *n* instruction
vejledning • *n* guide, instruction
vejr • *n* weather
vejrandøje • *n* wall
vejrhane • *n* weathercock
vejrmølle • *n* cartwheel
vejviser • *n* guide
vekselpenge • *n* change

vektor • *n* vector
velbevaret • *adj* well-preserved
velfærd • *n* welfare
velformuleret • *n* rhetoric
velkommen • *adj* welcome • *interj* welcome
vellystig • *adj* voluptuous
velmagtsdage • *n* heyday
velordnet • *adj* orderly
velovervejet • *adj* deliberate
velsagtens • *adv* arguably
velsigne • *v* bless
velsmagende • *adj* delicious, palatable
velstand • *n* money, wealth
veltalende • *adj* voluble
velvilje • *n* kindness
vemodig • *adj* wistful
ven • *n* friend
vende • *v* face, turn
vendepunkt • *n* crisis, inflection
vendt • *v* face
vene • *n* vein
veninde • *n* friend, girlfriend
venlig • *adj* cheerful, friendly, kind, sweet • *adv* kindly
venlighed • *n* kindness
venligsindet • *adj* friendly
venligst • *adv* kindly
venligt • *adv* friendly
venneløs • *adj* friendless
venskab • *n* friendship
venskabelig • *adj* amicable, friendly
venskabskamp • *n* friendly
venstre • *n* left • *adj* left
venstrefløjen • *n* left
venstrehåndet • *n* left-handed
venstreorienteret • *adj* left
vente • *v* wait
venteliste • *n* queue
ventil • *n* valve
ventilator • *n* fan
ventrikel • *n* ventricle
veranda • *n* veranda
verbum • *n* verb
verden • *n* world
verdensborger • *n* cosmopolite
verdslig • *adj* temporal
vers • *n* verse
versefod • *n* foot
versefødder • *n* foot
versfod • *n* foot
versfødder • *n* foot
version • *n* release
versus • *prep* against
vesir • *n* vizier
vest • *n* waistcoat, west
vestibule • *n* vestibule

vestlig • *adj* western
veteran • *n* veteran • *adj* veteran
veto • *n* veto
vi • *pron* we
viadukt • *n* viaduct
viaticum • *n* viaticum
vibe • *n* lapwing
vibrafon • *n* vibraphone
vibrator • *n* dildo
vid • *adj* ample, full, wide
vidde • *n* expanse
vide • *v* know
viden • *n* knowledge, science
videnskab • *n* science
videnskabelighed • *n* science
videnskabsmand • *n* scientist
vidne • *v* evidence • *n* witness
vidneskranke • *n* stand
vidneudsagn • *n* evidence
vidunder • *n* prodigy, wonder
vidunder- • *n* wonder
vidunderlig • *adj* wonderful
vielse • *n* marriage, wedding
vifte • *v* fan, wave • *n* fan
vigtig • *adj* important
vigtigste • *adj* prime
vikar • *n* temporary
vikariere • *v* supply
vikle • *v* wind
vild • *adj* wild
vildfaren • *adj* lost
vildlede • *v* mislead
vilje • *n* voice, will
viljestyrke • *n* character
vilkårlig • *adj* arbitrary
ville • *v* be, want
vin • *n* wine
vinballong • *n* demijohn
vind • *n* flatulence, wind
vinde • *v* reel
vindebro • *n* drawbridge
vinder • *n* winner
vindmølle • *n* windmill
vindrue • *n* grape
vindstille • *n* calm
vindue • *n* window
vindueskarm • *n* windowsill
vingård • *n* vineyard
vinge • *n* wing
vinke • *v* wave
vinkel • *n* angle
vinkelret • *adj* orthogonal
vinkle • *v* angle
vinstok • *n* grapevine
vinter • *n* winter
violin • *n* fiddle, violin
violinist • *n* violinist

virak • *n* incense
virke • *v* act, function, look, work
virkelighed • *n* fact, reality
virksomhed • *n* company, enterprise, factory
virtuel • *adj* virtual
virtuos • *n* virtuoso
virus • *n* virus
vis • *adj* sapient
visdom • *n* wisdom
vise • *n* song
visent • *n* wisent
viser • *n* hand
visk • *n* whisk
viske • *v* erase
viskelæder • *n* eraser
viskøs • *adj* viscous
vismuth • *n* bismuth
visne • *v* wilt, wither
visuel • *adj* visual
visum • *n* visa
vitalisme • *n* vitalism
vitamin • *n* vitamin
vittighed • *n* joke, wittiness
vod • *n* net
vodka • *n* vodka
vogn • *n* car, carriage, taxi
vognhjul • *n* cartwheel
vokal • *n* vowel
voks • *n* wax
vokse • *v* grow, wax

voksen • *n* adult
vokslys • *n* taper
volapyk • *n* gibberish
vold • *n* bank
voldelig • *adj* violent
voldeligt • *adj* fierce
volden • *n* rampart
voldgrav • *n* moat
voldsom • *adj* severe, violent
voldtægt • *n* rape
voldtage • *v* rape
volt • *n* volt
vorte • *n* wart
vortemælk • *n* spurge
vortesvinet • *n* warthog
vov • *n* woof
vrangforestilling • *n* delusion
vrangvillig • *adj* sullen
vred • *adj* angry, mad
vrede • *n* anger, wrath
vride • *v* wring
vrøvl • *n* gibberish, rubbish
vrøvle • *v* babble
vue • *n* vista
vuf • *n* woof
vugge • *n* cradle
vulgær • *adj* rude, vulgar
vulkan • *n* volcano
vulva • *n* vulva
vurdere • *v* appraise, price, value

W

walkie-talkie • *n* walkie-talkie
watt • *n* watt
wc • *n* toilet
weekend • *n* weekend
whisky • *n* whiskey

wienerbrød • *n* danish
wok • *n* wok
wolfram • *n* tungsten

X

xenofobi • *n* xenophobia
xenon • *n* xenon
xylofon • *n* xylophone

xylografi • *n* xylography

Y

yacht • *n* yacht
yak • *n* yak
yakokse • *n* yak
yams • *n* yam
yde • *v* supply
yderside • *n* face
ydmyg • *adj* humble, pious
ydmyge • *v* abase, humble
ydmyghed • *n* humility

yndig • *adj* delicious
ynkelig • *adj* pathetic
yppig • *adj* voluptuous
ypsilon • *n* upsilon
ytre • *v* utter
ytterbium • *n* ytterbium
yttrium • *n* yttrium
yver • *n* udder

Z

zar • *n* tsar
zebra • *n* zebra
zink • *n* zinc
zirkonium • *n* zirconium
zobel • *n* sable

zodiak • *n* zodiac
zombie • *n* zombie
zone • *n* zone

Made in the USA
San Bernardino, CA
27 October 2017